Indians and the American West in the Twentieth Century

The American West in the Twentieth Century
Martin Ridge and Walter Nugent, *editors*

Indians and the American West in the Twentieth Century

DONALD L. PARMAN

INDIANA UNIVERSITY PRESS
Bloomington and Indianapolis

The paper used in this publication meets the minimum requirements of
American National Standard for Information Sciences—Permanence of Paper
for Printed Library Materials, ANSI Z39.48-1984.

Manufactured in the United States of America

Library of Congress Cataloging-in-Publication Data

Parman, Donald Lee, date
    Indians and the American West in the twentieth century / Donald L.
Parman.
        p.   cm. — (The American West in the twentieth century)
    Includes bibliographical reference (p.   ) and index.
    ISBN 0-253-34289-9 (alk. paper). — ISBN 0-253-20892-0 (pbk. :
alk. paper)
        1. Indians of North America—West (U.S.)—History—20th century.
    2. Indians of North America—West (U.S.)—Politics and government.
    3. Indians of North America—West (U.S.)—Government relations.
    4. Land tenure—West (U.S.)   5. Water rights—West (U.S.)
    I. Title.   II. Series.
    E78.W5P37   1994
    978'.00497—dc20   93-48060

2   3   4   5   00   99   98   97   96   95

FOR OUR NUCLEAR FAMILY
Vince, Joanne, and Julia; Steven, Denise,
Jason, and Corey

Contents

Foreword

Scarcely more than a century ago, the American Indians were seen as a dying people. The last gasp of Indian resistance, the "Ghost Dance" had been extinguished at the Wounded Knee Massacre. The Census report in 1890 showed a Native American population that had fallen to fewer than 250,000 and was still declining. Artists, photographers, and ethnologists, anticipating the complete demise of the Indians, had for a quarter century been capturing their images and preserving their artifacts for posterity. Poverty was almost universal among Indians who lived both on and off reservations. Diseases such as alcoholism and tuberculosis took a dreadful toll, as did infant mortality. The expansion of the mining and agricultural frontiers had eroded the Indian land base. In fact, with few exceptions, the reservations had been so severely reduced during the nineteenth century that they were inadequate to maintain the Native American population, even if the Indians had been willing or able to accept the economic activities that the government urged on them. Moreover, combinations of businessmen and government officials often linked up to exploit reservation resources to their own advantage.

At the dawn of the twentieth century, both scientific racism and racial prejudice also contributed to the deplorable condition of native peoples. Ironically, both the white friends and enemies of the Indians often proposed the same solution to the "Indian Problem." The Indians must be acculturated as quickly as possible and moved into the mainstream of American society. Their friends feared that without acculturation the Indian would perish; their enemies looked greedily upon the economic resources that still remained in Indian hands. The Dawes Act satisfied both interests. It called for breaking up reservations, allotting lands to individual Indians but placing such holdings in trust for a quarter of a century. Since not all reservation lands were allotted, the remaining portions were opened to white settlement. Thus, because of both good and bad intentions, the Indian land base was reduced even further. Small wonder that by 1900 respect for Native Americans and their culture was virtually at a nadir.

This is the historical past against which Donald Parman begins his study of Native Americans and governmental policy in the West during the twentieth century. His book is neither sentimental nor a jeremiad. The author looks hard at the relationships between economic interests and the government in dealing with the Indian. In many cases the players are clearly identified individuals, who for reasons of national purpose, the best of intentions, or personal gain, sought control of the underdeveloped resources on reservation land.

Parman traces the changes in public policy and the impact of foundation studies that occurred prior to the election of President Franklin Delano Roosevelt. He offers a balanced analysis of the Indian New Deal under Roosevelt. John Collier, Roosevelt's eccentric and influential commissioner of Indian affairs, emerges as neither hero nor villain, and his contributions to the restoration of both Indian lands and Indian culture are seen in terms of their long-term effects. An assessment of Collier is placed in the context of accomplishments as well as hostile and friendly criticism.

The role of the Native American in the Second World War receives careful examination, not only in a military sense but also in terms of the social and economic revolution that the war and its aftermath had on younger Indians—both male and female—who had worked away from the reservations. Parman's discussion of the postwar world breaks new ground. He indicates the Indians' successes and failures in trying to develop their own landed resources and their on-going struggles before the federal and state courts for economic and political independence. President Dwight Eisenhower's termination policy and other programs are depicted in their historical contexts rather than as aberrations. Parman often demonstrates the ultimate irony in the policies of the Johnson and Nixon administrations, which acted with one goal in mind, only to see a result far different from their original intent. In bringing his study into the years of the Ronald Reagan presidency, Parman allows his reader to feel much a part of the story and to be informed about why current Indian programs and issues involve every citizen directly. Parman subtly differentiates between the genuine issues that confront Native Americans and the emotional and symbolic matters that receive popular attention.

When Parman's story ends, the status of the Indian has been revolutionized. The Native American population exceeded 1.5 million and is growing, the Indian land base is expanding, and the courts have repeatedly upheld the rights of Indians in ways that nineteenth-century whites would never have imagined possible. But for many Indians, little has changed. The publicity surrounding the recent fiasco at Wounded Knee highlights the complexity of current Indian-white relations.

Unlike other authors who have written about Indians and feel that their works must scream with moral outrage at every ill-conceived governmental policy or misdeed by a private corporation, Parman gets behind the policies and actions to explain their origins, implementations, and effects. Quite often he brings this down to the level of a single individual, a tribal faction, a government official, or the leadership of a private company. The result is refreshing and insightful. The reader comes away with hard evidence on which to make a decision rather then congeries of moral judgments and abstractions.

This book is one of a series dealing with the West in the twentieth century. It is a fine companion volume to two splendid earlier works in the series: Richard W. Lowitt's, *The New Deal and the West*, and William H. Mullins's, *The Depression and the Urban West Coast*. The series is intended to provide the general public and the scholarly reader with a deeper understanding of important aspects of the recent past of the American West.

Martin Ridge
Walter Nugent

Preface

One of the basic goals in this work is to examine the relationship of Indian affairs to the development of the American West in the twentieth century. Anyone familiar with Indian history during this period has encountered evidence that western vested interests sought and often obtained Indian property, blocked needed protections, and dictated the activities of the Bureau of Indian Affairs. The main object of westerners' interest in Indian affairs has centered on gaining Indian resources—land, minerals, water, timber, labor, etc. As the West developed after 1900, it changed from a region primarily devoted to farming, ranching, and production of raw or semi-processed goods to a mixed economy that fostered urban and industrial development. Obviously this transition led to a shift in what Indian resources whites regarded as valuable, but, more importantly, it changed the Indians' economic environment and created new opportunities and problems both on and off reservations.

I am not proposing an ironclad thesis of the West versus Indian resources. Indian-white relations are much too complex for such a simple thesis. The West, for example, has never possessed the political, economic, or philosophical unity needed to form a true regional consensus for dealing with Indians or much else except perhaps its strong hostility for federal controls. At best a kind of loose unity in economic and political matters has existed. In addition, the region's geographic diversities, its uneven economic development, and the marked differences in Indian cultures and reservation conditions frustrate any regional consensus. In more recent times, significant shifts in western public opinion and politics regarding Indians seems apparent. Instead of the traditional hostility toward Indians, some westerners since the mid-1950s have demonstrated considerable sympathy and concern. Indians have also learned how to manipulate the system. These changes doubtlessly account for the recent willingness of some western politicians to support Indian causes.

Federal intervention in such important areas as land reclamation, conservation, creation and operation of national parks and forests, regulation of grazing, and development of natural resources has been significant in the West because the region lacked capital and so much of it remains public domain. Such federal programs have also influenced Indian affairs in many ways. While western vested interests have usually dominated federal programs, both whites and Indians frequently found themselves helpless be-

fore the dictates of Washington officials. Because of the Indians' dependence on the Bureau of Indian Affairs, their fate was often determined by
the outcome of interagency battles, both within the Department of Interior
and between that department and other government agencies. Again, the
point is not to deny that important connections existed between Indian affairs and western development but to suggest that complexities preclude a
simple thesis.

A second basic goal of the study is simply to present a reasonably balanced and objective summary of twentieth-century Indian history. I would
not suggest that the results are definitive in any sense, but hopefully I have
provided an overview that captures the main elements of the subject and
points to needs that future scholars can address.

When I first undertook this study, I hoped to complete a synthesis of existing writings, but that has not been entirely possible. Previous publications on the subject do not always permit such a treatment. Much of the
historiography on Indians has centered on the 1920s and the New Deal periods because of the keen interest in John Collier's reform efforts. With few
exceptions, mainly tribal histories and general policy studies, historians
have usually slighted other periods. They have particularly neglected the
first two decades of the century. No one, for example, has completed a detailed assessment of the impact of progressive reforms on Indian affairs,
yet several books have been devoted to Collier's reforms. The coverage of
the period after World War II is somewhat fuller because a few younger
scholars have completed studies on termination and relocation policies of
the 1950s. Unfortunately, the literature on the period since the rise of the
Red Power Movement of the 1960s has tended toward polemics more than
objective studies. While an impressive body of scholarship on twentieth-
century topics has been produced during the past two or three decades, the
overall picture remains somewhat sketchy. My solution has been to syn-
thesize where possible and to fill the important gaps with my own research.

For the purposes of this study, the geographic limits of the American
West rest on political boundaries and start with the eastern borders of the
plains states—the Dakotas, Nebraska, Kansas, and Oklahoma. Texas can
be excluded from the "Indian West" because it contained no significant
population of Indians after 1900. Of the sixteen remaining western states,
Kansas, Nebraska, and Colorado have contained relatively small Indian
populations during most of the twentieth century. One, however, has to be
somewhat flexible in defining such matters since World War II because of
the shift of Indians from reservations to urban centers. Texas and Colorado, for example, now contain larger Indian populations because of urban
migration.

One of the overriding themes of twentieth-century western history has
been regional economic development. The West in 1900 was still underdeveloped by any standard. Three of the present sixteen western states,

Oklahoma, New Mexico, and Arizona, were still territories. In terms of agricultural production, even California, Kansas, and Nebraska lagged far behind the corn belt in agricultural production. The value of farm products for California, now the highest in the nation, was $131,690,606 in 1899 compared to Iowa farm production which totaled $365,411,528. The figures for six other western states and territories—Arizona, Idaho, Nevada, New Mexico, Utah, and Wyoming—reveal even greater disparities.

Manufacturing in the West lagged even further behind older states in the number of firms, in the amounts of employment, in the value of products, and in the level of technology. Despite the much heralded completion of railroad trunk lines through the West before 1900, the transportation system was still incomplete in many areas, and marketing would remain a critical problem until the completion of highways. Population density of western states and territories offers still another illustration of regional underdevelopment. The density ranged from a low of 0.4 persons per square mile in Nevada to a high of l8.0 in Kansas. These figures compare to a national average of 25.6 people per square mile.[1] Given these conditions, it is little wonder that the West was economically and politically subservient to the East.

The undeveloped state of the West in no way meant that regional leaders lacked confidence in future progress. Indeed, the settlement boom that started before the Civil War continued at a high level. All of the western states and territories in 1900 had experienced population growth of 50 to 90 percent during the previous decade and most were at the upper level. Western leaders saw unlimited potential in the future growth of settlement, exploitation of resources, and, above all, irrigated farming. All that was needed to realize full prosperity, regional spokesmen asserted, was for the West to escape the domination and restrictions imposed by eastern financial interests. Attitudes such as confidence in the future, the desire for economic growth, and active resentment against eastern exploitation had already become ingrained by 1900 and would affect how Indians were treated.

Indian population in the western states and territories was quite uneven according to the 1900 census. A few states and territories contained the bulk of Indians:[2]

Arizona Territory	26,480
California	15,377
Colorado	1,437
Idaho	4,226
Indian Territory	52,500
Kansas	2,130
Montana	11,343
Nebraska	3,322
Nevada	5,216
New Mexico Territory	13,144

North Dakota	6,968
Oklahoma Territory	11,945
Oregon	4,951
South Dakota	20,225
Utah	2,623
Washington	10,039
Wyoming	1,686

Except that Indians of the West overwhelmingly lived on reservations, their conditions in 1900 varied greatly. Part of the diversity resulted from marked cultural differences. The plains tribes differed from the woodland groups brought to the West during the 1830s. Similarly, the Pueblos' culture contrasted with the desert Indians who shared residence in the Southwest. In California and Nevada many small bands lived in rancherias and colonies or had been pushed into remote areas as landless squatters. The Indians of the Pacific Northwest had once enjoyed a prosperity based on fishing and hunting, but most had been been removed to small reservations by treaties in the 1850s. Their makeup and settlements, especially in the Puget Sound area, were little less complex than those in California and Nevada.

Legal differences also contributed to the diversity of western Indians. Past treaties and federal legislation aimed at specific reservations contained provisions that created major differences between Indian groups. State jurisdiction over Indians varied too because of enabling acts approved at the time of statehood. Such differences became more pronounced with the admission of Oklahoma in 1907 because of special stipulations made during its admission as a state. Increasingly in the twentieth century, Indians and western states clashed over such complex questions as taxation, law enforcement, voting rights, fish and game regulations, and eligibility to share in education and social programs.

This book has been a "cooperative venture" in which numerous people have had a hand. Chief among these has been Martin Ridge. His combination of good humor, encouragement, insightful comments, solid copyediting, and suggestions for cuts have significantly improved the final product. He has, indeed, been the ideal series editor. Richmond Clow has also been helpful in researching the more recent period. He provided newspaper clippings and other materials collected for his class on contemporary Indian affairs at the University of Montana and supplied important leads to further research. Richmond also read and commented on the final three chapters. I benefited from his knowledge of recent history and from our lengthy phone calls and conversations at conferences.

Donald J. Berthrong, a colleague at Purdue University until his retirement two years ago and a longtime friend, provided assistance in ways that he may not fully realize. He has heard a good deal of the book's content during my mid-afternoon breaks from the library, and it was very helpful to have daily access to someone with his knowledge and sound insights as my research and writing progressed. More directly, he suggested sources and allowed me to use the materials that he had collected from western Oklahoma newspapers for the World War I period.

The graduate students at Purdue have also been major contributors. Peter Booth, Danny Rowe, and Jason Tetzloff read several of the early chapters, and our informal sessions proved that criticisms can flow in both directions. While serving as my teaching assistant, Jason Tetzloff helped check the citations and bibliography. I am grateful that I could tap his expertise as a former newspaper photographer in locating and selecting the pictures that appear in the book. Peter Booth and Kasshawna Blamer both found photographs for the book while they were researching in western manuscript collections. Paul Burch provided a sounding board and made suggestions as the book progressed. Thomas Cowger's earlier work on the Klamaths and his preparation of a dissertation on the National Congress of American Indians proved very helpful at several points. The same was true of Grace Gouveia, who is completing a dissertation on the role of Indian women during World War II. I particularly appreciate the collegiate spirit that has prevailed among the graduate students in Indian history at Purdue during the program's relatively brief existence. I suspect that I have learned far more from the graduate students during seminars and informal contacts than I have conveyed to them.

Robert Kvasnicka of the National Archives helped in the early stages to find records that filled gaps in the secondary literature and answered several reference questions. David Brugge, now retired from the National Park Service, responded to several queries. John Aubrey at the Newberry Library reaffirmed his reputation as a master bibliographer in all things dealing with Indian history. All three are valued friends. The staffs at the Harry S. Truman and Dwight D. Eisenhower Libraries were helpful during my research trips to Abilene and Independence. The reference librarians at Purdue were important in checking citations and names.

Thomas Biolsi, now at Portland State University, generously let me read his dissertation on New Deal tribal politics on the Rosebud and Pine Ridge Reservations while it was still under preparation at Columbia University. Dorothy Parker, former graduate student at the University of New Mexico and now at Eastern New Mexico University, sent me an excerpt from her dissertation on D'Arcy McNickle. Alison Bernstein read my chapter on World War II, and I profited from her dissertation on the subject.

Two grants relieved me from classroom duties and materially hastened the completion of the book. The first was a Senior Ford Foundation Fellowship at the D'Arcy McNickle Center for the History of the American Indian at the Newberry Library. I relished the opportunity to meet such scholars as Denys Delage, Matthew Dennis, and Howard Harrod and to attend seminars and lecture presentations by historians and other specialists. Frederick Hoxie, director of the center, and Jay Miller, then assistant director, made my stay thoroughly enjoyable. In many ways my stay at the New-berry was like a return to graduate school, but without the pain of prelim-inary exams, language requirements, and dissertation. The other grant was from the Center for Humanistic Studies at Purdue. Although the center has no building, no research collections, nor, amazingly, any administrative staff, it has been enormously successful in helping faculty members like me pursue their research projects. John Contreni, head of the history depart-ment at Purdue, was supportive in working out the details and timing of the fellowships and combining them with a sabbatical. Joyce Good, the de-partment's administrative assistant, was able to penetrate the formidable maze of Purdue regulations and procedures and make the necessary ar-rangements. Like many of my colleagues, I benefited from her compe-tence, diligence, and loyalty.

Finally, I would like to express my appreciation to Nadyne, my marriage partner for over forty years. Although she was less directly involved in the preparation of this book than some of my earlier publications, she played a major role by being supportive, by gently prodding me on, and by reliev-ing me of various responsibilities. Most of all, she assumed the role of "his-torian's widow" during research trips and the fellowship at the Newberry and tolerated my cantankerous moods.

Indians and the American West in the Twentieth Century

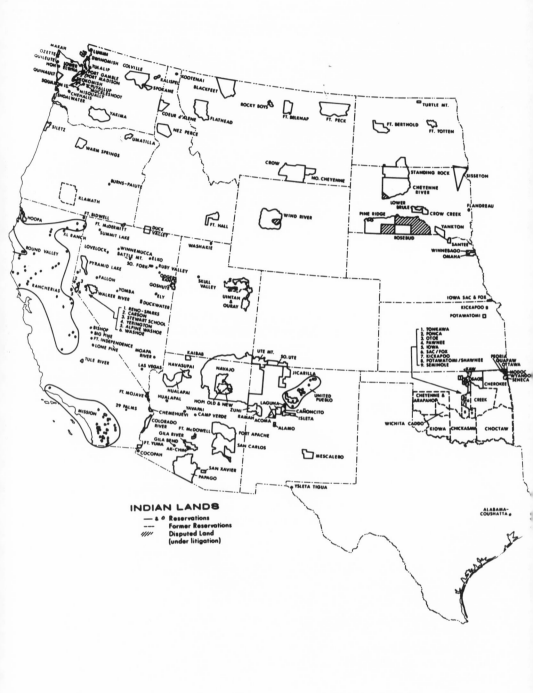

INDIAN LANDS
— & ᵒ Reservations
- - -   Former Reservations
///// Disputed Land
       (under litigation)

1.

The Heritage of Severalty

Without question the most important factor affecting Indians in 1900 was the 1887 Dawes Act. This legislation and later amendments instituted severalty or the distribution of tribally owned reservation land to individual Indians. Land allotment, however, embodied more than property rights. The architects of the policy aimed at broader goals, such as destroying tribal authority, eradicating native religions, and changing Indians into farmers. In short, severalty sought a complete transformation of Indian life.

In a sense, the Dawes Act offered little that was new. From the start, federal policy had been directed toward converting Indians from hunters to farmers and to a general acceptance of other aspects of white life. Tribal autonomy suffered a severe blow in 1871 when Congress prohibited future treaties with Indians. Reformers and federal officials repeatedly advocated severalty as the next logical step, but the general allotment bills introduced into Congress after 1879 failed to pass. Several tribes, however, had undergone allotment as a result of special federal enactments, and approximately 11,000 allotments existed prior to 1885. The importance of the Dawes Act, hence, was not that it embodied a new policy, but that it permitted individual assignment of lands on all reservations except for the Five Civilized Tribes (Cherokees, Creeks, Choctaws, Chickasaws, and Seminoles) and a few groups in Indian Territory, Nebraska, and New York.

The provisions of the Dawes Act authorized the president to allot any reservation considered suited to agriculture or grazing. Lands were to be distributed to all enrolled Indians: 160 acres to heads of families; 80 acres to single individuals over eighteen and to orphans; and 40 acres to unmarried persons under eighteen. These amounts could be doubled on reservations suited only to grazing. To guard against the sale of allotments, a common problem in earlier severalty experiences, the legislation placed the individual assignments under federal trust for twenty-five years. This meant that the allotments could not be encumbered, and courts later held that trust lands could not be taxed until patented in fee simple. The act, however, conferred immediate citizenship on adult allottees and made them subject to state and territorial laws.[1]

For white westerners, the most important result of the new legislation involved the surplus Indian lands remaining after allotment. The secretary of interior was authorized to negotiate a sale of such holdings with the allotted tribes. Although such transactions were supposedly voluntary, few tribes succeeded in retaining surplus lands if pressured to sell. The funds derived from the sales of such lands went into the national treasury for the benefit of the tribes involved. The money could be used for education and other civilization efforts, but it could only be appropriated by Congress. The land itself returned to the government for sale to "actual settlers."

Although access to surplus lands would seem to indicate a western role in passage of the Dawes Act, such was not the case. Senator Henry L. Dawes, sponsor of the measure and chairman of the Senate Indian Affairs Committee, was from Massachusetts, and the various Indian reform groups and leaders who had inspired earlier severalty bills, designed and lobbied the final measure to enactment. The role westerners played, if any, was indirect. Based on their knowledge that Indians who previously received fee simple titles to land had invariably sold their holdings to local whites at grossly low prices, the reformers inserted the trust provision. Even more important, the same spokesmen argued that western interests might entirely do away with reservations, dispossessing Indians of all their land. Allotment, according to the reformers, was a protective measure that would preserve adequate holdings for Indians to earn a livelihood. There is little evidence of any bargain in 1887 between the eastern advocates of severalty and land-hungry westerners lusting to open up reservations. Blaming the West for the Dawes Act grew out of the aftermath of 1887 when westerners took advantage of the legislation and its amendments to secure Indian land and resources.

One reason why the West failed to play a greater role in the Dawes Act was that it simply did not have much political influence in 1887. In the two decades after the Civil War, only two territories, Nebraska (1867) and Colorado (1876), gained statehood. A congressional deadlock prevented further admissions until 1889-1890 when South Dakota, North Dakota, Montana, Washington, Idaho, and Wyoming attained statehood. Utah became a state in 1896; Arizona, New Mexico, and Oklahoma won admission in the early twentieth century.[2] Even in the 1890s, Indian affairs remained secondary to much more pressing regional needs such as finding marketing outlets, competing with mass-produced goods of the East, and, most importantly, dealing with the economic and political turmoil after the panic of 1893. Only after 1900 with the admission of Oklahoma, New Mexico, and Arizona did western congressional delegations begin to dominate Indian affairs, irrigation, hydroelectric power, and the disposition of natural resources in the public domain.

Ironically, Colorado Senator H. M. Teller offered the chief criticism of severalty. In the only floor debate on severalty legislation, Teller in 1881 denounced allotment and warned that "in thirty years thereafter there will not be an Indian on the continent, or there will be very few at least, that will have any land." He further warned that severalty was "in the interest of the men who are clutching up this land, but not in the interest of the Indians at all. . . ." He accurately predicted "that when thirty or forty years shall have passed and these Indians shall have parted with their title, they will curse the hand that was raised professedly in their defense to secure this kind of legislation. . . ."[3]

The results of allotment more than realized Teller's dark predictions. Eastern advocates of severalty confidently anticipated that making Indians citizens and converting them to farming would solve existing reservation problems and, indeed, do away with the Bureau of Indian Affairs (BIA). Moreover, the most ardent reformers saw no real need to monitor the progress of allotment because, in their view, the legislation was self-fulfilling. Indians blessed with citizenship, they predicted, could protect all of their legal interests in white courts. In addition, education in English, conversion to Christianity, and acceptance of white standards of conduct and morality would sever the Indians' ties with their "savage heritage" and allow them to take their place in American society.

Only a small minority of observers cautioned against implementing allotment too quickly and stressed the Indians' need for practical education and assistance. BIA expenditures of the period show that Congress gave little heed to such needs. In 1884 it approved $25,000 for hiring more government farmers on reservations. The figure gradually rose to $70,000 in 1891 but fell to $65,000 five years later. In 1897 only 272 government farmers ministered to 185,790 Indians, exclusive of the Five Civilized Tribes. A similar pattern developed in federal expenditures for seeds, farm machinery, livestock, and draft animals. Although the allottees could not encumber land under trust, and practically none had any capital, Congress appropriated only $30,000 for agricultural aid in 1888. This figure represented less than ten dollars for every allotment made during that year.[4]

Most reformers seemed untroubled by such federal frugality and pinned their hopes on the education of the younger generation. Such idealists saw the twenty-five-year trust period as enough time for present adults to pass on and a new generation of educated Indians to assume control over allotments. In line with this idea, the reformers applauded the appointment of Thomas J. Morgan as Indian commissioner in 1889. The dynamic Morgan soon outlined a new educational program which stressed a standardized curriculum, compulsory attendance, and training in citizenship and Christian morality. His program, essentially the same schooling provided for white youngsters, gave little attention to practical education, especially for adult Indians.[5]

The actual allotment of Indian land increased steadily. In 1888 the BIA approved 3,349 allotments, but within four years the annual rate rose to

8,704. During the remainder of the 1890s, the figures declined somewhat, but in 1900 the government made 8,752 assignments. Somewhat surprisingly, allotment figures, although varying from year to year, remained generally high. As late as the early 1920s, for example, the annual rate stood at around 6,000 allotments. The figures are even more impressive considering the cumbersome nature of the allotment process. It involved appointment of a special allotting agent, survey of allotment boundaries, preparation of a tribal roll, assignment of individuals to the lands, and negotiations for the surplus lands. Completion of allotment often took several years.[6]

If western interests had no direct voice in passage of the Dawes Act, they nonetheless greatly influenced the conduct of allotment both before and after 1887. The quality of lands and density of white settlement were decisive in determining when allotment took place. The Santee Sioux, Winnebago, and Omaha lands in eastern Nebraska, for example, were located where rainfall rates were high and white settlement was already dense by the 1880s. Allotment of these reservations actually preceded the Dawes Act. Other reservations located in the eastern half of the northern plains, such as Devil's Lake, Sisseton, and Yankton, underwent severalty between 1887 and 1900.[7] Allotment of Indian lands in the western plains, where settlement was relatively slow and the land less arable, took place after 1900. White settlement doubtlessly created political pressures to implement allotment. Local settlers and leaders obviously wanted allotment agents friendly to their interests who would accomplish the process quickly so as to make the surplus lands available. Allotment personnel were urged not to give all the good land to Indians, so some choice holdings would be available to whites.[8]

Even though allotment progressed too rapidly for Indians to adjust to individual ownership or for the government to provide education and capital needs, the pace never satisfied whites. As a result, special legislation and agreements with individual tribes were used frequently after 1887 to open up reservations. Indian groups sometimes surrendered existing lands and moved to new reservations.

Several reservations never underwent severalty, or, if allotted, the Indians were never assigned. The reservations, however, were invariably isolated and of poor quality. The aridity of the Southwest and the Great Basin, in particular, forced even the strongest advocates of severalty to forego allotment. Thus the Navajos, various Ute groups, and other reservations escaped severalty, but those tribes with valuable agricultural or grazing lands were always allotted.

A significant 1891 revision of the Dawes Act permitted the leasing of allotments.[9] The circumstances behind leasing paralleled those of the Dawes Act. Western interests were not responsible for the new measure, but eastern reformers supported leasing because, in their eyes, it would protect and aid Indian allottees. The leasing proposal, too, aroused no debate in

Congress. Once passed, however, western interests quickly took advantage of it.

The chief rationale for leasing was that it would permit the young, old, or handicapped who could not operate their allotments to derive some income. To guard against abuses, only the secretary of interior, not local agents, could approve leases; the same official was directed to issue regulations for handling rentals. The legislation restricted leases of grazing and agricultural lands to three years and mining property to ten years.[10]

Revisions in the 1891 act and administrative policies led to widespread leasing of allotments by 1900, negating reformers' hopes that Indians would be forced to farm their individual holdings. Two years after its passage, the Indian commissioner ordered that agents would be primarily responsible for recommending leases, and thus approvals by Washington became pro forma. The 1894 Indian Appropriation Act liberalized matters by authorizing leases "by reason of age, disability, or inability." The addition of "inability" obviously afforded agents wider discretion. The same legislation extended the period of leases of agricultural and grazing land to five years and those for business or mining to ten years. In 1897 Congress restored the original restrictions of 1891, but in 1900 it again liberalized leasing terms by reinserting "inability" and extending agricultural and grazing leases to five years. After approving only six leases the first two years after 1891, the practice grew rapidly. By 1900 2,500 leases existed.[11]

The rental of Indian lands after 1891 probably became the chief source of collusion between agency officials and local white interests. Many whites undoubtedly had developed a tradition for illicit leasing prior to 1891 and continued it after the government assumed control. Real estate syndicates on the Omaha and Winnebago Reservations in Nebraska reportedly controlled virtually all leasing by direct arrangements with Indian owners. One firm on the Winnebago Reservation allegedly leased 47,000 acres illegally for which it paid the Indians from 10 cents to 25 cents per acre and subsequently sublet to white farmers for one to two dollars per acre. The local agent tried to evict unauthorized whites from the two reservations in 1895, but despite fifty extra police and seventy rifles, he failed in the face of local resistance and a state court injunction. The real estate interests had united the community against the agent, in part by taking notes from white tenants and then selling these to area banks.[12]

While this example may be especially flagrant, it by no means exhausted the types of illicit white practices used to gain control of Indian lease land. Agents, clerks, government farmers, and other agency personnel were often charged with rental schemes either for themselves or in combination with private citizens. Because agency workers knew the status of allotments, as well as when leases expired, and could certify that a healthy Indian was physically incapacitated, they could readily manipulate rentals. Similarly, local officials could ignore a real estate company that was evading regulations which limited the number of leases a single person could hold by allowing "dummies" to rent numerous allotments which were sublet at much higher prices. Such techniques were applied to tribal holdings too. Because of their large scope, illicit arrangements for renting tribal grazing land were much more tempting to whites than even subleasing farming allotments. When inspectors periodically uncovered leasing scandals, agency personnel who were dismissed quite frequently found employment with the same bankers, ranchers, and realtors who had been party to the conspiracies.

In the 1890s, Indian affairs in present Oklahoma took a somewhat different course because of historical factors.[13] Of the estimated sixty-seven tribes or tribal remnants who lived in the area in 1900, only a handful could claim residence prior to white contact.[14] From the 1830s until 1866, the general area had been set aside as Indian Territory for the exclusive use of the Five Civilized Tribes. Historians are rightfully suspicious of "golden ages," but that term is accurate when applied to the Five Civilized Tribes until the Civil War. Free from white settlement pressures, the Indians enjoyed an abundance of land that was held in common with fee simple tribal titles guaranteed by removal treaties. They enjoyed self-government with minimal federal interference.[15] The tribal governments developed after removal closely resembled those at state and federal levels with written constitutions and legislative, executive, and judicial branches. Although many full bloods maintained a traditional life, a variety of schools, supported by the tribes and missionaries, provided educational opportunities for many youngsters and became special objects of tribal pride.

The transition from a "golden age" to severalty and a loss of sovereignty by 1902 involved a long and complex set of changes created by war, federal legislation, reform agitation, and white economic pressures. The Civil War itself devastated tribal prosperity and intensified factionalism. Moreover, to punish the Five Civilized Tribes for their support of the Confederacy during the war, Indian Commissioner Dennis N. Cooley in 1865 announced to the Indian delegates gathered at Fort Smith that they had forfeited all rights guaranteed by earlier treaties, must abolish slavery and provide homes for former freedmen, and would henceforth come under a consolidated territorial government under close federal control. Convinced that such actions were illegal violations of treaty rights, tribal representatives stubbornly resisted Cooley's proposals for three weeks. Federal officials then ended the negotiations and scheduled a second meeting in the national capital in early 1866.

The final treaties concluded in Washington partly realized Cooley's initial harsh demands. Although the Cherokees retained the "Outlet," a sixty-mile-wide strip of land which ran east and west along the southern border of Kansas, they had to permit the settlement of other tribes in the area. The Seminoles were compelled to relinquish their previous land at 15 cents an acre and then to purchase a new reservation from the Creeks at 50 cents per acre. The Choctaws and Chickasaws received $300,000 for the "Leased District," a 7,000,000 acre plot between the 98th and 100th meridians. In addition to the loss of approximately the western half of Indian Territory, the 1866 treaties required the Five Civilized Tribes to grant two railroad right-of-ways across their remaining lands and to accept the future establishment of federal courts.[16]

Federal authorities wasted little time in finding uses for the vast cessions. The Treaty of Medicine Lodge in 1867 established three large reservations in western Oklahoma for the Cheyennes, Arapahos, Kiowas, Comanches, Caddos, and Wichitas. Other negotiations in the period provided reservations for the Kaws, Osages, Pawnees, Iowas, Sac and Foxes, Kickapoos, Pottawatomies, and Shawnees, who took up land between the plains groups and the area that the Five Civilized Tribes occupied.

Because of the significant cultural, legal, and geographical differences that marked Indian Territory reservations after 1866, federal administration varied considerably. The plains tribes to the west endured the general policies of the BIA. This meant that agency staffs permitted little or no self-government. The smaller groups living in the central area sometimes retained at least vestiges of tribal independence. The Osages, for example, in the early 1880s adopted a constitution with a legislative council, principal chief, and a supreme court patterned after Cherokee government. The Five Civilized Tribes, even after the treaties of 1866, retained tribal governments and common land title, but they faced an uncertain relationship with the federal government. The Dawes Act added more variations. Section 8 excluded the Five Civilized Tribes as well as the Osages, Miamis and Peorias, and Sac and Foxes, but allotment applied to all other groups.

The postwar period witnessed numerous additional challenges to the autonomy of the Five Civilized Tribes. The construction of railroads through their lands created towns, brought in white workers, and raised controversies over the railroad builders' use of timber and stone without paying for it or attempting to avoid full compensation. Tribal sovereignty received an especially serious blow in 1882 when Congress unilaterally granted the Frisco Railroad a right-of-way across Choctaw lands.[17] Federal officials allowed other white interests to enter Indian Territory to mine coal, cut lumber, farm, or graze cattle. Although the whites' attitudes and behavior varied, all sought to evade what they regarded as capricious regulations by tribal governments and federal officials. Railroads, in particular, sought to end the special status of Indian Territory and supported legislation which would place the area under territorial laws leading to statehood. Fifty bills for that purpose were introduced in Congress between 1866 and 1876 alone.[18]

By the 1880s the "pragmatic weight of numbers" threatened the final extinction of the sovereignty of the Five Civilized Tribes and the opening of Indian Territory to white settlement. Indeed, many non-Indians had already moved in. Some worked on railroads, others had married into tribes and were placed on the rolls, many rented farm land or worked for Indians, and still others were squatters. The main popular pressures for opening the area, however, came from prospective settlers and townsite developers in the adjoining states of Kansas, Missouri, Arkansas, and Texas. As much as farmers criticized railroads in the period, these "boomers" held no qualms about cooperating with railroad officials in demanding such an opening. David Payne, the colorful leader who repeatedly "invaded" the unassigned land with fellow boomers, reportedly received funds and backing from railroad interests.[19] Support for opening Indian Territory extended beyond the border areas of adjoining states and included newspaper and mercantile interests as far away as Kansas City and St. Louis. The latter, like the railroads, obviously saw great commercial potential in such an opening.

The example of the Dawes Act played a decisive role in ending Indian Territory.[20] In early 1889 Congress approved measures which awarded the Creeks $2,280,000 and the Seminoles $1,912,000 for relinquishment of their claims to the unassigned lands, and later the same year, the "89ers" made their famous run to occupy the area. The next year all the area west of the Five Civilized Tribes was organized as Oklahoma Territory and subsequently came under federal territorial jurisdiction. Four additional runs took place between 1891 and 1895 after more reservations were opened. All that remained was to impose severalty on the Five Civilized Tribes in Indian Territory and to dismantle their tribal governments.

The prospect of abrogating Indian Territory and merging it with Oklahoma Territory to achieve statehood united most eastern reformers and local whites. The two groups persuaded Congress to establish the Dawes Commission in 1893. Theoretically, the three-man body had only the power to negotiate with the Five Civilized Tribes, but it was given great discretion in making agreements to end Indian governments, institute severalty, and establish other procedures needed to achieve statehood.[21] Dawes, now retired from the Senate, acted as chairman, and Meredith H. Kidd of Indiana and Archibald S. McKinnon of Arkansas served as the other commissioners. To preserve their governments, tribal officials evaded, delayed, and resisted negotiations in the initial meetings. Incensed by such behavior, Dawes recommended that Congress simply overthrow existing treaties and terminate the tribal governments.[22]

When Dawes failed to get the needed legislation, he and other commissioners launched a publicity campaign that exaggerated the lack of legal protections for white residents of Indian Territory, the amount of violent crime, and the need to utilize untapped natural resources. Their statements were even more erroneous in depicting the poverty of full bloods pushed into the hills by a few wealthy Indians who enriched themselves by monopolizing the best lands. As one author observed, "unquestionably land hunger was the real motive behind most of the agitation to terminate the tribal regime, and a fairly good case could have been made out in the name of 'manifest destiny,' or in the right of the strong to dispossess seventy thousand easy-going Indians in favor of a million white people. . . ."[23]

Although the Five Civilized Tribes continued to resist negotiations, federal pressures forced their eventual surrender. In 1895 Congress authorized the Dawes Commission to survey the land, and the following year to draw up tribal rolls.[24] Fearful of harsh federal action, progressive Indian leaders then decided to treat with the commission, and all but the Cherokees drew up compacts. By 1898 the Seminoles had ratified an agreement, but the Creeks, Choctaws, and Chickasaws still resisted final approval. The 1898 Curtis Act terminated tribal land tenure without Indian consent, revised some of the previous agreements (but not that of the Seminoles), and laid out severe general provisions on such matters as enrollment, allotment, and land appraisal. To escape these punitive features, each of the Five Civilized Tribes by 1902 reached compacts or supplemental compacts, and the complex burden of administering enrollment, land distribution, tribal assets, and other matters came fully under the Department of Interior.

Severalty, whether brought about by the Dawes Act, special legislation, or the arrangements for the Five Civilized Tribes, created serious dislocations among nearly all Indians. Allotment was unsuited for many reservations which suffered from low rainfall and could never be farmed successfully. In such areas, especially the northern plains, the only hope for Indian self-sufficiency was large scale livestock grazing along communal lines, not in farming or family-sized ranches. The sale of surplus lands compounded the Indians' future problems. Despite the large size of many reservations and their low population densities, arid geographic conditions demanded the retention of all existing holdings for Indians to become self-sufficient. In addition, the actual assignment of land by allotting agents varied greatly, but procedures often served future needs badly. Accustomed to judging land quality by their own standards, many allottees, for example, selected plots along sheltered streams that were well suited for camp life but with little promise for farming.

The most striking feature of severalty was its contribution to the transfer of Indian land to whites in the final two decades of the nineteenth century. In 1881 the Indian estate amounted to 155,632,312 acres. By 1890 it had fallen to 104,314,349 acres and by 1900 to 77,865,373 acres. Not all of this decrease can be attributed to the Dawes Act and sales of surplus land, for the government also obtained Indian land through special legislation, agreements, and relocation. Regardless of the means, the staggering loss of land base fitted in with the severalty philosophy which demanded that the Indians make do with less land by reordering their traditional life.

Allotment was counterproductive as a means of encouraging Indian farming and ranching. Although reform propaganda emphasized that "closed" reservations obstructed progress, many Indians were making the adjustments necessary for successful agriculture prior to allotment. On thirty-three unallotted reservations, eighteen increased the acreage under cultivation over 10 percent annually and thirteen raised production levels over 10 percent. Because of allotment, Indian agriculture and ranching deteriorated after 1900, especially when compared to white operations in the same period. This strongly suggests that tribal ownership of land on closed reservations had never handicapped Indian farming and ranching, and might have been an appropriate means for Indians to adjust to reservation life.[25]

In sum, the philosophy of allotment was poorly conceived and implemented. It originated with eastern reformers who had little understanding of the western geographic, economic, and social environment and no concern for Indian traditions. The leasing legislation of 1891 sprang from the same idealistic and narrow impulses and created additional impoverishment for Indians. Once severalty and leasing became law, the reformers ignored the educational and financial needs of adult Indians. Instead they gave their attention to Americanizing the younger generation by providing formal education and destroying tribal authority. Although western economic interests had little direct role in either allotment or leasing legislation, they quickly took advantage of the new opportunities. In the dismantling of Indian Territory, western vested interests at several levels played a major part, but eastern reformers also lent their support. Despite the striking land losses and attendant problems facing Indians by 1900, the severalty philosophy remained unchallenged and would dictate the direction of Indian policy during the first two decades of the twentieth century.

2.
The Progressive Era, 1900-17

From 1900 to America's entry into World War I, important changes in the West affected Indians. One of these, the revival of settlement, increased pressures for Indian land. Another, the progressive reforms, affected westerners' perceptions about regional development and Indian matters. The West, however, took a very selective attitude toward progressivism. Regional leaders wanted no major obstacles that curtailed economic development, especially their access to Indian land and other resources.

During the early twentieth century, agriculture, ranching, mining, lumbering, and railroading continued to dominate the western economy. Similarly, the region specialized in the production of raw or semi-processed goods for outside markets. Despite sizeable railroad construction after 1900, transportation remained an obstacle to western development because of high costs and the incomplete internal transportation system. In short, the West remained a dependent region without a mature industrial base.

Nevertheless, population prior to 1910 increased sharply throughout all of the western states except Nevada, which experienced a loss. In large measure, irrigation and reclamation projects contributed to this rapid growth. But neither could increase the amount of water in the West, and battles over water rights became common. Because the federal government claimed total jurisdiction over reservation trust lands, legal conflicts with states over Indian water rights were inevitable, and court decisions became vital to Indian well-being.

The Indian was primarily a bystander, seldom a participant, often a victim, and rarely a beneficiary of the progressive reforms. While the western white community turned its attention to corporate abuses, government corruption, and efforts toward direct democracy, the Indian remained a voiceless outsider who had little role in determining his own fate. Indeed, as more western states were added to the Union, the influence of whites over Indian affairs increased, usually to the Indian's detriment.

Western influence received a major boost in 1901 when Theodore Roosevelt assumed the presidency. Roosevelt's experience as a Dakota

11

rancher and his participation in civil service reform exposed him to western problems and Indian administration and contributed to his presidential interests in western reclamation and conservation.[1] He also relied on his "Cowboy Cabinet" — Hamlin Garland, George Bird Grinnell, Charles Lummis, Frederic Remington, Owen Wister, and Francis E. Leupp. Except for Garland, the cabinet members were actually easterners acquainted with the West through visits.[2] Their lack of "born and raised" credentials never inhibited them from offering their ideas on Indian administration. Perhaps the major impact of the "Cowboy Cabinet" was its advice that the best approach to solving the Indian problem was to win the cooperation of white westerners. Leupp, as Roosevelt's Indian commissioner, 1904-1909, particularly sought to devise Indian policies that fitted in with westerner development.[3]

Western domination of Indian legislation and the Department of Interior that began during the Progressive Era had a far more lasting impact than Roosevelt's "Cowboy Cabinet." The addition of three new states with sizeable Indian populations, Oklahoma (1907), Arizona and New Mexico (1912), enhanced the western influence over Indian affairs. Oklahoma's role was particularly significant because its large population at statehood gave it five members in the House. Indian land and resources were inordinately important to the state, and its congressional delegation exercised extraordinary control over Indian legislation from the first.

Access to Indian land remained central to western interests. Allotment of reservations and opening of surplus land are most often associated with the 1890s, but the severalty program actually peaked during the first decade of the twentieth century, when western developers' publicity about dryland farming was widespread.[4]

Several congressional amendments to the General Allotment Act of 1887 made white acquisition of Indian land easier. A section in the Indian Appropriation Act of 1902, for example, dealt with the growing number of allottees who had died and whose land lay idle. The new legislation permitted the secretary of interior to remove trust restrictions and sell such holdings in behalf of adult heirs. The land of minor heirs could also be sold by guardians approved by "proper courts" and with the consent of the secretary.[5]

The Burke Act of 1906 amended the 1887 legislation by delaying citizenship for future allottees until the end of the twenty-five-year trust period. This legislation, however, permitted the secretary of interior to issue patents in fee and convey citizenship anytime during the trust period to individuals by issuing a "certificate of competency" to allottees deemed capable of managing their own affairs.[6] Little is known about the motivations behind the Burke Act except that Commissioner Leupp had serious misgivings about automatic citizenship and wanted some screening device to distinguish between allottees who needed trust protection and those who did not. Moreover, the Supreme Court in 1905 had ruled in the *Heff* decision that federal Indian liquor laws did not apply to allottees.[7] Leupp, alarmed about the ruling, wanted to maintain trust status over most allottees. Although his motive was to protect Indians against drinking, the administrative discretion to issue fee patents opened the way for future abuse.

Typical of progressivism, flexibility and administrative control also appeared in other legislation. The Indian Appropriation Act of 1907 permitted Indians under trust restrictions to sell portions of their allotments.[8] The purpose of the law was to allow allottees to gain sufficient capital to acquire machinery, livestock, and fencing needed to farm their remaining land. The following year Congress approved legislation that permitted Indians to petition the secretary of interior for the sale of all their trust land.[9] The rationale for the law—to allow the elderly, ill, or handicapped to convert allotments into needed cash—had merit, but its implementation demanded careful oversight.

The progressives' desire for administrative flexibility and control reached its zenith with the Omnibus Act of 1910, a lengthy statute that increased the secretary of interior's authority over probating Indians' trust property and allowed "competent" heirs unrestricted use of funds derived from the sale of inherited land.[10] The measure provided credit terms for white purchasers of heirship lands. Adult allottees could make wills and, while still alive, divide trust lands among their children. Because of the growing importance of irrigation, the new act authorized various sized allotments, depending on whether land was suited to irrigation, regular agriculture, or grazing. The secretary could also reserve power and reservoir sites for irrigation and other purposes. Finally, the act outlawed cutting, injuring, or destroying timber on trust lands and authorized the sale of timber on unallotted land under regulations devised by the Department of Interior.[11]

The general legislation of the period was not primarily the direct product of western political forces. Instead, the laws bore the stamp of the commissioner's office, especially during Leupp's administration, and they broadly reflected progressive philosophy by attempting to improve administrative efficiency, ending federal controls over certain categories of Indians, and expanding services in forestry, irrigation, and other areas. Much like the general allotment and leasing measures of the 1880s and 1890s, the new legislation opened up avenues for whites to obtain Indian land and resources. The enactments also greatly increased BIA authority over Indian property.

Westerners wasted little time in seizing the new opportunities for acquiring Indian land. In 1903 whites purchased 44,494 acres of heirship holdings, and the figure rose to 122,222 acres in 1904. From 1905 to 1911, annual sales averaged approximately 95,000 acres and then the average sales dropped to some 46,000 acres annually between 1912 to 1919.[12] The issuance of fee patents under the Burke Act also developed quickly, and in 1907 the Washington office received 881 applications for competency and approved 753. Within two years, however, BIA administrators recognized that local real estate interests were duping allottees into applying for competency and buying their allotments at bargain prices. The sellers generally squandered the funds quickly and became dependent upon relatives. The BIA then introduced more stringent regulations, which reduced the number of applicants and raised the percentage of disapprovals in 1909, but the danger of abuse remained.[13]

The West's influence on opening Indian land was primarily through congressional delegations' control over allotment of reservations and sale of the surplus land. The impression is often created that the executive branch alone implemented the allotment of reservations, but this is erroneous. Opening a reservation required ratification of an agreement and the appropriation of funds to carry out its terms, and these were congressional acts. Seldom were these vetoed. In addition, Congress could initiate its own legislation and disregard the procedures outlined in general allotment laws. Over thirty western reservations were affected by special allotment legislation between 1900 and 1910, and several were subject to more than one act.[14]

One case, *Lone Wolf* v. *Hitchcock* (1903), forcefully encouraged congressional intervention. The case involved an 1892 agreement between the Kiowas, Comanches, and Kiowa Apaches and a government commission to open a reservation in western Oklahoma and dispose of a huge tract of surplus land. Opposition by tribal leaders and their white allies at first blocked ratification, but in 1900 Congress not only approved the agreement but also unilaterally modified it, and refused to resubmit the changes to the Indians for approval as demanded by an 1868 treaty. The *Lone Wolf* ruling held that Congress had plenary authority over tribes and could alter treaty provisions without Indian consent. The decision probably did not establish a new legal precedent, but it informed western delegations that they could open reservations regardless of previous treaties or agreements. The ruling also gave the BIA added leverage in negotiating allotment agreements.[15]

The opening of the Flathead Reservation in western Montana in 1910 provides an excellent case study of western congressional influence over Indian land affairs. Representative Joseph M. Dixon skillfully manipulated the opening and used it to serve a network of business interests centered in Missoula, just south of the reservation, and to further his political career. Moreover, the 1,400,000 acre reservation offered varied and rich resources for potential exploitation by local whites.

The reservation's population was diverse and politically fragmented. According to a roll completed in May 1905, the Indians on the confederated reservation numbered only 2,133, divided among Pend Oreilles, Flatheads, Kutenais, Lower Pend Oreilles, Spokanes, and others. Over half were mixed bloods with the largest share descended from French fur traders.[16] Only one-fourth of the full bloods farmed or owned cattle, and most pursued traditional hunting and gathering. Some of the mixed bloods, however, owned large cattle herds and controlled the best lands.[17] The only factor uniting the Indians was their opposition to allotment.

Western Montana had experienced significant recent development. Missoula County, for example, grew from 2,537 residents in 1880 to 14,427 in 1890. The Northern Pacific Railroad, with Missoula as a divisional headquarters, attracted settlers, and James J. Hill in the early 1890s built a line west of Havre that brought more newcomers.[18] Montana politicians and newspaper editors repeatedly advocated opening reservations as vital to the state's future. This, they argued, would not only benefit whites, but it would also lead the Indians into a more "civilized" existence. Openings would, moreover, combat a practical problem. A Missoula newspaper in 1901 lamented that liberal land policies of nearby Canada were attracting settlers away from Montana.[19]

Dixon's opening of the Flathead Reservation demonstrated his mastery of politics at all levels. A North Carolinian, Dixon arrived in Missoula in 1891 and read law. He soon combined a lucrative legal practice, real estate interests, and ownership of a newspaper with a successful political career. Elected to the House of Representatives in 1902, he diligently cultivated Speaker Joseph Cannon for assignments to the public land and Indian affairs committees. He became one of Cannon's favorites and admonished the speaker and other Republican leaders that their party's future success in Montana depended on opening the Crow and Flathead Reservations.[20]

Dixon's network of family and business ties also favored the Flathead opening. A brother-in-law owned and operated a store on the reservation, and a sister-in-law was married to the secretary of Missoula Mercantile Company, who also served as a bank official and a member of Montana's Republican Central Committee. Dixon's close friend and business associate, C. H. McLeod, was vice president of Missoula Mercantile, which owned shares in a cattle company that rented winter pastures on the Flathead Reservation. Other Dixon ties were to a major Missoula bank and various real estate interests.[21]

The Confederated Flatheads received little BIA support against an opening. In 1897 William H. Smead became agent. A local resident and Republican stalwart, Smead two years earlier had sponsored a memorial in the Montana senate in behalf of an opening, and he advocated the same position as agent. There were serious allegations that Smead's grazing leases favored the Missoula Mercantile and that he ran his own livestock on reservation land. Dismissed after an investigation in 1904, Smead formed a real estate company in partnership with a former employee of the Missoula land office. The two produced a handsome promotional book extolling the potential of the Flathead Reservation and sold memberships to an organization that guaranteed to assist settlers select the best lands. Smead's successor also supported the Flathead opening.[22]

Dixon first worked to open part of the Crow Reservation because a strong lobby already existed in Billings and because he wanted to avoid charges that he favored western Montana. By adroitly trading votes and rallying local support, he secured House approval of the Crow bill in February 1904 and final enactment in April.[23]

In the midst of promoting the Crow bill, Dixon introduced legislation in December 1903 to open the Flathead Reservation. Given his rapport with Missoula business interests and the lack of effective Indian opposition, Dixon foresaw only one obstacle. He initially believed that the Indians had never approved allotment, and he feared that reform critics, despite the recent *Lone Wolf* decision, would block passage without Indian consent.[24] An attempt to win the support of key mixed bloods failed badly, but Dixon learned that the original Flathead treaty of 1855 contained provisions for allotment and sale of surplus lands. Armed with this, Dixon pushed the Flathead bill through the House without problem and then pressed Montana's two Democratic senators to support the bill. Dixon appeared before the Senate Indian Affairs Committee and secured the group's unanimous approval. The bill was signed on April 23, 1904.[25]

Although the Flathead episode received less attention in the national press than several more controversial openings, it demonstrates nearly all the major ingredients of local western influence over Indian affairs. Dixon's personal ambitions, his network of political, family, and business associations, and his energetic legislative work permitted him to open two major reservations in a single year. His successes were important in a state which regarded development as paramount. His return from Washington prompted a large rally, and he would in later years view the Flathead opening as "a particular accomplishment, an amalgam of moral principles and dedication to the interests of his constituents."[26] In addition, the episode illustrates the political impotence of Indians when, handicapped by factionalism and without allies or other means of opposition, they faced someone with Dixon's skills.

The pace of allotment slowed after 1910.[27] The white demand for land diminished because allotment during the previous thirty years had already given settlers access to the better Indian farming and grazing areas, and, except for irrigable land, the remaining unallotted reservations consisted of marginal or submarginal lands.[28] The emphasis after 1910 shifted toward leasing, purchasing heirship holdings, or freeing allotments from trust status.

The policy of "forced patents" became a major instrument during the second decade for white acquisition of Indian land. Robert Valentine, appointed commissioner in 1909, typified progressive thinking in his belief that Indians must "stand on their own two feet."[29] In addition, Valentine knew that the more capable Indians seldom applied for competency under the Burke Act. They recognized that citizenship meant paying taxes, potential confiscation of land because of bad debts, and the loss of government services. Valentine soon decided to force citizenship and fee simple titles on such Indians by a coercive application of the Burke Act. Instead of waiting for allottees to apply for competency, he decided to form special commissions that would visit reservations, determine which individuals were capable of ending their trust status, and issue fee patents to the competent.[30]

The first application of forced patents occurred in 1909 on the Omaha Reservation in eastern Nebraska. Local officials complained about the lack of taxable land because the Omaha and Winnebago Reservations took up nearly all of Thurston County, but earlier attempts at taxing allotments had failed. Moreover, the two tribes' lands were unusually valuable because dependable rainfall allowed high crop yields. What particularly attracted white interest in the Omahas, first allotted in 1884, was the expiration of the trust period and the issuance of fee patents scheduled for July 10, 1909. As that date approached, whites maneuvered many allottees into illegal sales agreements. These became so blatant that President William Howard Taft, at Valentine's request, ordered a ten-year extension of trust status, but with the understanding that the BIA would survey the tribe and issue fee patents to those deemed competent.[31] This amounted to a sop to appease those thwarted by the extension of trust status.

In October 1909, a three-man commission, consisting of the superintendent, a special agent, and a local resident, began screening the Omahas. The Indians supposedly appeared individually before the commissioners and answered seventy-five questions aimed at determining their competency. After five months, the evaluators classified the Omahas into three categories: fully competent who would receive fee patents; partially competent who could lease their land and control individual money but not gain full titles; and incompetent who would continue under trust status. Out of 605 Indians screened, 294 received full competency, and the BIA issued 244 patents in March 1910. Included were illiterates, others who had not been interviewed personally, and 107 who protested that they did not want fee patents.[32]

The commission obviously contributed to the frauds that followed. Impatient whites purchased allotments before the issuance of fee patents, and local merchants and bankers extended credit in the hope of getting land at bargain rates. One white acquired an allotment worth over $10,000 from an illiterate Indian woman who owed him $925. By the end of 1910, whites owned 60 to 75 percent of fee patented land.[33] Despite the Omaha fiasco, Valentine, in September 1910, dispatched a commission to the nearby Santee Reservation. Disturbed by reports that the commissioners had not examined individuals in person, Valentine ignored their report and returned to evaluating only those Indians who applied for competency. In 1912, he ordered a survey on the effects of fee patenting which confirmed his misgivings.[34]

Although the Omahas' grim experience gave ample warning about forced patenting, the policy was revived and accelerated during Woodrow

Wilson's presidency. This may reflect the increased influence of westerners in the new administration. Edward M. House of Texas served as Wilson's advisor for appointments from the West. He suggested Franklin K. Lane, a West Coast journalist and attorney as secretary of interior. Lane, in turn, named many westerners to top interior posts. These included Andrieus A. Jones of New Mexico as first assistant secretary—who supervised Indian affairs—and Cato Sells, a Texas banker and rancher, as the new Indian commissioner.[35]

Sells and Lane accelerated the issuance of fee patents immediately after taking office. This initially consisted of more liberal policies for processing competency applications, especially for mixed bloods whom Sells believed did not deserve trust protection. The following year, Lane received praise when he stated in his annual report that all competent Indians should be freed from trust.[36]

Certainly Sells knew the dangers in the forced patent policy. He requested the Omaha superintendent in late 1914 to report on the results of previous fee patenting. His unusually perceptive response traced the Omahas' transition from village farming to livestock raising and to modern agriculture. While they mastered barter and money exchanges in the first two stages, the report noted, they had failed to adjust to the credit economy of modern agriculture. The Omahas, he added, willingly mortgaged teams, implements, and crops to finance a feast or trip to another reservation and seemed oblivious of how they would repay the loans. Faced with the confiscation of personal property, they obtained a fee patent to their lands which they also mortgaged and eventually lost. He concluded that 13 percent of Omaha patentees had used their land well, 7 percent took care of money from land sales, and 80 percent lost everything. Other midwestern superintendents voiced similar concerns.[37]

Despite these warnings, Sells and Lane in 1915 revived forced patenting. Lane first broached the idea to Sells in 1914 and suggested the Flathead Reservation as an ideal starting point. Sells, endorsing Lane's suggestion, in 1915 named James McLaughlin, veteran inspector, and Frank A. Thackery, the Pima superintendent, as competency commissioners. The superintendent of each reservation visited served as the third commissioner. When the three met at an agency, they reviewed a list of prospects, interviewed the more likely at home, and then rendered decisions based largely on self-sufficiency and literacy. The names of those deemed competent were forwarded to Washington, and later fee patents were distributed to the Indians. The process was clearly involuntary, and when Indians refused to accept their patents, Lane ordered they be sent by registered mail.[38] Claiming success, Lane formed two additional commissions in 1916. By September, they had visited sixteen reservations and distributed fee patents on seven.[39] During fiscal 1916, the BIA issued 576 fee patents, which with 949 voluntary applications, covered 220,490 acres.[40]

But problems arose quickly. Lane received reports from the Yankton Reservation in South Dakota in May 1916, that whites, paying less than half market value, had illegally purchased allotments before Indians had fee title.[41] Lane himself visited Yankton in May to preside over a much publicized distribution of patents. Discovering that many patentees had already sold their land, he withdrew approval of twenty-five titles but still conducted the colorful three-hour ceremony.[42]

The squandering of sales money quickly followed. The *Washington Post* reported that the Yanktons purchased fifty new automobiles during a ten-day period.[43] A visitor from Milwaukee, incensed by widespread dissipation he had observed on the reservation, warned Lane that "schemers, sharpers, and bootleggers are fast getting the Indians['] land, [and] cheating and wronging them in every possible way."[44] Despite ample warnings, Lane continued the competency commissions.

The role of the West in the forced patent policy is somewhat ambiguous. Lane and Sells acted as the primary motivators, and the secretary took a personal interest in the competency commissions and insisted that they submit detailed weekly reports on their progress.[45] Local businessmen took advantage of Lane's policy. Representative Scott Ferris of Oklahoma, at the request of a constituent, asked the Indian office for a list of "competent Indians" at three agencies in western Oklahoma where commissions were scheduled to appear. When cold weather and bad roads slowed screening on the Yankton Reservation in January 1916, the BIA notified Lane that numerous congressmen, senators, and Indians had inquired about competency work. Lane ordered the commissioners to the Southwest, noting that "we cannot afford to waste time on this matter. . . ."[46] Westerners obviously welcomed forced patents because they "got Uncle Sam out of the Indian business" and provided access to the best remaining Indian land at bargain prices.

Somewhat surprisingly, BIA and interior department leaders sought to expand the Indian land base during the Progressive Era, either by allotting Indians on the public domain or securing land by executive orders. The best known example of adding land involved the Navajos in Arizona and New Mexico. When Navajos returned from exile in eastern New Mexico in 1868, their treaty provided a reservation of four million acres equally divided by the Arizona-New Mexico border.[47] The new reservation did not conform to Navajo land use, and many lived at off-reservation locations. An added complication developed when the government chartered the Atlantic and Pacific Railroad in 1866 with a land grant of forty sections of land per mile of right of way. When finally built in 1881, the line ran from Albuquerque through Gallup and westward south of the reservation. In typical fashion, the government gave the land in alternate sections (known as the checkerboard) to the south and to the east of the reservation. The checkerboard contained a sizeable portion of the tribe. The Navajo economy, meantime, underwent dramatic change when the railroad opened marketing outlets. Navajos' traditional herding subsistence became partially commercialized as tribesmen bartered lambs, wool, and other products for manufactured goods at trading posts. Livestock numbers rose because of this, resulting in an expansion of off-reservation grazing. In response, the government made several major extensions of the reservation by executive orders before 1900.

Frictions between Navajos and Spanish-Americans in the eastern checkerboard had been fairly commonplace after 1868, but after 1900 Anglo-American sheepmen began wintering large herds in the area. The Navajos were ill equipped to compete with the aggressive newcomers for grazing and water. The off-reservation residence of the Indians and lack of agency protections added to their problems. In 1905 white ranchers charged that Navajo sheep infected with scabies were spreading the pest to non-Indian herds.[48] The same year the New Mexico territorial legislature approved a memorial accusing the Navajos of taking all the water within twenty miles of their reservation, violating game laws, trespassing on the public domain, and stealing livestock.[49] The New Mexico livestock interests in 1906 unsuccessfully attempted to quarantine the Navajo Reservation because of scabies.

The BIA reactions to these problems were not totally effective. The government's dipping program against scabies was initially handicapped by shortages of funds, Navajo fears about the treatment, and long distances to dips. Within two years, however, the program successfully treated nearly all reservation and checkerboard herds, but complaints from whites continued. One Navajo superintendent who found no infestation on Navajo sheep in early 1907 angrily charged that white "agitation is for the purpose of driving the Navajos['] sheep onto the reservation to prevent them from using the grass and water off the reservation to which they are as entitled as the white people."[50]

To meet the Navajos' growing needs for land, the federal government continued to expand the reservation by executive orders. These included a large extension to the west in 1900, a smaller addition in the southwest in 1901, and a moderately sized extension in the south in 1907, as well as several minor additions and adjustments prior to 1917.[51] The government allotment of Navajos in the checkerboard started in 1906 after Commissioner Leupp visited the area. The allotments, never intended to promote agriculture, were aimed at giving Navajos the water holes and control of adjacent grazing land. In late 1907 President Roosevelt temporarily withdrew a huge area of public domain east of the reservation from entry while two allotment agents made assignments to 1,667 Indians.[52] By December 1908, the allotment of the eastern half of the withdrawn area was completed and the unallotted land was returned to public domain. President William Howard Taft restored the western portion in January 1911, but not all Indians had been allotted.

The Navajo allotments brought a vigorous response from New Mexico. Territorial Delegate W. H. Andrews in early 1908 forwarded letters and petitions from constituents who insisted that the Navajos did not need more land, decried the loss of tax revenues and stifling of development, and warned that reservation Indians would be given allotments. An unstated but likely cause of the protests was New Mexican hope for statehood and fear of losing more land to Indians. Despite repeated assurances that the 1907 extension was temporary, Andrews secured legislation in 1908 ordering a restoration after allotment.[53]

The Navajo allotments offered less than full protection. Surveyors mistakenly located Indians on railroad land; Navajos lost their allotment papers; illegal fences enclosed allotments; and whites commonly trespassed on Indian holdings. In at least one instance, county officials levied taxes on allottees' personal property. Perhaps the worst problem, however, was the General Land Office. Responding to white pressures, the Santa Fe office threatened to cancel numerous applications for allotments because Navajos failed to reside on their allotments and to meet other legal requirements. Although technically correct, the land office ignored the Indians' nomadic grazing habits and the equally illegal practices of whites.[54] Exactly how many Indian holdings were voided is unclear, but certainly the number was large.

To provide some protection to eastern Navajos, the BIA established the Pueblo Bonito agency in 1909 with Samuel F. Stacher as superintendent. As agency head without a reservation and burdened with endless squabbles, Stacher defended the local Indians' interests and tried to develop rapport with cooperative white ranchers. But he was frustrated by his inability to resolve the endless problems. Other Navajo superintendents faced the same dilemmas in the southern checkerboard.[55]

The attempts to secure more land for Navajos were not unique. Congress in 1910 permitted Indians living within national forests to be allotted if they were already residents.[56] The BIA established several small colonies in Nevada and California, usually in conjunction with irrigation projects, to provide for landless groups. Because the Turtle Mountain Reservation lacked sufficient land for allotment, some 650 adult males took public domain assignments in North Dakota and Montana after a 1904 agreement.[57] The largest acquisition, however, was the creation in 1916 of the two million acre Papago Reservation west of Tucson, Arizona. The executive order, however, made important concessions to mining and livestock interests.[58]

The government's efforts to add more lands by executive orders were blocked shortly after the creation of the Papago Reservation. In 1918 Interior officials began plans for an extension along the southern border of the Navajo Reservation. During a floor debate on the Indian appropriation bill in March, Senator Marcus A. Smith of Arizona proposed an amendment prohibiting additional executive order extensions in Arizona and New Mexico except by congressional authorization.[59] Bitterness about the new Papago Reservation and the prospective Navajo extension doubtless prompted Smith's action. With the support of Senator Henry Fountain

Ashurst, a fellow Democrat from Arizona and chairman of the Indian Affairs Committee, Smith won congressional approval for his amendment. The following year, Congress extended the ban to all states.[60] Although executive order lands did not fully meet Indian needs, they allowed the government to offer services and protections far greater than landless Indians enjoyed.

Perhaps no area of western Indian affairs better demonstrates progressive reform ideology and its failures than irrigation and Indian water rights. After 1867 Congress funded numerous specific projects, and in 1884 it first authorized a general appropriation of $50,000. General appropriations reached a peak of $335,000 in fiscal 1914-1916. The increases after the turn of the century undoubtedly demonstrated the progressives' interest in reclamation and Indian self-support. Starting in 1919, Congress returned to appropriating funds for specific projects.[61]

Early Indian reclamation was haphazard. Agents' limited expertise, poor engineering, and faulty materials resulted in numerous failures, reconstruction, and high maintenance costs. The BIA in 1899 employed two superintendents skilled in irrigation. Two years later the agency hired an irrigation engineer and seven inspectors to supervise construction.[62] During Leupp's administration, the BIA transferred control of projects on the Blackfeet, Fort Peck, Flathead, and Yuma Reservations to the Reclamation Service, but the cooperative arrangement ended early in the Taft administration.

Progressive leaders and westerners usually supported Indian irrigation. Reformers, belatedly recognizing the impossibility of farming in arid areas, saw irrigation as a marvelous opportunity to "civilize" Indians by converting them to agriculture. They hoped attracting white settlers to live in close proximity to Indians on or near reservations would also encourage their assimilation. Ironically, on reservations already surrounded by whites, reformers argued that irrigation projects would prevent settlers from monopolizing local resources. Much like allotment, however, westerners supported Indian irrigation as an aid to white development. New projects meant that Indians needed less land and that the surplus would become available to white settlers. Because irrigated allotments were generally subject to the same controls that governed regular allotments, they could be leased to whites, sold as heirship land, or patented in fee.[63]

The irrigation projects varied greatly. Some projects were small in size and involved minimal construction. Larger works demanded large reservoirs, complex distribution systems, and extensive maintenance. The more important projects were part of even larger off-reservation works. Irrigation on unallotted reservations were freed of many legal and practical problems that confronted projects on allotted reservations with mixed populations. Indians themselves reacted differently toward irrigation. The Pimas were already skilled irrigationists, but most groups were inexperienced and almost totally disinterested in their projects. For these, irrigation mainly afforded employment during construction, and white lessees normally farmed the land.

A major turning point in irrigation funding developed after 1905 with the authorization of a 45,000 acre project on the Wind River Reservation. In 1906 Congress approved the irrigation of a projected 200,000 acres on the Uintah Reservation and a major new development on the Yakima Reservation. Congress authorized projects on the Blackfeet and Flathead Reservations the following year. In all five instances, Congress provided no gratuitous funds but appropriated tribal funds derived from recent openings and sales of surplus land. The Indians, in effect, financed not only their own irrigation works but also subsidized white farmers who purchased the surplus lands.[64] Given these circumstances, it is easy to see why Congress favored the five projects.

Friction between white settlers and Indians over water rights arose at virtually every major project. The Pimas' water rights problems were probably the oldest and most complex of any tribe.[65] Many clashes arose during the 1905 drought. On the eve of the Uintah opening that year, several whites, who were already taking water from the Strawberry River, entered the reservation supposedly to clean and repair their canals but were accused of enlarging the outlets so they could increase their water quota after the opening.[66] On the Walker River Reservation, ranchers above an Indian project diverted all the water from a stream. More serious problems developed on the Yakima Reservation. Commissioner Leupp requested that a patrolman be hired because the whites in one area had constructed dams and taken all the water. Leupp mentioned that the local Indians "have been so terrorized by the white intruders that they dare not exert themselves and destroy those dams. . . ."[67] The same day Leupp asked that a U.S. attorney take action because unknown parties had destroyed a BIA dam on the Yakima River. A local irrigation company then received a temporary restraining order against Indians taking any water until a state court could determine which side held rights to the river.[68]

The basic problem for safeguarding Indian water rights was the BIA accedence to state water codes based on prior appropriation and beneficial use. Because of special conditions on reservations, especially tardiness in putting land into cultivation, Indians needed their own water code, but this was politically impossible. To gain some protection, the BIA filed water claims with state officials. As the time to demonstrate beneficial use approached, agency workers frequently leased irrigable land to whites to avoid cancellation of claims. But fulfilling state codes did not alleviate all problems. Interminable legal suits often arose in state courts, where Indians customarily fared poorly, and U.S. attorneys seldom defended Indian rights aggressively. Perhaps most importantly, the water conflicts, in effect, pitted the BIA against the Reclamation Service, and the latter agency's large constituency and influence gave it a decided advantage. Its star was rising while the BIA's influence was diminishing.

The 1908 landmark decision by the U.S. Supreme Court in *U.S.* v. *Winters* offered a potential setback to the state water codes, but the case produced limited results. The background circumstances typified many reservations. In 1888 the Gros Ventres and Assiniboins entered an agreement that created the Fort Belknap Reservation in northern Montana. The Milk River skirted the northern border of the reserve. White settlement followed, and both the Indians and upstream farmers and ranchers tapped the stream for irrigation. Because of increased white use and the severe drought in 1905, the Fort Belknap Indians had no water for their crops, and in June the superintendent appealed to Washington for "radical action."[69]

A response quickly followed. Within two weeks the Justice Department ordered the U.S. attorney in Montana, Carl Rausch, to defend the Indians. Rausch won a temporary injunction against the settlers from the federal district court in Helena. His bill of complaint asked that the Indians receive 11,000 miner's inches of water from the Milk River based on "prior use."[70] Somewhat ironically, Rausch's subsequent research revealed no clear evidence that an Indian claim had been filed or how much water they actually used. Moreover, Montana's water code permitted filing claims under either prior appropriation or riparian doctrines,[71] and Rausch decided to use a riparian water claim but added "other rights" to broaden his grounds. In late June, Judge William H. Hunt issued a temporary injunction against the white settlers' use of any water from the Milk River, but he soon modified his stance, allowing them any surplus above 11,000 inches.[72]

Rausch experienced new problems in preparing for the next hearing but still managed to win a permanent injunction. He learned that the Fort Belknap project diverted only 5,000 inches, not 11,000, and even worse, the settlers had a prior use claim well before any Indian application for water. Despite this, Judge Hunt granted a permanent injunction guaranteeing the Fort Belknap Reservation 5,000 inches. Although the 1888 agreement establishing the reservation made no direct reference to water rights, Hunt believed that an "implied right" to water existed. He based his opinion on the fact that the agreement called for Indians to become self-supporting through agriculture and that, given the arid conditions, they must enjoy sufficient water to farm. He added that the 5,000 inches was a minimum figure and might be raised in the future.[73]

Irate settlers appealed Hunt's decision to the Ninth Circuit Court of Appeals in San Francisco. The arguments remained the same except the plaintiffs' attorney attacked Hunt's "implied right" and maintained that the injunction would "lay waste to thousands and thousands of acres made fertile by the labor and expenditure of settlers, who had gone upon them under express authority from the government."[74] In unanimously rejecting the appeal, the court stressed the Indians' "reserved rights," which meant that they retained whatever rights they had not specifically given up in earlier treaties or agreements. The Gros Ventres and Assiniboins thus retained water rights because they had never ceded them.[75]

The Winters case in 1908 came before the U.S. Supreme Court which upheld the permanent injunction. The opinion did not vary significantly from earlier rulings, but it left unclear whether the Indians, the government, or both had reserved water rights. The issue was more than academic. If the Indians reserved water rights, then they held an indisputable legal position similar to the "right of occupancy." If the government reserved water rights, however, they existed only from the time that a reservation was created and would not have legal standing over claims non-Indians established earlier.[76]

Although the Winters ruling obviously strengthened Indian water rights, it is virtually impossible to generalize about its later impact except that it did not guarantee a "clear and unquestioned right to water." Certainly the decision did not abrogate state water codes on reservations. Agency officials continued to file claims with states after 1908, and, worried about beneficial use, they still leased irrigated land to whites. In the absence of a federal code for Indian water rights, the BIA was forced to initiate prolonged suits based on the Winters doctrine. Fort Belknap reflects the frustrations Indians experienced. The 5,000 miner's inches became the ceiling, but whites in the area increased their water supply many fold.[77]

The need for an Indian water code was obvious, but even a piecemeal effort in 1914 was defeated by strong western opposition. In June, a group of senators, headed by Carroll Page of Vermont and Joseph Robinson of Arkansas, proposed an amendment to the Indian appropriation bill to guarantee Indian water rights at Fort Hall regardless of the Idaho water code. Assistant Commissioner Edgar Meritt, Robinson's brother-in-law, undoubtedly inspired the amendment because he knew that some 90 percent of the water claims at Fort Hall would expire at the end of year.

During the ensuing debate, Senator William E. Borah of Idaho attacked the amendment as an illegal invasion of his state's jurisdiction, arguing that "white settlers of the State are entitled to have that water when no one else is using it." After the amendment was defeated, its supporters moved to strike $50,000 from the Fort Hall project because it would not benefit the Indians. Borah and his western allies responded angrily. Borah denounced the outside interference by "some clerk in the [Interior] department" and restored the appropriation. A later amendment to protect Indian water rights at the Flathead Reservation prompted equally hostile reactions but caught the westerners off guard and passed. When the Senate debated the conference committee's report in July, western figures killed the Flathead amendment by a vote of forty-five to seven.[78]

Western influence over Indian irrigation also appeared in provisions dealing with the financing of projects in the 1914 appropriation bill. Always reluctant to use gratuitous funds for Indian irrigation, Congress had charged project costs against tribal funds after 1905, but in 1914 it ordered that projects be financed by reimbursable loans charged to individual allottees. In other words, the government "loaned" the Indians money for projects and expected each user to pay back a share of the costs. Since Indians seldom requested irrigation, this amounted to forced indebtedness.

Despite sizeable appropriations for irrigation prior to World War I, the progressive hope that projects would lead to Indian self-support and assimilation seldom succeeded. Water rights had little bearing on the failures. Projects suffered because Indians proved indifferent or they lacked the capital and expertise that irrigation demanded. Some used irrigation to raise hay but not other crops. On the more important projects, such as Yakima, whites actually controlled most of the irrigated land, either by renting or acquiring title through various avenues. Based on how Indian irrigation was financed, it seems clear that Yakima and other important works were designed primarily for white settlers' benefit.

Management of Indian forest resources in the West was not a major aspect of the progressive era, but some developments had important consequences.[79] There were several reasons for the neglect of western timber resources. The BIA focused on Minnesota and Wisconsin at the turn of the century because the industry was better developed there, logging technology was well suited to local conditions, and marketing costs were relatively low. With few exceptions, logging on western reservations presented obstacles. Much of the timber was at higher elevations and on inaccessible terrain, which made it expensive to log. The lumber, once sawed, had to bear the high transportation costs to outside markets. In short, western timber resources suffered from typical regional handicaps.[80]

In addition, lumbering posed legal problems. Most of the early Indian timber contracts in Minnesota and Wisconsin were negotiated in the 1860s by tribal leaders, lumbermen, and agents without statutory authority.[81] In 1874 the Supreme Court ruled that Indians held only a right of occupancy to reservations and that the government, not the Indians, owned the timber.[82] Because of the graft in 1880s midwestern timber sales, Congress in 1889 ordered that only "dead and down" timber could be sold on either allotted or unallotted land.[83] Finally, the BIA lacked expertise for modern forestry management. A superintendent of logging, appointed in 1899, supervised sales, but he lacked training in conservation, fire protection, and scientific forestry techniques.

Anything resembling modern forestry management had to await the Leupp and Valentine administrations. Leupp and Valentine (then secretary to the commissioner) met Gifford Pinchot, head of the Forest Service, in January 1908, and negotiated an interagency agreement that gave Pinchot's agency control over timber management on several reservations. Pinchot claimed the arrangement "worked admirably." The corrupt and inept BIA had completely mismanaged Indian timber, but during the next eighteen months, according to Pinchot, the Forest Service instituted systematic cutting on thirteen reservations, fire control on six, and land-use surveys on eleven. Unfortunately, Secretary of Interior Richard A. Ballinger abrogated the agreement, claiming it lacked statutory authority.[84] Pinchot later used the cancellation as one of the major charges against Ballinger during the famous joint investigation of the secretary.

The cooperative agreement had not worked well. The fact that the BIA funded the forestry work but agency superintendents had no control over Pinchot's young foresters caused friction. Moreover, Forest Service workers overstepped the agreement by dealing with grazing and became angry over the lack of funds for fire protection. Perhaps most important, the zealous young foresters never adjusted to BIA trust roles such as operating tribal sawmills, using Indian labor, and dealing with the "dead and down" law.[85]

Commissioner Valentine decided to assemble a staff for a forestry division within the BIA, using a recent appropriation of $100,000. Among the first hired was J. P. Kinney, a graduate forester, who became the pioneer of modern BIA forestry management. The Omnibus Act of 1910 also provided badly needed authority for the sale of both dead and green timber. This not only encouraged better management but also, for the first time, gave Indians title to live timber. The same act permitted the sale of timber on trust allotments with the receipts credited to the allottees.[86] These efforts typified progressivism: timber should be used for Indian support and advancement, revenues from sales should bear administrative expenses, and the resource should be conserved through wise use.

In the summer of 1910, Kinney visited twelve western reservations to conduct surveys and devise methods for timber management. The allotment of timberland with no agricultural potential perplexed him. Scientific management was impossible on allotments, and Indians were invariably victimized by local timber buyers. He also objected to designating timber areas as surplus lands and opening them to settlement. White homesteaders, who had no intention of farming, simply sold the timber and left the area. Clear-cutting resulted. If stands could be kept intact, Kinney argued, controlled cutting would provide sizeable long-term income to the Indians.[87] Unfortunately, Congress never approved the necessary legislation.[88]

Administrative turmoil within the BIA hampered the forestry program. After serious organizational and staff problems, much delayed regulations won approval in 1911.[89] Finally in 1913 Commissioner Sells appointed Kinney as supervisor. He held the post for nearly two decades.

Kinney pursued a conservative approach to timber sales. He knew that his superiors favored large sales to defray reservation administrative costs, but he believed that weak demand and low prices warranted delay. Until World War I, when markets improved significantly, he made few sales. Demand was low even on the Klamath Reservation, where conditions were optimal. The Klamaths owned an estimated 8,000 million board feet of western yellow pine, a new branch of the Southern Pacific reached Klamath Falls, Oregon, in 1910, and rivers of the area permitted floating logs to sawmills. The forestry division made several sales between 1912 and 1917, but bids were at the minimum figure or slightly above.[90] Although differences in tree species make comparisons difficult, obviously stumpage prices in the West remained well below those of Wisconsin and Minnesota before 1917.

Although scientific forestry management first developed during the Progressive Era, Roosevelt and Pinchot's cavalier use of executive authority did not always operate in the Indians' interest. As the end of the Roosevelt administration approached, Pinchot became fearful that the incoming Taft administration would not continue his conservation programs, and he lobbied for major withdrawals of public lands with valuable natural resources. As part of these last minute efforts, Roosevelt issued eight proclamations which transferred some fifteen million acres of Indian timber on executive order reservations to adjacent national forests.[91] The sweeping withdrawals included practically all the marketable timber at Fort Apache, Mescalero, Jicarilla, San Carlos, Zuni, Hoopa Valley, and Tule River Reservations as well as considerable Navajo timber. The 1909 proclamations rested on a legal theory that could do enormous harm to Indians. Roosevelt's proclamations held that Indians had no legal claims to executive order lands and occupied them only at the sufferance of the president.[92] Roosevelt somewhat softened the impact by allowing Indian occupants to retain the income from the timber and Interior Department services for twenty-five years, but the Department of Agriculture held overall control. At the end of the twenty-five years, Indian residents lost all privileges unless they held allotments.

Although the legal status of executive order reservation land remained unsettled for many years, the proclamations were blatantly unfair to Indians. This was not another instance of private malfeasance, but a powerful federal agency arbitrarily taking control over a resource worth an estimated $23,000,000. J. P. Kinney, with characteristic understatement, noted that "the Indian Service was disposed to question the efficacy of the Executive Orders of March 2, 1909. . . ."[93] Fortunately, legal opinions by the Department of Agriculture and the attorney general's office in 1910 and 1911 led to executive orders in 1912 that returned the timber tracts to the Indians.[94]

In reviewing western development prior to World War I, western influence over Indian affairs sharply increased. Western congressional delegations may not have shaped the general Indian legislation, but, as Dixon did in the Flathead opening, they controlled the specific cases. Indeed, western senators and representatives demanded and received a veto over any Indian legislation that affected their state or district. In addition, western influence prevailed when men from the West headed the agencies in the Interior or Agriculture Departments. The establishment of the Reclamation Service in 1902 as a dynamic federal agency which encouraged western development initiated a trend which would grow in the future.

The impact of progressive reforms on Indian affairs was mixed. The commissioners of the period, starting with Leupp in 1905, tapped reform ideology by instituting scientific administration, offering more technical services in forestry and irrigation, implementing administration decentralization, and upgrading health and education; but their ultimate goals remained almost identical to the eastern reformers who designed and secured passage of the General Allotment Act of 1887. Captives of a white, Christian, and middle-class outlook, and unwilling to perceive a different cultural perspective, progressives sought the assimilation of the Indian as an ultimate goal. Even more than the older reformers, however, the progressive generation encouraged the removal of trust protections from Indians in a head-long drive for assimilation in such programs as forced patenting. Yet the BIA leadership after 1905 tried to protect Indians by providing more land by executive orders and by defending Indian water rights. But western congressional leaders abolished the future use of executive order land additions in 1919, and the passage of a much needed federal Indian water code proved politically impossible. Of all the shortcomings of progressives, certainly their greatest was their failure to preserve the Indians' land for future generations.

Blackfoot Indians, using "fresnos," at work on an irrigation canal on the Blackfoot Reservation in 1911. National Anthropological Archives, Smithsonian Institution, Negative 44,888.

Lone Wolf, seated on the left, accompanied by the Kiowa delegation that visited Washington in 1903 when the Supreme Court rendered its decision in *Lone Wolf* v. *Hitchcock*. National Anthropological Archives, Smithsonian Institution, Negative 1434-A.

Henry Roe Cloud, perhaps the best known Indian leader of his generation, served on the Meriam Commission and held other prominent positions during a long career. Federal Personnel Records Center, Henry Roe Cloud file.

Carlos Montezuma, a Yavapai and Chicago physician, strongly advocated assimilation and abolition of the Bureau of Indian Affairs until his death in 1923. National Anthropological Archives, Smithsonian Institution, Negative 53,534.

Jim Thorpe, a Sauk-Fox from Oklahoma and famous
Olympic and professional athlete in several sports, played
football at Carlisle Indian School. National Archives,
00000126.PCX.

A flag-raising ceremony staged by Joseph K. Dixon in 1913 at Otoe, Oklahoma, during a "Citizenship Expedition." Dixon Collection, Mathers Museum, Indiana University, Catalogue W 6338.

Oklahoma Choctaws serving in a special "Telephone Squad" transmitted in their own language during World War I, thereby reducing the risk that messages would be intercepted. The white officer on the right served as commanding officer. Dixon Collection, Mathers Museum, Indiana University, Catalogue W 6451.

James Black Hawk, a Cherokee from Bliss, Oklahoma, served as Fireman 2/C on the *U.S.S. North Dakota* during World War I. Dixon Collection, Mathers Museum, Indiana University, Catalogue W 6357.

Chief Plenty Coups, former Crow warrior, participated in the dedication of the Tomb of the Unknown Soldier in 1921. Dixon Collection, Mathers Museum, Indiana University, Catalogue W 7804.

John Collier, on the right, worked as an Indian reformer and Indian
Commissioner from the early 1920s to the 1950s to reshape Indian policy.
He poses here with Henry Taliman, a Navajo leader, in the 1930s.
Photograph from E. R. Fryer.

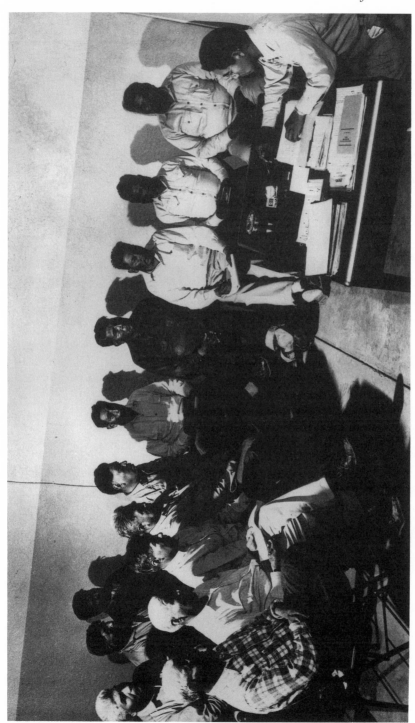

Thomas Segundo, a young veteran, presiding over the Papago Tribal Council shortly after World War II. Newcomer Collection, Arizona Historical Society/Tucson.

Navajo CCC-ID enrollees took part in the highly controversial roundup of surplus horses on the Navajo Reservation in the late 1930s. Photograph from E. R. Fryer.

Indicative of the greater tolerance for Indian culture and religion during the New Deal, Pete Price, noted Navajo medicine man, and colleagues participated in the dedication of a new government hospital at Fort Defiance, Arizona, in 1938. Photograph from E. R. Fryer.

Ira Hayes points to the famous photograph taken at Iwo Jima that propelled him into an unwanted hero status and his ill-fated participation in a war bond drive. United States Marine Corps (courtesy of Albert Hemingway).

This "Victory Dance" on the Pine Ridge Reservation in September 1945 was one of numerous similar ceremonies on western reservations after World War I and World War II. National Anthropological Archives, Smithsonian Institution, Negative 55,455.

Indians fishing with dip nets at Celilo Falls around 1942. Oregon Historical Society, Negative Or.45964.

Two Chinook Indians rest at Celilo Falls shortly before the last major Indian fishing site on the Columbia River was flooded by the construction of the Dalles Dam in the 1950s. Oregon Historical Society, Negative Or.55460.

Helen Peterson served as executive director of the National Congress of American Indians during the organization's struggle against termination. National Anthropological Archives, Smithsonian Institution, Helen Peterson Papers.

D'Arcy McNickle, Indian novelist, historian, and reformer, pursued a varied career inside and outside government from the New Deal until his death in 1977. National Anthropological Archives, Smithsonian Institution, Helen Peterson Papers.

Senator Arthur V. Watkins of Utah acted as the chief architect of termination and relocation policies during the Eisenhower administration. Senate Historical Office, Negative 5442-16A KLC.

Representative E. Y. Berry of South Dakota cooperated closely with Senator Watkins during the termination hearings in 1954. National Anthropological Archives, Smithsonian Institution, Helen Peterson Papers.

Charles Curtis, vice president during the Hoover administration, repeatedly told audiences that he was "one-eighth Kaw and one-hundred percent Republican," but he ignored his Indian heritage except when it benefited his political career. Kansas Historical Society, B Curtis, Charles 10.

Senator Ben Nighthorse Campbell of Colorado has consistently emphasized his Northern Cheyenne heritage both in his political stances and personal appearances. Office of Senator Ben Nighthorse Campbell.

A young Navajo drilling in a uranium mine in the early 1950s on the Navajo Reservation. Newcomer Collection, Arizona Historical Society/Tucson.

Phillip Deere, a Muskogee-Creek spiritual leader, addressing a rally on the steps of the national capitol during the 1978 "Longest Walk." Photograph from Dick Bancroft.

Displaying an American flag with an image of an American Indian superimposed on it became an important symbol for Wisconsin Indians during protests over spear fishing. Great Lakes Indian Fish and Wildlife Commission Collection, Chippewa Valley Historical Museum.

3.

Dissolving the Five Civilized Tribes

The dissolution of the Five Civilized Tribes of eastern Oklahoma stands as the most important instance of Indian land loss in the twentieth century. The abrogation of tribal governments and the allotment of tribal land violated long-standing treaties. Clearly, more was at stake—for Indians and whites—than opening reservations in thinly populated and remote parts of the West. The Five Tribes owned approximately half of present Oklahoma, an area enormously rich in agricultural land, timber, coal, asphalt, oil, and natural gas. Moreover, the Indian population was also sizeable. According to the 1890 census, Indians numbered 50,055, Negroes 18,636, and whites 109,393. The tasks of enrollment, land appraisal and allotment, as well as disposing of townsites, timber resources, and other tribal property, overwhelmed federal officials. The process produced incredible corruption at all levels, national publicity about the scandals, and ineffective investigations by both government and private agencies. In the end, the tribal dissolutions, allotment, and new white population forced adjustments on the Five Tribes, especially full bloods, that proved traumatic.[1]

The Dawes Commission after 1893 tried to dissolve the Oklahoma tribal governments and implement severalty, but it had not succeeded, except for the Seminoles. The Curtis Act of 1898 then ordered the termination of tribal governments by April 26, 1906, and unilaterally prescribed procedures for enrollment, allotment, and land appraisal. The legislation had also ordered that an inspector, who reported to the secretary of interior, handle the details of liquidating the Five Tribes. J. George Wright held the post until 1907, when his duties were combined with those of the commissioner to the Five Tribes at the union agency in Muskogee. Meantime, a sizeable bureaucracy developed at the agency to carry out the complex tasks.

Although the resulting forced agreements with the Five Tribes differed somewhat, they were basically the same. Wright accepted the Dawes Commission's rolls and rejected those of the tribes. The agreements, however, permitted officials to add or strike names before closing the rolls. Thousands of individuals, aided by attorneys, "besieged" the roll makers to gain free allotments. The Choctaws and Chickasaws, alarmed about unmerited additions, hired a law firm to negotiate a supplemental agreement to establish a tribunal in 1912 to hear appeals. Obviously, many claimants had committed perjury and forgery to get on the rolls. Of 263 cases involving 3,403 individuals, the tribunal rejected all but 156 claimants, saving the two tribes some $16,000,000. Litigation and controversy over the rolls continued for years.[2]

At the same time as enrollment, the Dawes Commission appraised the land to insure an equitable allotment. The appraisers, however, assigned arbitrary monetary values well under market prices. Later whites tried to buy the land at appraisal figures, and the government also used the low evaluations in paying off a claims case. Also before allotment, the government isolated several categories of property (Choctaw-Chickasaw coal and asphalt holdings, townsites, land for schools, churches, tribal buildings), which the Department of Interior managed, leased, or sold.

The allotments to individuals varied. The Creeks, for example, lacked sufficient land and money to give each enrollee a full share of land or in-lieu money. The Cherokees ran short of land, and some received no allotments. The Choctaws and Chickasaws agreed to 320-acre allotments and the sale of surplus land, but the 320-acre figure was based on average value, and the actual assignments ranged from 160 acres to 4,165 acres. Most Indians received two different allotments, a "homestead" assignment where the person already lived and "away land" at another location. The Indians, however, received little assistance in removing white squatters from the "away" allotments.[3]

Federal legislation in 1904 gave the Department of Interior more control over land sales and ordered the liquidation of 1.5 million acres. Congress also authorized the department to prepare regulations to remove individual trust status. Anticipating the Burke Act, the regulations allowed mixed bloods to apply for fee patents by completing a form on which they recorded their age, sex, blood quantum, and business experience. During the first three years, the government issued some 6,000 fee patents to applicants.

In 1906 Congress approved the McCumber amendment which affected land sales. The new legislation placed full bloods' land under trust for twenty-five years, but allowed several categories of Indians to sell all but their homesteads without government supervision. Inherited lands could be sold freely, but full-blood owners needed federal approval for sales.[4]

The agreements and legislation opened massive opportunities for corruption. A major scandal broke in 1903, when Samuel Brosius of the Indian Rights Association charged that federal court officials had conspired with land companies and that Dawes Commission employees had participated in land speculation and worked for real estate firms. The Board of Indian Commissioners dispatched Charles J. Bonaparte, later U.S. attorney general, to investigate the Dawes Commission, and the Justice Department sent three individuals to examine the courts. Although the investigations did not always reveal clear-cut malfeasance, they demonstrated many improprieties. The punishments, however, were mild. Interior Secretary Ethan Allen Hitchcock merely prohibited future speculation, and Congress approved a similar ban in 1904.[5]

Astute mixed bloods shared in the graft. Robert L. Owen, a well-known Cherokee leader and later U.S. senator, held some 10,000 acres under the Cherokee government, and he manipulated matters so that his former holdings were assigned to allottees as their "away land." Owen's agents then rented the allotments with a stipulation that he could buy them when they became alienable.[6] Most mixed-blood grafters, however, worked for white real estate interests, receiving fees for translating or other assistance.

Certainly the most numerous and blatant irregularities were committed by whites who acquired allotments on their own. Many mixed bloods, who applied for fee patents after 1904, were unqualified for the most rudimentary business and credit transactions. Their applications for removal of trust were actually the work of whites who already held sale contracts of some sort. Another tactic allowed a potential buyer to secure special legislation removing the trust status from a full-blood's allotment without the owner's knowledge, and then purchase the land. It was not uncommon for the whites to "kidnap" an owner and take him or her to another state or shift the person from town to town while a deal was in progress so that no one could interfere. As a rule, the more valuable the Indian's property, the more extraordinary were white efforts to obtain title.

The scandals over land sales eventually diminished because whites gained most of the Indians' property, but guardian abuses continued into the 1920s. The appointment of guardians, in theory, had some legitimacy because Indian parents frequently sold or leased their children's allotments for a pittance. County probate courts in 1903 began appointing white guardians for Indian children. A class of professional guardians arose as bankers, lawyers, and businessmen recognized a source of potential income. Unethical guardians reaped profits by leasing a minor's property at a low rate to a real estate firm which then sublet the land to a farmer at a much higher figure. The guardian, who probably received a kickback from the real estate firm, also charged the minor for various fictional services, leaving little or no income from the property. If the minor had individual money, the guardian either used it himself or loaned it to relatives or associates at low interest rates. By the time a minor became of age, the estate seldom had any assets left.

Adult Indians, particularly those with oil income, were also declared incompetent by the courts and subjected to the same treatment. In a few cases, a legally competent adult, who became rich when oil was discovered on an allotment, was brought before a court and declared incompetent. After the guardian had secured the ward's wealth, the Indian was returned to the same court and declared competent. Guardians usually did not realize much income from a single Indian, but by overseeing a large number of wards, a guardian could amass a fortune.

Why the nightmarish despoliation of Indian property in eastern Oklahoma continued without major correction is a simple question with complex answers. The outrages received national publicity; formal investigations often took place; and legislative and policy changes followed. But at least part of the difficulty can be attributed to the massive task of enrollment, allotment, and disposition of tribal property, which permitted little time to protect individual Indian assets. Bonaparte, for example, complained that allotment personnel should have made assignments in the field in order to meet individual needs, but this meant far more trouble than making allotments from the union agency. The few government attorneys assigned to probate courts could do little more than intervene in the worst guardianship scandals. Federal solutions, at best, afforded temporary relief. Commissioner Sells in 1913 increased funding for probate attorneys and reached an agreement with state judicial officials in 1914 to safeguard Indian wards, but within a few years corruption was as rampant as before.

The central factor behind the scandalous treatment of Indians of eastern Oklahoma were white leaders and their "booster ethic." Scholars differ somewhat on interpreting the group's makeup, but most agree on several major points.[7] The despoliation of Indian property was seldom done by actual settlers who lacked the money and influence needed to acquire Indian land. Instead, the aggressive community leaders acquired the bulk of Indian land. While researching *And Still the Waters Run* in the 1930s, Angie Debo found that many of the individuals involved in land or guardianship scandals had become the leading citizens of Oklahoma. Their names littered the society pages of newspapers, indicating their "respectability." Later, the grafters somewhat lost status.[8] The "boosters" held few qualms about leaving Indians landless and impoverished or imposing harsh adjustments upon the full bloods. As elsewhere in the West, the opportunists depicted themselves as self-sacrificing citizens trying to better their communities and state. A unity obviously existed among the white community leaders. County probate judges undoubtedly knew that the guardians they appointed were systematically robbing Indian wards, but they ignored the problem because their courts were already swamped, the guardians were their friends and associates in civic clubs, and the judges needed their support to win election. Indians, in short, simply suffered from the traditional "courthouse gangs" typical of many rural areas.

One common trait of the "boomers" was their intense hostility toward any federal attempt to obstruct their acquisition of Indian land or money. Other factors, however, motivated "boomers" too. They shared resentments over the long struggle to achieve statehood, the control of territorial patronage by Republicans, and a host of other grievances. During the dissolution of the Five Civilized Tribes, for example, Oklahoma newspapers repeatedly vilified Secretary Hitchcock whenever he intervened to protect the Indians or sought to conserve natural resources. The "boomers" attacked the Indians themselves when they refused to sell land or, as sometimes happened, they sold their allotments several times.

Western congressional leadership certainly placed no major obstacles in the way of local elites. In late 1906, on the eve of statehood and during the worst scandals, a Senate select committee held hearings in eastern Oklahoma. The five senators included four westerners: Clarence D. Clark of Wyoming, chairman, Chester I. Long of Kansas, Henry M. Teller of Colorado, and William A. Clark of Montana. Frank B. Brandegee of Connecticut served as the "token" easterner. The investigators sampled a wide cross-section of white and Indian opinion, but most of the witnesses were white attorneys or businessmen who wanted to remove all restrictions on Indian land sales. A few, however, admitted that the full bloods should remain under trust. Although settlers made up a huge majority of whites living in Indian Territory in 1906, few testified before the committee. Ironically, the settlers were victimized by real estate interests almost as badly as the Indians.

Indian opinion at the hearings varied greatly. The most fascinating witnesses were the full bloods, who refused to take allotments because they saw the removal treaties as the handiwork of God and, therefore, immutable. Sincere, uncowed, and totally honest, they believed in the ultimate good faith of American government and, with misguided confidence, thought that somehow the current tragedy would stop and the previous conditions would return. Clearly, the senators had as much difficulty comprehending such perspectives as these traditionalists had understanding recent events. Some mixed bloods, claiming to represent their people, seconded the position of white witnesses. Most, however, displayed considerable sympathy for the full bloods and recommended a continuation of federal trust.

Throughout the hearings the senators demonstrated their regional bias. Audiences applauded their denunciations of Hitchcock and witnesses who advocated development. An exchange between Senator Teller and Dr. J. S. Murrow, a longtime missionary, demonstrated the conflict between western development and the need to protect the Indians. Teller argued that current land frauds would not continue beyond statehood because public opinion would not tolerate such abuses. Murrow strongly disagreed and warned that "inside a year . . . these full bloods would be deprived of almost every bit of their property." Even after Teller and others tried to browbeat Murrow into changing his opinion, he doggedly maintained his ·original position.[9] Fortunately, the committee's recommendations that all restrictions be removed from Indians and their protection be given to the state were not enacted.

An interesting sidelight to Oklahoma statehood in 1907 was federal litigation to void illegal sales of Indian land and other property. The most important of the suits dealt with the legality of over 27,000 individual conveyances before 1907. By 1911 whites had formed at least two protective associations to fight against the federal suit. Both organizations hoped to win passage of a federal law which would affirm their titles before the courts could act. One group, the Seminole Protective League, was formed at Shawnee in 1910, and the second, the Indian Land Protective League, was organized somewhat later. By 1911 the latter group issued a "Circular Letter" with an attractive cover sheet containing a photograph of a prosperous farm house with the words, "PROTECT YOUR HOME," boldly inscribed across the top of the picture.

Leaders of the Indian Land Protective League appeared at Wewoka to recruit members in June 1911, and a transcript of their proceedings reveals much about their attitudes. The controversy over clouded titles, one speaker announced, had reduced land values and ended the flow of investment funds into Oklahoma. Another lamented "the fact that the State was being retarded" by a "cloud . . . hanging over the lands." Although federal officials denounced league spokesmen as "active land grafters," all of them denied that they had ever been major speculators, claiming that they had obtained their present holdings honestly. One speaker expressed indignation "that every man that had bought a piece of Indian land was [considered] a grafter and a forger." Another expressed the belief that a law affirming the clouded titles would benefit the Indians by raising the values of their land; and a third stressed that Indians and Negroes would never develop Oklahoma, and declared that "the white man deserves the credit for making the development that has been done. . . ." The league's leadership hoped to win the support of actual farmers by setting membership fees at $2.50, but based on the small audience, the tactic had failed.[10]

The white organizations were unsuccessful in their attempt to secure a legislative resolution for their clouded titles, and in 1912 the federal district court in Muskogee heard the cases. The court lumped the suits into three groups based on legal issues and then ruled on each. The first decision dealt with forty-six suits involving 3,715 Cherokee conveyances. The court voided all the sales as a direct violation of federal law. In its two later rulings, however, the court affirmed the remaining disputed titles to white purchasers. After the second ruling, Wewoka citizens staged a celebration with band music and speeches by leading citizens.[11]

What happened in eastern Oklahoma during the Progressive Era was not the piecemeal opening of reservations but something awesome in its scope. In successfully fighting off earlier federal attempts to open the area to white settlement, the Five Tribes had only forestalled an inevitable tragedy. Most whites knew that the stakes were high. The other Indian reservations being opened at the time were far to the west and in areas so arid that all but the most optimistic whites recognized their limited potential. In comparison, eastern Oklahoma was lush and bountiful, truly the last major garden spot left in the West. Other factors that contributed to the dissolution of the Five Tribes included sizeable recent settlement in western Oklahoma and the desire for statehood among the new settlers and those whites who already lived among the Five Tribes.

Since statehood in 1907, Oklahomans have taken a somewhat euphoric view of Indian-white relations and see themselves as a model for other areas of the West. They like to remind outsiders about the important part that Indians have played historically in Oklahoma politics, fine arts, business, and professions. In truth, pride in being Indian is important to many state residents, not something to hide. A good portion of Oklahoma college students, for example, will unhesitatingly raise their hands when an instructor asks how many possess some Indian blood. But all this, unfortunately, tends to ignore the harsh realities of a past era when treaties were violated by the federal government, corruption ravished innocent Indians of wealth, and full bloods experienced severe adjustments during the transition from tribal authority to statehood.

4.
The War to Assimilate All Indians

Although American participation in World War I lasted only nineteen months, it brought immediate and profound changes to the American West. The war allowed the western economy to overcome its traditional handicaps and establish firms which could, for the first time, compete with eastern manufacturers in finished products. Urbanization developed simultaneously as cities such as Seattle, Portland, and San Francisco attracted thousands of workers to fill war jobs. Because of this and young men entering the military, Indians and other minority groups found new employment opportunities. Wartime food needs led to the notorious "Great Plow-up" that affected several Indian reservations.[1]

Since the federal government traditionally exercised a high degree of control over reservations, in many ways the war effort affected Indians more than the general population. Indeed, Commissioner Cato Sells's enthusiastic support for the war caused him to turn every BIA program toward victory. Sells believed the war represented "the difference between a despotic and an altruistic spirit; the difference for *Deutschland über alles* and America for all." The commissioner also saw the war as a unique opportunity to benefit all mankind. Americans were "proving democracy's excellence and stability and commending . . . its liberty and justice to all governments."[2] Thus, instead of reassessing prewar policies of Indian self-support, citizenship, and assimilation, Sells sought to use the war in every possible way to accomplish these goals.

Sells urged Indians to enter the military forces and to realize their opportunity to assimilate. An unknown, but probably small, number of young men had already responded by enlisting in the Canadian armed services.[3] Once the United States declared war, a large number of Indians enlisted. Registration for the draft occurred in June 1917, and it included all Indian males, both citizens and non-citizens, between twenty-one and thirty-one years old. The provost marshall general instructed the BIA to establish draft boards at each agency, but Sells preferred that regular selective service officials handle registration, deferments, and inductions. Where selective service machinery did not exist, agency employees administered the process.[4]

Although all Indian males in the proper age bracket were required to register, only citizen Indians could be drafted. The guidelines used to distinguish citizens from non-citizens conformed with existing legislation. Anyone allotted prior to the Burke Act of 1906 or who had taken up separate residence was eligible for conscription. The same was true of children of citizens, individuals who received fee patents after 1906, and those declared citizens by legislation. Non-citizens included the unallotted and those who received allotments after 1906 and remained under federal trust. Although the guidelines seemed clear, BIA officials faced considerable difficulties in explaining to Indians why non-citizens must register but would never be drafted.[5] Estimates vary, but from one-third to one-half of Indians were citizens at the time. Perhaps the legal distinctions between citizens and non-citizens were somewhat meaningless because approximately 75 percent of Indians in the military enlisted rather being drafted. Sells estimated in 1918 that some 8,000 Indians served: 6,500 in the army, 1,000 in the navy, and 500 in other military positions. He revised these figures to 9,000 and later to 10,000.[6]

One of the major issues early in the war was whether Indians should be placed in segregated units or integrated with other servicemen. Precedents for segregation were readily available. The British and other European nations had frequently formed special units made up of colonial subjects, and starting in late 1915, Canada formed Indian companies and battalions. Indeed, several individuals proposed special Indian units before the United States entered the war. Edward E. Ayer, a wealthy Chicago lumberman and member of the Board of Indian Commissioners, in February 1917 proposed the enlistment of ten to fifteen regiments of Indians. He argued that Indians could not readily adjust to integrated service and that their progress and self-respect would be enhanced if they served with other Indians. Ayer won the support of several prominent figures, including fellow Commissioner Frank Knox, who badly wanted to command an Indian unit.[7] The idea aroused sufficient interest that several bills to organize separate units were introduced in 1917.

The House Committee on Military Affairs held hearings on one bill in late July. Dr. Joseph Kossuth Dixon appeared as the main spokesman for the measure. A colorful type, Dixon was described by the veteran Indian inspector James McLaughlin as "the most unique example of misdirected energy I remember having seen." A former minister, Dixon had come under a cloud at each of his pastoral assignments. In his last charge, the trustees literally barred the church doors to him, and his wife divorced him on grounds of adultery. Sometime later Rodman Wanamaker, a wealthy Philadelphia merchant, employed Dixon to give public lectures on various subjects, and he began to specialize on Indian topics. Always interested in dramatic and patriotic projects, Dixon had persuaded Wanamaker to finance three "citizenship" expeditions to Indian reservations before 1914 as well as to support a "National Indian Memorial" in New York harbor. A ground-breaking ceremony was staged for the latter, but the project was never built.[8]

Dixon's statements before the committee amounted to an eloquent but simple minded compound of stereotypes. He held an Edenic view of Indians, but he somehow linked this with a belief in assimilation. He liked to portray Indians as hapless prisoners on reservations, and he believed the only solution was taking politics out of Indian administration and encouraging Indians to develop a sense of American patriotism. In his testimony before the House committee, Dixon proposed the organization of ten Indian regiments to serve on the Mexican border, and, in return, each enlistee would receive American citizenship. Repeatedly, he expressed the idea that Indians had innately superhuman qualities. "The Indian is not a professional scout," he proclaimed, "he is a born scout. He is a scout from the cradle up." Despite Dixon's praise for Indians' "strength, courage, intelligence, loyalty, power of endurance, stoicism, sagacity, persistence, and relentless of purpose," he recommended they be consigned to duty on the Mexican border. Congress never approved the bill.[9]

The idea of separate Indian units aroused strong opposition. The Society of American Indians, a group composed of largely middle-class Indians, firmly endorsed Indian participation but denounced segregated units as "an affront to Indian dignity." The Society saw separate units as undoing earlier assimilation.[10] Commissioner Sells adamantly opposed separation of the races. Interior Secretary Franklin K. Lane, after initially supporting segregated units, reversed himself. The decisive opponent, however, was Secretary of War Newton D. Baker who rejected separate Indian units early in the war and refused to change his position.[11]

Regardless of Dixon's defeat, his image of the Indians as scouts endowed with superhuman fighting qualities continued in the publicity about their role in World War I. Although Sells placed major emphasis on how military service contributed to assimilation, he too used the "scout image" in one annual report.[12]

Government publicity also stressed that Indians gave unqualified support for the war. Different tribes and individuals, however, reacted to the war with remarkable diversity. On the more isolated reservations of Arizona, New Mexico, Utah, Nevada, and California, the largely non-citizen and unacculturated Indians took little interest. The superintendent of the White River Apaches in 1917, for example, noted that only two out of 152 males registered for the draft had enlisted.[13] When Sells circulated a questionnaire to all agencies in 1920 requesting information on individuals who had been in military service, superintendents from isolated reservations usually reported that few men had served.[14]

Although little information exists in autobiographical materials to show Indian reactions to the war, some expressed serious misgivings. One Indian father from Millard County, Utah, complained that he did not want his sons sent to war. They were required for farm work, were too young, and still needed their mother's care. Like several other Indians, who believed it unfair to dispatch Indians overseas to fight, the father added: "We don't want to send our boys across the ocean; it is going *too far to war!*" He also pointed out the inconsistency of past white admonitions for Indians to be peaceful and the present war.[15] Three young Indians stationed at Camp Lewis, Washington, voiced different complaints. They noted that whites had asked why Indians participated in the war when they owned nothing and had no income. They also resented discrimination they had experienced in white business establishments. The three concluded by saying, "We ain[']t talking to get out of this at all; all we want is a fair deal after this, and we want our rights."[16]

The first registration for the draft in June 1917 aroused more suspicion than any other event. With one exception, Indian protests came from the more remote reservations. Unrest was reported at Fort Hall, Idaho, the Navajo agencies in Arizona, the Goshute Reservation on the Nevada-Utah border, and among the Creeks in eastern Oklahoma.[17] The most serious protest developed among the Goshutes. After countering opposition in earlier attempts to register Indians, the government in February 1918 sent troops to the agency. The detachment arrested three individuals believed guilty of inciting the resistance and forced the others to register. Clearly the uprising was the product of confusion over registration, but it also reflected past grievances against the superintendent. Unfortunately, newspaper stories about the episode falsely claimed that German agents had inspired the "uprising."[18]

Registration confused both Indians and draft officials. Many Indians assumed registration automatically meant they would be forced into the armed services, although only citizens could be drafted. Draft officials were often baffled by missing birth records and frequent changes of residence. BIA workers were not always certain whether individuals were citizens or not. Part of the problem with the Goshutes, for example, was that they did not regard themselves as citizens because they could not vote, and they did not understand that states decided voter eligibility. Their superintendent initially insisted that those who lived on the public domain were citizens, but by mid-1918 he was uncertain himself.[19]

Local newspapers in the Cheyenne and Arapaho areas of western Oklahoma reported both a willingness to enter the military and a significant increase in ceremonies, especially following the war. Shortly after the armistice, local Indians held a large victory dance at Watonga.[20] During the next year or so, the small weeklies reported numerous other victory or scalp dances honoring returned Cheyenne and Arapaho veterans. Both the former soldiers and their communities took these events seriously. One young veteran, honored for his war feats, was renamed and given the title of chief.[21] Although whites traditionally had been repulsed by Indian scalping, newspapers gleefully reported stories of Indians bringing home German scalps.[22]

Several newspaper accounts indicate that the war united the Indian and white communities in western Oklahoma. Residents of Watonga, for example, donated beeves and other food at the armistice dance, and whites invited Indians to perform a scalp dance at a county fair. Community reaction to the death of Harvey Goodbear, a young Indian from Thomas killed in France, provides more telling evidence. Two thousand people attended burial services when Goodbear's body was returned to Thomas in 1921. When veterans formed an American Legion post a few months later, they named it after Goodbear and a white who had also died in France.[23]

Navajos reacted to the war very differently from the Cheyennes and Arapahos. Not over a dozen Navajos entered the armed forces, and probably all were students or former students at boarding schools.[24] Although the non-citizen Navajos could not be drafted, the war created unrest in the more remote areas of the huge reservation. According to Hilda Faunce, wife of a trader near Black Mountain, Arizona, local Navajos reluctantly registered for the draft, and then they became upset when a rumor spread "that the registered Indians were to be compelled to go to war and would be put in front and shot first to save the white men." The Indians began buying ammunition and discussed plans to kill all the traders, burn their posts, and then attack the border towns to the south if the registrants were called to duty. Alarmed traders sent their families off the reservation. Mrs. Faunce's husband, who spoke Navajo, averted the threatened rebellion by promising that he would lead those asked to report for military duty.[25]

The Navajos' tightly circumscribed world gave them a unique outlook on the war. Mrs. Faunce regularly showed her customers copies of the *New York Times,* and the Indians were fascinated by war pictures. Their visits to border towns had familiarized them with automobiles, soldiers, and buildings in the photographs, but they were baffled by depictions of airplanes and warships. When they despaired counting the huge mass of people seen in one crowd shot, one clever individual used a soda bottle to draw circles all over the photograph. The onlookers then counted all the faces inside the circles, estimated the number outside the circles, and had Mrs. Faunce add the totals. When shown long casualty lists, the customers asked if enough white men would be left to care for their women.[26]

A very different reaction to the war developed among acculturated groups. In responding to Sells's 1920 questionnaire, superintendents in Kansas, Oklahoma, Nebraska, Wisconsin, and Minnesota reported large numbers had served and often requested more questionnaires from the Washington office. The Five Civilized Tribes were especially prominent with an estimated 4,000 men in the armed forces.[27] This figure partly reflects a high enlistment rate, but many were already members of the Thirty-Sixth Division, a national guard unit sent to France.

There was no typical Indian serviceman. Again diversity based on several factors—acculturation, tribal culture, and education—figured importantly. Increased ceremonialism among plains tribes suggests that the war rekindled past traditions among such groups. Moreover, young plains tribesmen viewed their participation as a modern substitute for past means of gaining prestige by individual valor, an avenue missing since the reservation period. This obviously explains why several Southern Cheyenne veterans formed the new "War Band" or joined existing warrior societies after the war. Several gained tribal leadership roles in the 1930s and 1940s after older traditional chiefs died, and the same was true in many other tribes.

The experiences of James McCarthy, a twenty-two-year-old Papago student at Phoenix Indian School, offers several insights into Indian experiences in the military. Because boarding schools became recruiting centers, practically all eligible males at Phoenix volunteered "right away," but Mc-Carthy and a Cherokee friend were rejected because they were too short. The superintendent then intervened and got them in a national guard unit assigned to border duty. Later sent to La Jolla, California, for training, Mc-Carthy, his Cherokee friend, and another Indian volunteered for overseas duty in June 1918. Army life had caused little problem for the three because they were already accustomed to military discipline, uniforms, and drills in boarding school.

After arriving in France, the three Indians joined the same company in the Twenty-Eighth Infantry Division and went to the front lines. Although always addressed as "Chief" by whites, the nickname carried no racist connotation for McCarthy. Still he mentioned that when his unit entered combat, "more than ever, we Indian boys stuck together." The "scout image" manifested itself when McCarthy's unit was pinned down and ran out of water. After a sergeant unsuccessfully asked for volunteers to bring water from a nearby stream, he turned to McCarthy and asked, "What about you Chief?" The Papago and a white comrade then crawled to the stream and filled canteens for the other men. After being gassed and sent to a hospital, McCarthy became so "lonesome for my company and my Indian friends" that he tried to leave for the front. A military policeman, however, intercepted McCarthy, still dressed in his pajamas, and returned him to the hospital. McCarthy later was wounded, captured, and sent to a prison camp in Germany. His low-key account of military service does not indicate the patriotism typical of whites, but more a quiet and intelligent desire for adventure and new sights.[28]

Much the same attitudes seemed to guide McCarthy's decision to reenlist. He had not thought about remaining in the army until he returned to the United States, "but I made up my mind that I wanted to go someplace." After signing up for a tour in the Far East, McCarthy spent a month at home. He received no great fanfare upon his return, nor did his family stage a ceremony, although Papago tradition called for a purification ritual for those wounded in war. His pride in his military service, however, seems indicated by his statement that "most of the time I stayed in my uniform."[29]

McCarthy's decision not to return home may indicate a fairly common pattern among both Indian veterans and perhaps those who found off-reservation jobs. One California field official, who admitted that he lacked precise data, in 1921 concluded: "A great many who went from this public domain [area] have not yet returned, and we often hear even now of some Indian who is in Germany with the soldiers still there."[30] In McCarthy's case, he came home permanently only when forced to by the Great Depression. It appears likely that World War I set a minor precedent for the more sizeable off-reservation exodus Indians made during and after World War II.

The government's publicity about Indian support for the war on the home front was more realistic than its depiction of their military role. Indians responded enthusiastically to campaigns to buy war bonds and stamps. In the five subscriptions between 1917 and 1919, Sells reported that the Indians had purchased $25,000,000 in war bonds and an additional $1,000,000 in war stamps, or approximately $75 per person.[31] These figures were somewhat misleading, as Sells acknowledged, since some of the money came from individual trust accounts. In other words, superintendents simply encouraged Indians to transfer their trust money to bonds. Here again, Sells viewed the war as a means of realizing assimilation. He hoped that the purchase of bonds and stamps would instill a habit for thrift.[32]

Without much government prompting, Indians also engaged in the many other programs related to the war effort at home. Indian school children and adults, working mostly through the Red Cross, raised funds by contributions and auctions of handiwork, made up Christmas boxes for soldiers, and produced thousands of sweaters, socks, and other articles. Some surprising changes resulted. A missionary reported that the Standing Rock Sioux associated both the Red Cross and the Sun Dance with healing, and during the war, the Sioux paid their Sun Dance vows by donating horses to the Red Cross and wore the organization's badges during the ceremonies rather than cutting their breasts.[33] Volunteer war work may have unified Indians of varying levels of acculturation with local whites. The superintendent of the Five Civilized Tribes noted in 1918 that Indians and whites commonly joined in war work and patriotic meetings.[34]

The war obviously created new employment opportunities for Indians. In several instances, the war simply increased opportunities in jobs Indians already performed. This was true of the cotton picking in Arizona, cultivation of sugar beets, and other migratory farm labor. Some Indians no doubt found additional jobs on local farms and ranches. Unlike World War II, relatively few Indians found employment in major war industries.[35] The widespread displacement of BIA employees during the war doubtlessly offered some agency jobs for Indians in education, nursing, and minor positions.

Unfortunately, the economic impact of the war seriously restricted BIA services to Indians. Numerous resignations of field workers curtailed supervision for irrigation, agriculture, livestock production, and home extension. Similar problems appeared in Indian education as school administrators coped with shortages of teachers and other personnel. The prestigious

Carlisle Indian school closed permanently in 1918, when the War Department converted the facility to a rehabilitation center. Staff shortages forced other school closures. The wartime resignations of doctors and nurses reduced the BIA medical staff by approximately one-third. This not only reduced already inadequate medical care for Indians but also coincided with severe epidemics of typhus, measles, and pneumonia. None of these, however, rivaled the virulent influenza pandemic that struck Indian reservations and schools with terrifying effect in 1918 and 1919.[36]

Wartime inflation also hampered the BIA. Prices rose approximately 105 percent from 1917 to 1920, and this meant that government services and goods were cut drastically when Congress froze BIA funding for fiscal 1918 and 1919 at approximately $11,000,000. Although appropriations increased after fiscal 1919, the BIA never came close to offsetting wartime inflation.[37] Sells retrenched services rather than aggressively seeking higher appropriations.

If he viewed the war as an opportunity to assimilate young Indians who entered the military, much the same applied to Sells's general wartime policies. Such prewar goals as self-support, ending individual trusts, and encouraging Indians to assume a white lifestyle were, if anything, intensified during the war. Unfortunately, several of his policies led to new inroads on Indians' resources.

The best illustration of prewar goals carried into wartime was the "Declaration of Policy in the Administration of Indian Affairs" of April 17, 1917. In the statement, Sells announced that his first four years had focused on health, liquor suppression, economic improvements, vocational education, and property protection. It was now time "to take the next step" of ending guardianship over the competent Indians and making the incompetent competent. His "Declaration" outlined new guidelines to end wardship. All Indians of less than one-half blood quantum would be given full control of their property, and the same would be true for those of one-half or more Indian blood if judged competent. In addition, graduates of boarding schools would be granted citizenship when they came of age. Other provisions included more liberal guidelines for the sale of Indian land, control over individual money, and the payment of pro-rata shares of tribal funds to unrestricted Indians.[38]

Sells confidently depicted the "Declaration" as a final solution for the Indian problem:[39]

> It means the dawn of a new era in Indian administration. It means that the competent Indian will no longer be treated as half ward and half citizen. It means reduced appropriations by the Government and more self-respect and independence for the Indian. It means the ultimate absorption of the Indian race into the body politic of the Nation. It means, in short, the beginning of the end of the Indian problem.

In reality, of course, the "Declaration" complemented the competency commissions, active since 1915, by offering new criteria for ending the trust status. Sells could now notify superintendents to submit lists of Indians of less than one-half blood and then forward these to the secretary of interior for automatic approval. The competency commissions henceforth concentrated on screening Indians of one-half or higher blood quantum.

Not surprisingly, an overwhelming majority of Indians who received land in fee patent and full control of individual monies under the "Declaration" soon lost both. Reports from such reservations as the Crow, Fort Peck, and Pine Ridge indicated that some 90 percent or more sold their allotments or mortgaged them at ruinous interest rates. Indians quickly squandered money from land sales and loans. The Crow superintendent wryly remarked that Henry Ford and John D. Rockefeller should support fee patenting because it lined their pockets.[40] Indian servicemen reportedly received fee patents and returned home to find that their allotments had been sold for taxes. Despite the evidence against wholesale fee patenting, Secretary Lane and Sells doggedly maintained the policy.

The "Declaration" elicited interesting but mixed reactions. The Board of Indian Commissioners applauded the new approach because "it is in line with policies which the Board . . . has advocated, consistently and continuously, for more than a quarter of a century."[41] The conservative Indian Rights Association also endorsed the "Declaration." Western congressional leaders approved the new guidelines but complained that Sells was still not moving fast enough. In 1918 Representative Charles Carter of Oklahoma introduced a bill to remove restrictions from all Indians of one-half blood or less, and he later wrote Secretary Lane that the BIA was ending restrictions too slowly to suit the House Indian Affairs Committee.[42] Sells strongly defended his policies, maintaining that many Indians of the Southwest would require government supervision in the foreseeable future, but in 1919 he announced that all Indians of one-half blood would automatically lose their trust status.

The "Declaration" and the continued work of the competency commissions clearly worsened the already disastrous effects of earlier forced patenting. Sells in 1919 exulted that in the three previous years the BIA had issued 10,956 fee patents, 1,062 more than conveyed before 1917.[43] The transfers of property to whites seriously reduced the land base needed for Indians' future survival. Moreover, it added to an already large body of landless Indians dependent on the the charity of families and friends. Forced patenting finally ended after Lane resigned in 1920, and his successor canceled the "Declaration" guidelines, disbanded the competency commissions, and accepted only applications from allottees who requested fee patents.

The BIA actively cooperated in the government's wartime crusade to increase food production. Sells again saw the national emergency as a means of carrying out prewar goals. Since his first tour of reservations in 1913, he had believed that much reservation land was under-utilized and Indians should develop more farming and ranching. With the wartime food emergency, Sells announced that conservation of Indian property had become secondary because "when a nation is at war[,] ordinary considerations do not govern."[44] To increase food production, the government followed two principal avenues: encouraging more Indian agriculture and giving whites greater access to reservation land.

The campaign for increased food production actually preceded American entry into the war. Sells in January 1917 asked superintendents to encourage more farming by providing seeds and implements through reimbursable loans. Two months later he admonished field personnel that thousands of acres remained uncultivated and asked that government farmers concentrate more on agricultural instruction than on clerical duties.[45]

Shortly after the nation declared war, Sells telegraphed all superintendents and instructed them to redouble their efforts. He asked that field workers see "that every tillable acre" was cultivated and ordered meetings of government farmers and Indian leaders to organize farming operations. Previous restraints on agricultural loans were eased. A virtual crusade resulted as agency workers staged innumerable meetings during the planting season and urged Indians to give all their energies to averting the food crisis. Speakers appealed strongly to patriotism and declared that failure to participate in the food campaign was tantamount to treason.[46]

Field workers used compulsion and persuasion to win Indian participation. The superintendent of the Cheyenne and Arapaho Agency noted that some of the local Indians had always boasted that "the whole United States army could not make them work," but he had used the war to counter such recalcitrance. He applied the slogan, "work or fight," literally by canceling the draft deferments of a "few incorrigibles."[47] But Indians generally responded positively without BIA threats. As with other war work, the results often proved surprising. The Nighthawks of the Cherokees, the most traditional faction, cooperated fully with the food campaign and surprised their superintendent by requesting more land to farm. According to Sells, the increase of acres Indians farmed in 1917 averaged 34.4 percent. The low starting base of some reservations, however, makes the statistic somewhat misleading.

Field workers held meetings well before the planting season and were better organized in 1918. The results paralleled 1917 with an increase of 31.6 percent in acreage farmed. The successes were not uniform. Some reservations suffered crop failures due to weather and insects. The Rosebud superintendent, for example, reported that all his efforts produced limited improvements. A drought and an early freeze in 1917 had destroyed wheat and potato crops. He noted further that a large planting of fall wheat for 1918 had failed because of winter kill, but the spring wheat looked promising.[48]

The second means of growing more food, allowing whites greater access to Indian land, was initially approached cautiously. Sells wanted every acre farmed, preferably by Indians, but if not by them, then by whites. His caution, however, lasted only briefly, and by the end of 1917, both the Washington office and superintendents adopted a more liberal outlook toward leasing.

The most spectacular leasing operation involved Thomas D. Campbell, a native of Grand Forks, North Dakota, who had grown up during the bonanza era of the Red River Valley and later supervised large-scale farming in California.[49] When Campbell first contacted the BIA about a major lease to grow wheat, his offer was rebuffed; but a letter to President Wilson put him in touch with Secretary Lane. In April 1918, Lane and Campbell concluded an agreement which called for leasing up to 200,000 acres on the Crow, Fort Peck, Blackfeet, and Shoshone reservations. Their agreement deviated considerably from standard BIA contracts. Some of the basic terms included the right to lease both unallotted and allotted land and dry-land and irrigated areas. Campbell hoped that the leases would run for ten years, but this proved impossible for non-irrigated land, which by law could only be contracted for five years. Instead of the normal cash rental, Campbell agreed to pay 10 percent of the crop as well as a share of the straw. The agreement stipulated that Campbell must fence all tracts farmed and leave the land in a tillable condition with at least one-fourth sowed to alfalfa.[50] After concluding the agreement, Campbell and Louis W. Hill of the Great Northern Railroad negotiated a loan of $2,000,000 from Wall Street bankers. He then formed the Montana Farming Corporation under New York laws in mid-May. The *New York Times* acclaimed the firm as "the largest farming concern ever organized."

Although Campbell's leasing scheme was tied to the food campaign, its actual operations belong more to the postwar period. BIA officials managed to win the consent of the Crows for a lease in May 1918, but they encountered problems at Fort Peck where the Indians successfully demanded a five-year lease and cash payments.[51] In late June, Campbell's massive tractors began breaking Crow grasslands, and by fall 7,000 acres were planted in wheat. A year later Campbell placed 45,000 acres in cultivation and by 1923 110,000 acres.[52] Drought and low wheat prices forced the sale of the Montana Farming Corporation in 1921, but Campbell purchased the equipment and lease rights. He abandoned operations at Fort Peck the following year but continued large-scale farming on the Crow Reservation until 1930.

The Montana Farming Corporation was unique only in its size. On the Colorado River Reservation, the BIA approved three major new leases, two for growing cattle feed and one for cotton. The Great Western Sugar Company leased 4,000 to 5,000 acres of Crow land for sugar beets.[53] In his 1917 report, Sells mentioned that because Indians could not farm all their land, the BIA had liberalized leasing regulations and taken "aggressive steps" to bring surplus land under cultivation. He estimated "that more than 200,000 acres of additional land have been or will be leased by the next crop season."[54] Evidence from several reservations suggests that the government's leasing policies seriously harmed Indians and undid earlier progress toward self-sufficiency. The Pine Ridge Reservation provides one illustration. A new superintendent in 1900 encouraged cattle operations with excellent success. Not only did the number of livestock increase, but the Sioux also relished the lifestyle, dress, and work of ranching. With price increases after 1914, however, local white cattlemen wanted to lease Pine Ridge grazing lands, and the Indians were encouraged to sell their animals. By 1916 few Sioux cattle remained, and within two years, white lessees controlled the entire reservation. The Indian ranching economy never recovered, and the sale of cattle was "the greatest disaster that had befallen the Pine Ridge Indians since the vanishing of the buffalo."[55]

But the war created important economic changes even when government leasing and controls were absent. The war, for example, had little direct impact on the more isolated Navajos, but it brought major increases in the prices they received for their wool, lambs, cattle, and other products. Wool prices in New York jumped from 16.6 cents per pound in 1914 to 57.7 cents in 1918. Traders paid Navajos more than 50 cents per pound for wool in 1918 despite its low quality, and prices for other products rose accordingly.[56] Unethical traders urged the Navajos to sell off female stock needed to maintain their breeding herds, arguing that they would never again receive such high prices, and many unwisely followed the advice.[57] Indeed, sales of livestock by whites and Navajos in the eastern checkerboard so depleted numbers that competition for grazing land was temporarily eased. As with whites, the wartime inflation rate offset much of the higher prices Navajos received for their livestock.[58]

The war's broader impact on Indians was not so much a product of western development as it was from the overall war effort. If any common denominator existed, it was wartime economic development and inflation. Otherwise, the changes varied from tribe to tribe and from individual to individual based on such factors as levels of acculturation, geographic conditions, and legal status of Indian males. In many ways, the war was the crest of unchallenged assimilation. This not only resulted from the "Declaration of Policy" in 1917, but from Indians entering the military and off-reservation jobs and from the cooperation of many Indians and whites in the home front campaigns. In other ways the war led to a revival of traditions, although usually adapted to fit new circumstances. For a minority of Indians the war offered a chance to break away from their reservations and experience life on the outside. This most likely changed their personal perceptions but qualified some for leadership roles in postwar years. The war, in sum, was a time of important but often contradictory changes.

5.
From War to
Depression, 1919-29

During the 1920s, the West experienced changes that reshaped its basic character. Although western progressives and agrarian spokesmen formed the Senate bloc known as the "Sons of the Wild Jackasses," conservatives in the form of the Ku Klux Klan and more moderate types gave the region a diverse political makeup.[1] Population generally increased only slightly in the Great Plains and Mountain states, but the growth of the West Coast states, especially California, was sizeable.[2] This intensified the trend toward two "Wests": a heavily populated and urbanized coastal region and a huge but far less developed interior. Numerous older midwesterners moved to California, Arizona, and New Mexico because of a warmer climate.[3] Automobile ownership in the West increased dramatically during the decade, and by 1927 twelve western states had one automobile for every three to five residents.[4] The increase in automobiles, particularly in California, created assembly plants, dealerships, repair shops, filling stations, and more tourism.[5] In the 1920s trucks emerged as a partial solution for the West's internal marketing bottlenecks, aided by highway construction and improved vehicle design. Unlike railroads, the lowly trucks operated with few restrictions and were especially well suited for marketing perishables.[6]

Western irrigation grew during the 1920s, but not at the spectacular pace experienced at the turn of the century.[7] Despite this, western water needs remained high. More water was needed for the growing urban population, but also water development was increasingly tied to flood control, hydroelectric power, and river navigation. Meeting these more complex demands required large-scale projects and the damming of major streams. The prototype for multi-purpose water development was the lower Colorado River and the construction of Boulder Dam. When completed in 1941, the new dam, renamed Hoover Dam in 1947, controlled flooding, provided electricity for southern California, and supplied water for irrigation and for domestic use in the Los Angeles metropolitan area.[8]

Indian water rights were almost entirely ignored during the long controversies over water development of the Colorado River. The issue arose

71

when Secretary of Commerce Herbert Hoover presided over the negotiation of an interstate compact at Santa Fe in 1922, but the participants made no attempt to determine how many Indians lived in the Colorado basin or their water needs. Article VII stated that "Nothing in this compact shall be construed as affecting the obligations of the United States of America to Indian tribes." Hoover evidently had two motives in inserting the article. First, he knew that treaties existed, and he wanted the obligations recognized. He hoped additionally that the statement would defer possible criticism from Congress. Arizona later demanded that Indian reservations receive sufficient water from the lower basin quota to develop their irrigable land, but California rejected this stipulation and insisted that water for Indian needs be taken from the quotas assigned to each state.[9]

In the midst of the early struggles over the lower Colorado, Congress moved decisively toward future water development in the West. The 1925 Rivers and Harbors Act authorized surveys of all navigable rivers in the United States, except the Colorado, to study their potential for hydroelectricity, navigation, flood control, and irrigation. The detailed surveys contained a wide range of data but emphasized how various river improvements would affect the economic development of river basins. The reports laid the groundwork for the huge improvements built during and after the New Deal.[10]

The postwar economic development in the West helped reshape Indian affairs. Land for settlement continued as a secondary concern, but other Indian resources increased in importance. There were unbridled attempts to exploit reservation resources after the Harding administration took office in 1921. New Mexican Albert B. Fall, secretary of interior, was an attorney-rancher who had served in the Senate from 1912 until his appointment by Harding. An arch foe of conservation, Fall during his Senate career repeatedly but unsuccessfully tried to end federal controls over the public domain. He enjoyed greater success, however, with Indian land matters. In 1913 he joined with the Arizona delegation to prohibit Indian allotments on the public domain in the two states, and when this act was circumvented, he backed legislation in 1918 which ended executive-order extensions and the patenting of public domain lands to Indians. Fall's hopes for private exploitation of public domain resources received a serious setback when the General Leasing Act of 1920 made the federal government responsible for leasing and general administration of the public domain. Fall's appointment rested on his long record as spokesman for pro-development interests and his friendship with Harding, a "poker-playing crony."[11]

Fall's involvement in the Teapot Dome scandal overshadows his attempts to exploit Indian lands for mining and petroleum interests that were thwarted by the General Leasing Act. His machinations focused on the executive order reservations of New Mexico and Arizona, and, had his plans succeeded, business interests and the two states would have realized tremendous benefits. Fall, moreover, manipulated Mescalero affairs to advance his own personal interests.

Although the BIA did not actively conspire with Fall, it offered few obstacles to him. The new commissioner, Charles H. Burke of South Dakota, had served in the House of Representatives some thirteen years before he retired from politics in 1914.[12] His experience on the House Indian Affairs Committee familiarized him with his new duties, but he avoided problems by bowing to the strongest pressures of the moment. Critics charged that Assistant Commissioner Edgar B. Meritt, a Sells holdover and brother-in-law of Senate Minority Leader Joseph Robinson, actually ran the BIA.

The first furor over Indian affairs during Fall's administration arose in 1922 over a bill introduced at the secretary of interior's request by Senator Holm O. Bursum of New Mexico. The measure attempted to resolve long-standing land and water disputes between the Pueblo Indians and non-Indians in the Rio Grande Valley. Under the Treaty of Guadalupe Hidalgo of 1848, the United States accepted Pueblo land grants and citizenship as recognized by Spain and Mexico. Non-Indian intruders on Pueblo grants received a major advantage in 1876 when the Supreme Court ruled that, as citizens, the Pueblos were not entitled to federal protection against land alienation. Losses continued until 1913, when the Court declared that the Pueblos were entitled to federal protection. Very tangled legal problems resulted. Some of the non-Indian claimants had legitimately purchased their land, but others were outright trespassers. Virtually all titles remained clouded. Unfortunately, both the Pueblos and largely Hispanic residents badly needed the land and water rights for subsistence.

The Bursum bill was heavily biased against the Indians. The early sections of the bill established the jurisdiction of the federal courts over the Pueblos and the disputed land titles. Later sections gave non-Indian claimants title to the land if they could demonstrate possession before June 10, 1910, and compensated the Indians in either land or money for their losses. The Pueblos, however, received no additional water rights for any of the new lands acquired unless they brought suits in notoriously unfriendly state courts. Another provision upheld the validity of questionable earlier land surveys in the Pueblo as evidence for title. Last and most prejudicial, non-Indians who could show purchase and occupation after 1900 were allowed to have a federal court define their boundaries and fix the value of the land. Clear title to the land then could be obtained by payment of the resulting figure.[13]

The Bursum bill initially did not arouse a furor, but it attracted the attention of Stella Atwood of Riverside, California, a leader in the General Federation of Women's Clubs who was interested in Indian causes. Atwood repeatedly protested to Commissioner Burke and tried unsuccessfully to enlist the Indian Rights Association (IRA) against the bill. Fall gave the appearance that all interested parties supported the measure, but the House failed to bring it to a vote.[14]

Fall's dealings with the Mescaleros, aimed at his personal enrichment, dated to 1906 when he acquired the Three Rivers Ranch, which bordered on the reservation. In 1910 he concluded an agreement with the BIA by which he received part of the Mescaleros' water in return for building a dam and water distribution system for the tribe. The scheme was completed in 1914 after Fall entered the Senate. In 1920 he backed Mescalero Superintendent Ernest Stecker's plan for a $500,000 timber sale and a reimbursable loan of $500,000 for the purchase of a tribal herd and other purposes. Fall's support very likely rested on his son-in-law's need to renew a grazing lease on the reservation. The Mescaleros approved the lease, but the Senate failed to authorize Stecker's general plan.[15]

Once Fall became secretary of interior, he turned the office to personal gain. In April 1921, he ordered an investigation of an earlier water-rights dispute, and in October he transferred Stecker, who had insisted on a strict interpretation of the 1910 water agreement with Fall. In December, Fall used bribe money from Edward Doheny to buy out a ranching competitor, giving the Three Rivers Ranch a free hand over water rights and land in the western portion of the reservation.[16]

Fall's long and complicated campaign to create national parks in southern New Mexico was not only linked to the Mescalero Reservation but also indicates how he used his office to overcome earlier Senate defeats. Soon after entering the Senate in 1912, Fall introduced bills to create two national parks: one within the western portion of the Mescalero Reservation and the other at Elephant Butte, a Reclamation dam on the Rio Grande. Much to his dismay, the BIA and Reclamation blocked both bills. Hoping for better luck with the new Wilson administration, Fall reintroduced the park bills in 1914. Although a copy of the Mescalero proposal has not been found, criticisms that it aroused suggest its contents:[17]

> In effect, it called for the allotment in severalty of the reservation, the withdrawal of the Mescalero title to an estimated three million dollars worth of timber, the opening of the area to mining with no payment to the Indians, and the lease of lots to whites for "summer homes or cottages."

Protests to Commissioner Sells by the IRA and a local missionary, particularly over lack of mining royalties, blocked passage of the bills. Fall managed a partial victory in 1919, when an amendment to the appropriation bill opened all executive order reservations to metaliferous mining leases. His daughter-in-law, son-in-law, and ranch manager secured ten of seventy-three leases approved on the Mescalero Reservation before Fall, as secretary of interior, terminated all future leasing.[18]

As secretary, Fall also renewed efforts to create a national park from the Mescalero Reservation. To avoid criticism, he arranged public meetings in New Mexico to demonstrate popular support. The hodge-podge bill of 1922 called for the creation of an "All Year National Park" consisting of portions of the reservation, White Sands, the Malpais Lava Bed, and the Elephant Butte Reservoir. A companion bill that Fall authored a year earlier proposed that states be allowed to auction 10 percent of the public domain within their boundaries and to use the revenue to build roads. The second bill specifically authorized a road between Elephant Butte and the Mescalero Reservation, benefiting Fall's ranch. When opposition to both bills developed, Fall posed as an opponent to the All Year National Park bill, rigged a Mescalero council meeting, and altered the transcript of the deliberations. Although the Senate approved the park bill in 1922, it failed in the House. More formidable opposition killed the proposal in 1923.[19]

Although Fall's machinations show a cynical abuse of public office, they were far less important than his campaign to open executive order reservations to oil and gas developers. The question of oil and gas leasing on Indian land had first arisen thirty years earlier. Congress enacted legislation that permitted leasing on land "bought and paid for by Indians." Secretary Richard A. Ballinger refused to apply the act to executive order reservations in 1909, and such lands were closed to oil and gas development when Fall took office.[20] The recent discovery of natural gas in southern Utah on the Navajo Reservation led to intense interest in exploration in the San Juan area and requests to negotiate leases with the Navajos. Potential Navajo leases, however, posed several problems. The huge reservation contained both treaty and executive order lands, its administration was divided among five agencies, and the tribe lacked any governing body. Nevertheless, Commissioner Burke authorized an informal council meeting at the San Juan agency in May 1922, where the group rejected all applications. A second council in August approved one exploratory lease and refused all others, and a third in March 1922 turned down all applicants.[21]

Frustrated, Fall turned to a legislative solution. After learning that executive order lands covered twenty-two million acres, mostly in Arizona and New Mexico, Fall prepared a bill permitting oil and gas leases on the Navajo Reservation under a variation of the General Leasing Act. Introduced in May 1922, the proposal authorized Fall to negotiate leases and divide the revenues equally between the reclamation fund, the state in which the lease was made, and the tribe involved.[22] After testifying for the bill in early June, Fall four days later announced that executive order lands would be developed under the General Leasing Act. Like many westerners, he apparently reasoned that Indians held no title to such land and resided there only at the sufferance of the government.[23] Fall's order, which may have been a political ploy, would have denied the Navajo any revenue, and it touched off a five-year controversy over title to executive order lands.

The Omnibus bill was the final measure of the Fall administration and the only one not closely linked with either his personal interests or to allowing westerners to exploit reservation resources. It was a carryover from Sells's "Declaration of Policy" of 1917 and numerous postwar proposals to free Indians from federal wardship. Despite the disastrous impact of Sells's competency policies, the House Indian Affairs Committee in 1920 recommended liberal standards for granting citizenship and leases of unallotted land and the transfer of BIA services to other government agencies. Critics, however, warned that such abrupt changes would seriously harm the Indians.[24]

In 1922, advocates and critics reached a compromise. They agreed to extend citizenship to all Indians. Competency standards, however, were to be employed to decide which Indians would receive an individual share of their tribe's assets in return for a quitclaim to future federal services. The first element eventually became the Indian Citizenship Act of 1924, but with several guarantees for Indian rights. The House approved the Omnibus bill for a pro rata division of tribal assets in 1923. The Senate would have passed it, but Robert La Follette objected to a unanimous consent vote. Although western delegations doubtlessly supported the Omnibus bill, major supporters included the conservative IRA and the Board of Indian Commissioners.[25]

John Collier's emergence as an Indian reformer in 1922 marked a turning point in Indian affairs. His espousal of cultural pluralism challenged a longstanding consensus on assimilation. Collier's militancy, intelligence, propaganda skills, and direct attacks on the BIA differed greatly from the tactics of earlier reformers, who tended to blame shortcomings on dishonest or incompetent BIA personnel and to be satisfied with their dismissals or transfers. Collier, in contrast, focused on general matters, insisting, for example, that allotment had been ruinous and must be repealed.

Collier's path to Indian reform was circuitous. Born in 1884, he grew up in Atlanta where his father was a prominent banker, businessman, and civic leader. His mother's death in 1897 and his father's apparent suicide in 1900 marred his adolescence. In 1908 Collier began working at the People's Institute in New York City. His basic duties involved helping recently arrived immigrants adjust to urban life. He frequently staged dances, pageants, and other activities to preserve immigrants' customs and worked on educational and recreational projects. He also associated with political radicals whom he met at the home of the free-spirited socialite Mabel Dodge. After several setbacks to his work, Collier left New York in October 1919 to work for the California Housing and Immigration Commission.[26]

Collier organized a series of "institutes" to train people who would then teach Americanization to the immigrants. His own lectures dealt with "the European cooperative movement, the Russian revolution, St. Francis of Assisi, and Havelock Ellis's theory of sexuality." The commission assigned Collier to develop a program of adult education for immigrants, to train teachers for Americanization classes, and to establish community centers. Eighteen months after his arrival, however, hostile criticism and budget cuts led Collier to resign.[27]

Collier's first contact with Indians developed after he and his family embarked on a camping trip to Sonora, Mexico. Mabel Dodge, who now lived in Taos, New Mexico, invited the Colliers to visit on their way, and they arrived in time to witness the impressive Christmas rites staged at Taos Pueblo. Collier found that the ceremonies "entered into myself and each one of my family as a new direction of life—a new, even wildly new, hope for the Race of Man."[28] Collier had accepted the "prevailing anthropological view" that the Indian way of life was doomed, but he now recognized that the small group at Taos had maintained their "personality-shaping institutions" through "repeated and immense historical shocks. . . ."[29] When he left Taos in 1921 for a teaching job in San Francisco, Collier believed that Indians should not be lost to the onslaught of white pressures.

Like many contemporary thinkers, Collier believed that the industrial revolution, conservative Social Darwinism, and rampant individualism had created a society that made people isolated, alienated, and anomic. By reinstituting voluntary associations, Collier hoped to renew a sense of community and shared obligations that he believed once existed in European traditional communities.[30] He saw Indians in the same way. By preserving tribal cultures, they would not only continue an attractive life but also offer valuable lessons for other Americans.[31]

Although an idealist, Collier was pragmatic. He identified Indian survival with retention of their land base. He also recognized that Indians would change, but he rejected the forced assimilation and demanded cultural pluralism or individual choice. Realism also marked Collier's lobbying tactics. His stinging denunciations of opponents often went beyond truth and condemned individuals whose worst sin was difference of opinion, but such propaganda brought results. He drew financial support from New York or California intelligentsia. But Collier confronted some of the most powerful interests in the West with a highly varied set of congressional allies. Several were western progressives—Senators Burton K. Wheeler of Montana, William Borah of Idaho, and Lynn J. Frazier of North Dakota—but others—Senators Charles Curtis of Kansas and William H. King of Utah—were conservatives. Collier's strongest congressional ally was Representative James A. Frear of Wisconsin, a maverick Republican who in 1924 had supported the Progressive Party.[32]

Collier's switch from academe to Indian reform took place in May 1922, when he met Stella Atwood and her wealthy friend, Mrs. Kate Vosburg, at Azusa, California. Atwood wanted Collier to conduct an independent investigation of Indian conditions under the sponsorship of the General Federation of Women's Clubs, and Vosburg agreed to finance his work for two years. A month before Collier's departure for New Mexico, Atwood learned about the second Bursum bill, and after an unsatisfactory exchange with Burke, she decided to oppose the measure. Collier, meantime, had completed a study of federal Indian policy which he believed was flawed from its inception.[33]

Collier's arrival in Santa Fe in September initiated a hectic campaign to defeat the Bursum bill, which the Senate had approved. Collier initially cooperated with white sympathizers of Santa Fe and Taos who organized the New Mexico Association on Indian Affairs (NMAIA) to protest the bill. Collier and Antonio Luhan, a Taos Indian and Mabel Dodge's future husband, toured the northern Pueblos organizing support. Collier and Francis Wilson, a Santa Fe attorney, also drafted an anti-bill "blue book," which they distributed widely. After raising funds in California to employ Wilson, Collier visited the southern Pueblos.[34]

On November 5, 1922, 121 representatives from twenty Pueblos met and formed the All-Pueblo Council. According to Collier, the new group represented the first Pueblo confederation since the revolt of 1680.[35] The council adopted a memorial against the Bursum bill, and a copy of it soon appeared in the *New York Times*. A stream of news stories, editorials, and petitions followed. On December 21, Senator Borah recalled the Bursum bill from the House.[36]

The resulting furor led to a spirited but ineffective government defense. Fall threatened to start legal proceedings to evict all non-Indians from Pueblo lands. He also drafted a letter to Borah arguing that a quick solution was needed to avoid possible bloodshed and that whites deserved consideration because they paid taxes and Indians did not. The Harding Administration in January announced that Fall would leave the government in March.[37]

Although Borah's recall killed any chance of an immediate passage, Collier decided to prepare for the next session by bringing a Pueblo delegation to Washington. In early January 1923, he escorted seventeen Indians from New Mexico to Chicago and then to New York. Collier arranged several appearances, including a session of singing and drumming at the New York Stock Exchange. The colorful delegation was a huge success. In mid-January the Pueblos appeared before the Senate Committee on Public Lands and Surveys.

To provide an alternative to the Bursum bill, Collier and Wilson drafted the Jones-Leatherwood bill. The measure proposed that a three-man commission would arbitrate disputed claims, award titles, and determine compensation if both parties agreed. If arbitration failed, the federal district court would decide disputes, with the Indians represented by an attorney of their choice. The bill also sought $905,000 in federal funds to reclaim some 20,000 acres, which would be used to compensate unsuccessful claimants.[38]

Collier's cause fared well at the Senate hearings in mid-January 1923. Wilson testified about the Pueblos' loss of autonomy under the Bursum bill, its bias in giving whites titles, the unfairness of compensating Indians with worthless public lands, and their loss of water rights. Colonel R. E. Twitchell, government attorney for the Pueblos and co-author of the Bursum bill, admitted under sharp questioning that most provisions should be rewritten. Fall denounced the Jones-Leatherwood bill as too expensive.[39]

The House hearings in early February hearing went badly. After Wilson's testimony, committee members grilled Mrs. Atwood about her authority to represent the General Federation of Women's Clubs. Collier then criticized committee members for unfairly attacking Atwood and furiously condemned the Bursum bill and Pueblo health conditions. Assistant Commissioner Meritt countered Collier's testimony as the final witness.[40]

Collier's lobbying in 1923 was not flawless. Confident that he had blocked the Bursum bill, Collier left Washington in mid-February to organize more support. Unfortunately, he was unaware of impending hearings on the Omnibus bill and of Fall's recent order placing executive order lands under the General Leasing Act. Nor was Collier aware that Wilson and the Eastern Association of Indian Affairs (EAIA) were trying to effect a compromise on Pueblo lands before adjournment.[41]

Senator La Follette took the lead in defeating the Omnibus bill. During hearings in mid-February, the Wisconsin senator questioned the pro rata division of tribal assets by recalling the Sells competency policies. Collier first heard of the bill while visiting Chicago, and he contacted supporters in New York who met EAIA leaders and arranged some adverse publicity, but La Follette averted passage by objecting to a unanimous consent on the Senate floor.[42]

Collier's belated awareness of the compromise on Pueblo lands is even more puzzling. Roberts Walker, a New York attorney and EAIA leader, contacted Fall during the House hearings in early February and suggested that the two sides "forget the chatter and get down to brass tacks." Fall consented to a compromise only after Walker repudiated Atwood and Collier. Burke met with the Senate Committee on Public Lands on February 18, 1923, to draft what became the Lenroot substitute bill. Wilson, by Fall's orders, was not present but submitted a statement on needed changes.[43]

The Lenroot measure called for a three-man Pueblo land board to determine the validity of contested claims and bring suit in federal district court to quiet title. Two classes of non-Indians could gain title to land within the Pueblo land grants by appealing to the court: first were those who could prove occupation under "color of title" for twenty years, and second were persons with a "claim of ownership" for thirty years. The board would recommend compensation to losing claimants, but the bill did not authorize such awards. The Senate approved the measure on February 28, but a representative from Kentucky blocked passage in the House by objecting to unanimous consent.[44]

After the 1923 session ended, Collier and Wilson broke over the attempted compromise. To Collier, all non-Indian encroachment since 1848 had been illegal; Wilson believed that purchases before the 1913 *Sandoval* decision were valid. Collier attributed the worst motives to Wilson: he had compromised himself, willfully disobeyed orders, and deliberately deceived Collier. Despite Wilson's argument that the Lenroot bill corrected the major flaws in the Bursum bill, Collier dismissed him in late April.

During the 1923-1924 congressional session, the Lenroot bill and a measure drafted by Adoph A. Berle, Jr., Wilson's replacement, were introduced. Berle's bill stipulated that the Indians owned all the land they held in 1848, and their permission and compensation were required for all sales to non-Indians. The revised Lenroot bill contained two key provisions drafted by Wilson. One gave non-Indian claimants title if they had occupied the land continuously since 1902, and the other gave title to those who could show a "claim of ownership" since 1889. Berle's protests led to a compromise. The non-Indians could receive title only if they had paid taxes continuously since the two dates, and the Pueblos could appeal the board's rulings before the local federal district court. All unsuccessful claimants were entitled to compensation. In June 1924, the Pueblo Lands Act finally passed. Collier played little role during the session because of illness.[45]

Unfortunately, the implementation of the act fell short of Collier's expectations. Those appointed to the Pueblo Land Board rendered decisions that invariably favored the settlers, and the district court interpreted the continuous payment of taxes so loosely that the requirement was virtually negated. As his correspondence amply demonstrates, Collier's efforts to pursue legal remedies against the Pueblo Land Board's decisions proved too time-consuming and expensive to be effective.[46]

The issue of Indian rights to oil and gas revenues of executive order lands proved equally difficult to resolve. Not only were the revenues important, but they also could well determine the Indians' title to the land itself. The federal government tackled Navajo rights on two fronts after Fall placed the executive order lands under the General Leasing Act. Misgivings about leasing through the local councils and superintendents apparently led Fall to restructure Navajo administration and governance. In early January 1923, he placed Herbert J. Hagerman of New Mexico in charge of leasing and forming a tribal council to approve new leases.[47] After a briefing in Washington, Hagerman conferred with the Navajo superintendents on the procedures for organizing the tribal council. With some adjustments in the latter, the Navajos elected delegates, and the tribal council met in July, authorizing Hagerman to make future oil and gas leases.[48]

The task of resolving the oil and gas revenues issue fell to Hubert Work, a prominent Republican and former postmaster general, who replaced Fall. Work's reputation as a competent and honest administrator doubtlessly led to his appointment. Even though the Teapot Dome scandal had not yet broken, Fall had left the Interior Department in chaos because of internal divisions and criticisms of conservationists.[49]

In dealing with the executive order lands, Work froze both the exploratory permits already granted and the processing of new applications under the General Leasing Act. He asked the attorney general in 1924 for an opinion on what title Indians held to the executive order lands and whether those holdings came under the General Leasing Act as Fall had ruled. The resulting opinion denied that the executive order lands were still public domain and added that neither Congress nor the courts had ever made any distinctions between lands ordained by treaty, executive order, or legislation, and the attorney general warned that the issue would remain unresolved until the courts or Congress acted.[50]

The legislative battle that followed offered a striking example of the conflict between white regional interests and Indian protection. The extreme western position would have denied Indian title and kept them from receiving any revenues. The opposite view would have guaranteed Indian title and total revenues. Obviously, Congress was unlikely to approve either of these positions, but the Indian Oil Act of 1927 came surprisingly close to a full realization of Indians' interests.[51]

Secretary Work, seizing the initiative, introduced legislation in both houses in December 1923 to place the leasing of oil and gas on executive order lands under the General Leasing Act but awarding all revenues to the tribes. Even so, Work's proposed legislation implied that the federal government retained title to the lands and gave control of leasing to the General Land Office rather than the BIA.[52]

The bills failed; Congress approved the Indian Oil Leasing Act of 1924, amending the 1891 act for treaty land leases. The new measure enacted existing leasing regulations into law, dropped the ten-year limit on leases in favor of contracts that ran until the oil or gas was depleted, and allowed the states to tax production on reservations at the same rate as non-reservation production. Even though the act did not apply to executive order lands, it served as a precedent for future legislation.[53]

Work reintroduced bills on executive order lands in the next session, but they again failed. One conference amendment, however, gave 37.5 percent of the revenues to the states. In the following session, Representative Carl Hayden of Arizona introduced a bill that placed all leasing of executive order lands under the Indian Oil Leasing Act of 1924. The Hayden bill also gave the states 37.5 percent of revenues with the proviso that the money be spent on Indian education or roads. Commissioner Burke endorsed the measure because the states' share would benefit Indians, but, perhaps more importantly, because he favored leasing under the BIA rather than the General Land Office. Neither reformers nor westerners wanted a compromise bill. A minority report filed by three members of the House Indian Affairs Committee recommended placing executive order lands under federal title and complained that the wealthy Navajos did not need any new revenues. Collier and Representative Frear agreed with placing leasing under the 1924 act because this strengthened Indian title, but they also wanted the 37.5 percent tax replaced by the same taxing arrangements of the Indian Oil Act of 1924.[54]

A controversy over the Lees Ferry Bridge during this same period gave Collier an ideal cause to develop support for his views. In February 1925, Congress had authorized a $100,000 reimbursable loan to the Navajos to build a new bridge across the Colorado River at Lees Ferry, if Arizona contributed an equal amount. Collier and his allies quickly denounced the project. The new bridge would not benefit the Navajos; it only served the needs of white promoters who wished to link the upper and lower rims of Grand Canyon. The Navajos, Collier complained, had more pressing needs such as land acquisition, water development, and improved live-stock breeding. Moreover, the tribal council had never been consulted about the $100,000. Collier's publicity, in short, created an image that the reimbursable loan was a blatantly unfair attempt to loot the tribe of recently acquired oil money. Even though Hayden and Senator Ashurst obtained funding for the bridge in 1926, the adverse publicity helped secure favorable legislation on oil and gas leasing.[55]

Meantime, sentiment in Congress shifted toward reform. Senators Wheeler and La Follette, in particular, endorsed the idea of awarding all oil and gas revenues to Indians subject only to the taxing arrangement of the 1924 act. Help came from a somewhat surprising source when Senator Ralph Cameron of Arizona introduced a bill that not only awarded Indians nearly all revenues but also stipulated that tribes must be consulted on reimbursable loans. Despite considerable opposition in both houses, the provisions of the Cameron bill were amended into the Hayden bill and approved by Congress. President Calvin Coolidge initially vetoed the bill, but he signed a slightly revised version in March 1927. Remarkably, the act retained the provision for Indian consultation on reimbursable loans. Although it was "the most important single piece of general legislation in the 1920's," ironically no oil was discovered in the executive order portion of the Navajo Reservation, and, because of overproduction and low prices, the government did not encourage new leases after 1927. The fact that the new act did not specifically grant Indian title to executive order lands has not been a major problem.[56]

A controversy over Flathead rights to royalties to hydroelectricity further illustrates problems of protecting Indian resources. In early 1927 Burke met with representatives of the Montana Power Company and the Flathead irrigation district. No Indians were invited. The meeting dealt with an important power site on the Flathead River six miles south of Polson, Montana. A "gentleman's agreement" in February gave Montana Power the right to generate 175,000 horsepower of electricity at an annual rental of one dollar per horsepower. The company promised to supply the irrigation district 10,000 horsepower of electricity at one mill per kilowatt hour and an additional 5,000 horsepower at two and one-half mills per kilowatt hour. The low rates would allow the irrigation district to pump water to lands presently too high to supply by gravity. Montana Power also agreed to pay the federal government $101,000 for the abandoned Newell tunnel. Finally, the federal power commission was to receive 25 percent of all rentals for its earlier survey and field expenses. Whites would receive two-thirds and Indians one-third of the remaining royalties.[57]

Secretary Work's hopes for a quick congressional approval of the power agreement faded. Representative Louis C. Cramton of Michigan, chairman of the Appropriations Subcommittee for the Interior Department, incorporated the agreement into an amendment to a deficiency bill. Cramton, ignoring any Indian claims to the site, saw the arrangement as vital in rescuing local white settlers from economic distress.[58] Collier, however, attacked the Flathead agreement. In a widely distributed bulletin, he maintained that the terms violated the treaty of 1855 that had guaranteed Indian title to land and timber around Flathead Lake. Moreover, the Federal Water Power Act of 1920 had promised Indians all royalties from reservation lands. Collier also complained that revenues should be three times higher, that the settlers did not deserve electricity at cost, and that the government should not be reimbursed for the tunnel.[59]

Once again, progressive senators aided Collier. Frazier, La Follette, and Wheeler successfully defeated Cramton's amendment to the deficiency bill, and the bill fell into limbo. Even before the Flathead controversy, Collier had developed a working relationship with Senator Wheeler and his friend, A. A. Grorud of Helena, Montana.[60] The Montana senator, a strong advocate of public power and a bitter foe of both the powerful Anaconda Copper Company and Montana Power, which supplied electricity for processing copper ore, saw the Flathead controversy as an ideal opportunity to strike a blow at his political enemies and to bring larger royalties to the Indians. He took the lead in killing the agreement in February 1928. This, in turn, placed the responsibility for any lease on the Federal Power Commission.[61]

Collier's efforts during the next two years centered on securing competitive bidding for the Flathead power site. Unfortunately, the thin population, market domination by Montana Power, and weak industrial potential in Montana were not conducive to producing increased royalties. Indeed, the only other bidder was Walter H. Wheeler, a businessman and consulting engineer from Minneapolis.[62] Wheeler proposed that he would develop 214,000 horsepower of electricity annually and pay a royalty of $240,000. His bid, however, was seriously weakened by his lack of immediate customers for the electricity. Although he maintained that new industries would purchase the electricity, his lack of specific details aroused serious doubts. Collier made imaginative but unsuccessful efforts to find some way to determine a fair royalty. Although he favored public power development, he backed Wheeler's offer as a lesser evil. The onset of the depression made the Wheeler bid even more tenuous. Ray Lyman Wilbur, secretary of interior, in 1930 endorsed the Montana Power proposal, and later in the year the Federal Power Commission granted the utility a license. The benefits given the Flatheads marked a major improvement over those offered originally. The Indians were to receive $60,000 annually for 50,000 horsepower during the first five years, and during the succeeding five-year increments the payments would increase to $125,000, $150,000, $160,000, and $175,000. Montana Power also supplied 15,000 horsepower to the irrigation district and paid the government $101,000 for the Newell tunnel.[63]

Collier's criticisms after 1922 led to the Meriam investigation of 1926-1927, perhaps the most significant inquiry into Indian conditions and administration during the twentieth century. The inquiry resulted from con-

versations between Thomas Jesse Jones of the Phelps-Stokes Fund and
Lewis Meriam and W. F. Willoughby of the Institute for Government Research of Washington, D.C.[64] Agreeing on the need for a study, the three
men began talks with Secretary Work and his staff. In June 1926, Work formally asked the Institute to conduct a study, and in September the Rockefeller family funded it.

Meriam meantime had largely completed organizing and appointing a
staff of ten investigators. Besides himself as technical director, Meriam included specialists in legal aspects, economic conditions, Indian migrants to
urban areas, health, existing records related to Indians, family life and activities related to women, education, and agriculture. Henry Roe Cloud, a
noted Winnebago educator, served as "Indian advisor" and intermediary
between the commission and Indians.[65] Meriam failed to name specialists
for irrigation or forestry, although both fields required considerable technical expertise.[66]

Meriam's normal quantitative approach for social and economic studies
was seldom attainable. Despite the BIA penchant for record keeping, data
on several vital topics were either missing or unreliable. The pace of visiting ninety-five jurisdictions and logging 25,000 miles in six months did not
permit a deliberate and scientific approach.[67] Staff members often split up
as individuals or small groups during their field work. Later they conferred
and exchanged impressions while traveling or in their lodgings. Nevertheless, the Meriam group visited nearly every important BIA facility in the
West and the Great Lakes regions. They returned to Washington in mid-
1927 and drafted their report, which was published as *The Problem of Indian
Administration* in early 1928.

The report showed a cautious stance toward Collier's cultural pluralism.
It recognized that many Indians wished to preserve their heritage but
warned that "Indians are face to face with the predominating civilization of
whites," and they had lost the original "economic foundation upon which
the Indian culture rested."[68] The commission criticized the dictatorial assimilation policies of the past, especially allotment and forced patenting,
but it warned against hasty or drastic changes such as abolishing the BIA or
ending all federal protections and services. Solutions would require
money, careful planning, and time rather than radical changes.[69]

The findings related to education, health, and poverty received the most
public attention. The report stressed that BIA education was grossly inferior to public schooling, and it failed to prepare youngsters for life on reservations or in general society. Moreover, the underfunding of boarding
schools led to the practice of students spending half of their days perform-
ing duties needed to operate the institutions. This seriously interfered with
educational opportunities and proved overly strenuous for younger students. The Meriam report was equally critical of the living conditions at
many boarding schools, particularly overcrowded dormitories, inferior facilities for personal hygiene, and inadequate nutrition.[70]

The report raised similar complaints about BIA health care. Indians suffered extraordinarily high rates of tuberculosis, trachoma, and other diseases, but BIA treatment facilities were grossly inferior to those maintained by federal and state agencies for non-Indians. Low funding discouraged employment of competent doctors and nurses and failed to provide proper medical equipment. Preventive medicine, except for smallpox vaccinations, was lacking. BIA medical facilities often failed to keep accurate health records.[71]

The report noted that "too many of them [Indians] are poor and living below any reasonable standard of health and decency," and statistics certainly confirmed the assertion.[72] Approximately two-thirds of the Indian population survived on an economic base (or total assets) valued under $2,000 per capita. Almost half held personal property worth less than $500. Some 71 percent of Indians earned less than $200 annually from both tribal and individual properties, and survived only by hunting and gathering. Even so, commissioners often asked, "How can these people eke out an existence?" Experienced BIA field workers admitted that they had never found a satisfactory answer.[73]

Mistaken government policies, the report stressed, were partially responsible for Indian poverty. Particularly harmful were allotment and forced patents. But Indians also had never adjusted to modern economic conditions. The commissions warned against Indians converting their remaining land or natural resources into cash by sales. Such transactions only eroded an already weak economic position. Indians were also adversely affected by the unearned income they derived from leasing of lands and interest from tribal funds. Such money kept them idle and impoverished. The report concluded that the remaining Indian assets—tribal and personal—needed to be protected and used in a manner which would encourage self-support.[74]

Although the commission's findings stressed ending Indian poverty by improved use of agricultural resources, some of its most interesting findings dealt with off-reservation migrants. It identified three basic categories of such people.[75] The first involved squatter camps located outside Needles, California, and Kingman, Globe, and Miami, Arizona. The residents lived in crude shacks and found occasional employment. They were extremely poor and isolated from adjacent communities.[76] The second group, mostly Pueblos, worked in repair shops of the Santa Fe Railroad at Winslow, Arizona, and Gallup, New Mexico. Although their wage levels varied considerably, they lived in company housing, their children attended public schools, and they participated in company social affairs. Most, however, maintained strong ties with their Pueblos by frequent visits back and forth.[77]

The final category involved Indians who lived in cities but were not colonized. The survey found great diversity among such Indians. Many were white in personal appearance and life style, although they identified themselves as Indians.[78] Many complained that boarding schools had failed to prepare them for a career, separated them from their families, and exposed them to hard work and poor living conditions. They contrasted their background struggles with the educational opportunities enjoyed by their own children. As a group, the urban Indians were more assertive about the BIA's failures to answer questions or explain such matters as enrollment or allotment rights.[79]

If any theme typified the non-colonized urban Indians, it was their belief that they could not make a living on a reservation. Some, indeed, advocated drastic measures for ending reservation poverty, including the abolition of the BIA, giving fee patents to everyone, and removing all children from parents. When asked about the impact of breaking up Indian families, they asserted that many reservation homes were "unfit or practically nonexistent." Some interviewees showed concern about reservation conditions because they wanted to help fellow Indians, still had children living with relatives on reservations, or planned to return later in life.[80] It seems clear that the 1920s urban Indians previewed the numerous Indians who moved to cities during and after World War II.

The Meriam report also noted that white employers often compared Indian job performance and personal traits with those of Mexican-American workers. Most white employers judged the Indians equal or superior because of their literacy in English and their steady work habits. Evidence demonstrated that Mexican-Americans and Indians often competed for the same low-paying, unskilled jobs.[81]

Most of the recommendations of the Meriam Commission centered on improving the efficiency of the BIA by more funding or increased expertise. The commission, for example, agreed that Congress should appropriate $1,000,000 as an emergency measure to improve the diet of boarding school children. The BIA also needed to upgrade the quality of its personnel and provide better health, education, and other services. The commission, in short, ignored a radical restructuring of federal Indian administration and sought to make existing programs more effective. Much of the commission's hopes rested on the creation of a division of planning and development within the BIA. The new office would provide continuity of policy both in Washington and in the field by designing long-term programs rather than changing policies with every shift in administration personnel. It would also produce technical and scientific advice that the BIA presently lacked.[82]

Collier's lobbying for a Senate investigation of Indian affairs while the Meriam report was still being prepared, in late 1927, seems puzzling.[83] With Collier's urging, Senator William H. King of Utah introduced a resolution for a Senate inquiry in December. At hearings the following month, Collier argued that a second investigation was needed to expose and fix responsibility for BIA shortcomings. The study, he added, would also reveal the need for new legislation to reverse land policies and end further losses.

Collier additionally claimed that the BIA had covered up serious health conditions and tolerated overcrowding in schools.[84] Collier probably already knew that the Meriam report would be too moderate for his tastes, and he may have believed that a second inquiry, coming soon after the Meriam report, would produce basic changes.[85] Regardless, the Senate approved the second investigation in February 1928.

A subcommittee of the Senate Indian Affairs Committee started its first hearings in late 1928 and continued until 1943. The "Survey of Conditions of the Indians in the United States . . . ," would eventually total over 23,000 pages in forty-one parts. The hearings provide an unstructured but invaluable body of data about reservations and Indian administration. During its early and most active years, the subcommittee spent most of its time in the field when Congress was not in session. Regardless of party affiliation, the early subcommittee members were men who had little affection for current national leadership.[86] Senator Wheeler's forceful examination of witnesses easily made him the dominant member. Although Collier held no official capacity with the subcommittee, he traveled with it frequently and cooperated closely with the special investigator on exhibits, witnesses, and related matters.[87]

One major event associated with the subcommittee's early work was the removal of Commissioner Burke during a probe of the Jackson Barnett case. Barnett was a full-blood Creek from eastern Oklahoma who had suddenly become a millionaire from oil royalties on his allotment. The case had gained notoriety because of Jackson's 1920 marriage to a white adventuress and former prostitute, Burke's consent to giving half of Barnett's estate to the Baptist Home Mission Society in 1922, and endless legal wrangling between state and federal officials. Indeed, Burke's role had been probed several times before the subcommittee in early 1929 opened hearings. A Justice Department attorney testified that Burke would have been among those indicted after a grand jury hearing in Oklahoma except that higher officials ordered the proceedings postponed. That afternoon Burke angrily charged Senator Pine with a conspiracy "to destroy me." He claimed that Pine sought revenge because of a patronage defeat and that the Oklahoma senator had enlisted government attorneys in a conspiracy against Burke. Collier, "a notorious Indian agitator," was also involved. During a later appearance to support his charges, Burke repeatedly softened his earlier statements, and Wheeler eventually forced him to admit that he had no direct evidence or knowledge of a conspiracy. Burke's resignation soon afterward, however, was foreordained. At sixty-eight and in ill health, he had little chance of retaining his post in the new Hoover administration.

John Collier's role in Indian affairs of the 1920s challenged the assimilationist strategy pursued since the 1880s. His cultural pluralism, militant lobby tactics, propaganda skills, and intelligence gave Indian reform a prominence it had lacked since the Dawes Act. Despite this, the regional context in which Indians lived merits a good deal of attention. The changing demography of the West, especially the diminished farm migration, was particularly important. Indian land for agriculture no longer commanded the attention of non-Indians as it had before World War I. The only major reform involving land that Collier pursued was the long fight over the Bursum bill, and this dealt with an attempt to recover holdings lost in the past. Collier's other struggles either dealt with policy matters or Indians' natural resources. Ultimately, the latter became the chief focus of concern.

6.

Depression and the New Deal

The stock market crash of 1929 and the depression which followed had a staggering impact on the American West. Reduced farm prices were nation-wide, but a large portion of the West experienced dust bowl conditions, which added to the distress of regional agriculture. Many of the intermountain areas had skimmed off mineral wealth earlier and failed to develop alternative enterprises. Personal income levels in western states generally fell below the national average in the 1930s. The industrial gains of World War I had not resulted in permanent jobs, and even San Francisco, Tacoma-Seattle, and Los Angeles had a low percentage of population involved in manufacturing.[1] Traditionally, western prosperity had depended on population growth. Despite all the attention given to migration to California during the 1930s, the figures fell well below those in the 1920s.

If the West had always been Uncle Sam's stepchild, the region became a full-fledged member of the family after 1933. The pace of federal efforts speeded up as unprecedented spending on the regional infrastructure completed projects that normally would have required decades to accomplish. The New Deal programs included construction of major dams and irrigation systems, road building, improvement and expansion of national parks, and prevention of wind and water erosion and other conservation efforts. Moreover, rational planning by an endless variety of national, regional, and state bodies studied problems and considered programs. Although some westerners disliked the "federal presence," most recognized that only the national government possessed the ability to meet the economic and natural disasters that decimated the region. In a span of some seven years, New Deal programs transformed the region from a preindustrial stage to a level where a "take off" could take place during World War II.[2]

Despite its numerous successes, the New Deal in the West also experienced serious failures. Perhaps the worst was Secretary of Interior Harold L. Ickes's inability to regulate the oil industry. The same oilmen who pleaded for federal controls in 1933 became adamant foes of regulation once their industry revived. Similarly, the small but effective western "silver bloc" managed to secure legislation that raised silver prices over the opposition of Ickes and President Franklin D. Roosevelt.[3] Although New Dealers often voiced the goal of helping the "little man," various special interests often manipulated programs for their own benefit. Coordinated planning by various levels of government and private organizations seldom worked well except in the Pacific Northwest. Partly because of this, but also because of squabbling between the Interior and Agriculture departments, New Deal programs were often piecemeal, wasteful, and overlapping.[4]

If economic woes affected Indians less than whites, it was simply because most reservations were chronically depressed. As one South Dakota Sioux commented, "we're all on the same level now. The white man is in the same shape we are."[5] Nevertheless, many Indians faced additional distress after 1929. Jobs vanished, and the lack of migratory work drove people back to reservations, further burdening relatives.[6] Revenues from land, oil, gas, timber, and other sources dropped disastrously.[7] The sale of arts and crafts fell as tourism declined. On the Navajo Reservation, wool prices dropped in 1930, and many owners kept their unmarketable fall lambs, thus aggravating overgrazing. Blizzards and subzero temperatures during the winter of 1931-1932 killed thousands of sheep and other livestock and even aroused the sympathies of traders long accustomed to Indian destitution. When spring came, Navajos pulled "dead wool" from sheep carcasses and sold the foul stuff to traders. Repeatedly they inquired if "Uncle Sam had gone broke."[8]

Prior to 1931, the Hoover administration seemed indifferent to the Indian problem. This changed when drought and locusts ravaged the Great Plains. The BIA, with few resources, turned to the Red Cross, which supplied $192,000 and sizeable amounts of flour and crushed wheat. The army donated fifty-five carloads of surplus clothing. A new session of Congress appropriated $410,000 for Indian relief, and they received seed loans from the Department of Agriculture.[9]

The Hoover administration after 1929 sought to implement the reforms of the Meriam report. Ray Lyman Wilbur, president of Stanford, became secretary of interior, and he appointed Charles J. Rhoads as Indian commissioner and J. Henry Scattergood as assistant commissioner.[10] Both men were Philadelphia Quakers and active in the Indian Rights Association (IRA) and other philanthropic work. Meriam remained available to advise the new administration, and, through his efforts, Collier agreed to "let minor things ride" and work on a common program.[11]

Rhoads endorsed Collier's suggestions on education, the need for an arts and crafts bill, and the protection of Indian civil liberties. The appointment of W. Carson Ryan as education director was regarded as a special victory. A nationally known leader in progressive education, Ryan had served on the Meriam commission, and his appointment indicated the administration's dedication to school reform, particularly to improved living conditions in boarding institutions.

In consultation with Matthew K. Sniffen of the IRA and Meriam, Collier drafted four letters to Lynn J. Frazier, chairman of the Senate Indian Affairs Committee, suggesting needed changes. The letters called for a repeal of the General Allotment Act, the authorization for tribes to incorporate themselves, additional agricultural credit, and enlargement of tribal control over real estate. The letters further asked for a ban on financing irrigation from tribal funds, the transfer of existing projects to the Reclamation Service, and settling Indian claims against the federal government.[12]

The two major achievements of the Hoover administration, the reorganization of the BIA and major increases in funding, stemmed from the Meriam report. The reorganization in 1931 separated field work into five divisions: health, education, agricultural extension, forestry, and irrigation. Each was headed by a director who reported to one of two new assistants to the commissioner.[13] Despite Meriam's urging, Rhoads never established a division of planning.[14] BIA appropriations rose from $16,000,000 in 1929 to $20,000,000 in 1932. But reorganization and larger budgets produced problems. Older BIA employees complained that higher employment and promotion standards jeopardized their future opportunities. The use of virtually all additional money to raise salaries of BIA workers and to add new positions did not relieve the severe distress among Indians.[15]

By 1930 Collier's disagreements with Rhoads and Scattergood led him to revert to his role of vocal critic. He denounced Scattergood's negotiation of the Flathead power lease and the BIA's failure to demand legislation that they had earlier endorsed. He was especially upset by Rhoads and Scattergood's acceptance of a compromise over the food budget for boarding schools. The Hoover administration had requested 37.8 cents per day for each student, but Representative Louis C. Cramton pared the increase by 75 percent. Incensed at this, Collier was furious when Rhoads refused to fight for a restoration of the original figure.[16]

Once Collier made his break with Rhoads and Scattergood, he employed the same tactics used against Burke. The Senate progressives, no more pleased with Hoover than they had been with Coolidge, cooperated with Collier's renewed campaign against the BIA. Herbert J. Hagerman offered an ideal target. In 1923 Secretary Fall had placed Hagerman in charge of organizing the Navajo council to approve oil leases, and he later served on the Pueblo Lands Board. In the latter post, he had, in Collier's eyes, acted prejudicially against the Indians.

At Senator Frazier's invitation, Collier prepared evidence against Hagerman and served as a virtual prosecutor throughout the long Senate hearings in early 1931. The inquiry first dealt with complaints against Hagerman's work on Pueblo land claims, including low compensation, underappraisals, failure to protect water rights, and bias in rewarding land titles to whites. When the subcommittee took up Hagerman's supervision of the Navajos, Collier unfairly linked Fall's appointment of Hagerman with the Teapot Dome Scandal. Collier also charged that the early Navajo oil leases were let when prices were low and favored large firms over independents. After Hagerman returned from the hearings, friends escorted him into Santa Fe and hanged Collier in effigy in front of the Governor's Palace. But more was involved in the episode than Collier's overly zealous persecution of Hagerman. Non-Indian settlers in the Rio Grande Valley, who had spent large sums on legal fees, supported Hagerman's low rewards to the Indians and bitterly denounced Collier's recent suits to eject non-Indians from their land. Perhaps more important, the real estate market collapsed because of imperfect land titles.[17]

In a final blow in Collier's battle against Wilbur, Rhoads, and Scattergood, Senator William King of Utah on March 9 presented a Collier petition on the Senate floor. It castigated Wilbur's retention of Hagerman as insulting to the Indians and lashed his administration for not fulfilling the reforms he endorsed in 1929. The following day, Wilbur blamed congressional inaction for failure to achieve needed reforms. The secretary characterized Collier's accusations as "misrepresentations almost approaching blackmail."[18]

The gains in education and increased funding during the Rhoads-Scattergood years were overshadowed by their failures. Both men were moderates and novices. Although they accepted the goals outlined in the Meriam report, they had little chance of achieving these without the strong support of Hoover and Wilbur, which was never forthcoming. Despite the rhetoric of cultural pluralism that appears in BIA *Annual Reports* after 1929, how fully Rhoads and Scattergood really believed in the philosophy and were prepared to implement it is questionable. As for Wilbur, he was an assimilationist who wanted the BIA abolished in twenty-five years. The obsessive interest of the Hoover administration in reorganization may have led Rhoads and Scattergood to believe that revising BIA administration in 1931 was an important advance, but the changes, however efficient, did not meet the pressing needs of Indians during the depression, nor did they respond to the basic legislative enactments Collier demanded. The inquiry on Hagerman was more a vehicle for Collier to embarrass the Hoover administration and to insure that it did not win reelection.

Crucial decisions on Indian affairs took place after the election of Franklin D. Roosevelt and the appointment of a new secretary of interior and Indian commissioner. Shortly after Roosevelt's victory, Harold L. Ickes let it be known that he wanted the commissionership. The Chicago attorney was a sometime ally of Collier and close friend and supporter of Senator Hiram Johnson of California. During the recent presidential campaign Ickes had worked to enlist fellow progressive Republicans to support Roosevelt.[19] During Ickes's trip to Washington to lobby for the commissionership, Collier, Meriam, attorney Nathan Margold, and others advised him to seek the more powerful post of assistant secretary of interior. Collier's real motive, however, was to steer the Chicagoan away from the BIA post. Collier regarded Ickes as too inexperienced and temperamental to head the BIA. Roosevelt eventually offered the secretary of interior post to Bronson Cutting and Hiram Johnson, but neither wanted to give up their Senate seats. In a surprise move, the president-elect named Ickes to head the Interior Department. Collier meantime had been working behind the scene to become Indian commissioner. Besides Collier, Margold and Meriam were regarded as likely reform candidates, but Ickes appointed Margold as a solicitor in the Interior Department, and Meriam rejected the job. This left Collier in competition only with former Assistant Commissioner Edgar Meritt who had the support of his brother-in-law Joseph T. Robinson, Senate majority leader. In a showdown with Ickes and Robinson, the president chose Collier over Meritt.[20]

The appointment was unorthodox in several ways. Roosevelt acted not so much on political grounds as from a reform impulse. Collier, moreover, carried into office a strong belief in cultural pluralism, which many BIA employees opposed, and his prolonged agitation had offended many of the top staffers. Nevertheless, no previous incoming commissioner knew so much about Indians or BIA administration and, once in office, displayed as much skill in bureaucratic manipulation.

Collier's agenda in 1933 had broadened considerably from his original ideas about Indians. Cultural pluralism remained central, but economic welfare had grown in importance. Few Indians could find non-reservation jobs, and Collier, out of necessity, placed a good deal of emphasis on economic development of reservations. Collier hoped to achieve Indian self-sufficiency through improvement and conservation of remaining Indian land, ending allotment and the constant loss of holdings, replacing white lessees with Indian farmers and ranchers, consolidating checkerboarded allotments into larger and more manageable units, and providing credit for economic development. Finally, Collier planned to revamp the role of the BIA from one of prosecuting attorney and judge to that of defender of the Indians' interests.

With Collier's appointment came new personnel. Assistant Commissioner William Zimmerman handled many day-to-day details of the bureau; Walter V. Woehlke, longtime ally of Collier, served in various capacities; and Ward Shepard, a forester, advised Collier on land policy. Given the past acrimony between the new commissioner and the BIA, Collier removed remarkably few bureau personnel.

Much of the administration's initial work dealt with organizing the Indian Emergency Conservation Work Program, popularly known as the Civilian Conservation Corps (CCC). Congress had approved the national CCC program even before Collier assumed office, and authorized conservation projects on federal, state, and private lands, including Indian reservations. J. P. Kinney, longtime director of forestry, and Ickes asked for a separate program for Indians, and the national CCC office and its several affiliated agencies approved the request. The Indian program afterward operated almost independently from the parent organization. In late April, the White House announced that the Indian CCC would receive $5,875,000 during the next six months for projects on thirty-three reservations. Hard pressed BIA workers had to recruit enrollees and supervisors, to design projects, and to buy equipment before the project work started in July.

The CCC gave reservations a much-needed economic boost in 1933. Some undernourished enrollees collapsed after starting work. Even the low wages permitted many Indian families to survive the drought and economic despair which gripped reservations. CCC projects also pleased local merchants who supplied equipment, and trading post operators were equally delighted that Indians had money to spend and to pay off old debts.[21]

If the CCC and other early emergency programs aroused little hostility in the West, the same was not true of Collier's Indian reorganization bill, sometimes known as the Wheeler-Howard bill. Several reorganization bills were introduced in early 1933, but none could be considered during the press of the One Hundred Days. Indian reformers during late 1933 began to discuss reorganization and the need to link self-government with land reforms and resource development. Representatives of several organizations met in Washington in early January 1934, with Lewis Meriam presiding and Collier and Ickes in attendance. They approved resolutions to end allotment, consolidate land holdings, create tribal governments, and replace existing Indian courts. Collier, meantime, conferred with Zimmerman, and Nathan Margold and Felix Cohen of the solicitor's office, to draft a reorganization bill. The result was sent in February to Senator Wheeler and Representative Edgar Howard, chairmen, respectively, of the Senate and House Committees on Indian Affairs.

The forty-eight-page bill was divided into four titles. Title I permitted Indian groups to establish tribal governments that could exercise numerous powers such as the chartering of business corporations and securing loans from a revolving fund. Title II endorsed the belief that Indian education should prepare students to assume positions in the BIA and to help preserve the Indian heritage. Title III repealed the General Allotment Act and outlined a complicated system for land consolidation by giving individual Indians shares in tribal lands rather than titles to specific holdings. The bill also authorized $2,000,000 per year for acquiring additional land. The most controversial provision allowed the secretary of interior to force the sale of allotments or exchanges of land to effect consolidation. Title IV called for the creation of special Indian courts, using traditional law, to exercise original jurisdiction on reservations.[22] Although the bill assigned numerous powers to tribal governments, many required the approval of the secretary of interior.

Hearings on the reorganization bill opened in the House committee on February 22. Although Chairman Howard supported the bill, it came under fire from several members who believed it would isolate Indians from the rest of society. The powers assigned to the tribes and the secretary of interior to force land consolidation raised even stronger misgivings. Undoubtedly, repairing the damage of allotment and consolidating trust lands into more manageable units required extraordinary measures, but the procedures in the bill varied so much from normal property rights and government roles that Thomas Werner of South Dakota and Isabella Greenway of Arizona raised strong objections.[23]

In the midst of the House hearings and during the Senate committee's early deliberations, Collier and his top assistants left Washington to conduct ten Indian congresses on the reorganization bill. The unprecedented consultation with tribal representatives reflected both Collier's altruism and his desire to win over Indian opposition. The first congress opened at Rapid City, South Dakota, on March 2, and congresses continued at various locations until they concluded at Hayward, Wisconsin, in late April. Collier or one of his assistants opened each congress by discussing how the bill addressed reservation problems. The government leaders then responded to written questions from the Indians. The sessions closed with the delegations giving their reactions to the bill.

The responses varied. Indians in the Pacific Northwest were more interested in fishing rights than land, while delegates of the Southwest and California raised questions about water rights. Neither subject was covered in the bill. Indian concerns generally focused on a few basic issues. They particularly raised questions about land consolidation. Most Indians had adjusted to the allotment system and viewed the arbitrary consolidation of land, at best, as overly abrupt, and, at worst, as confiscation of their only secure wealth. The land provisions also threatened to exacerbate existing divisions between full bloods and mixed bloods. Most full bloods still retained their allotments in trust, and they intensely resented the prospect that landless mixed bloods, who had lost their allotments after obtaining fee titles, would now gain new holdings. Many of the delegates rejected Collier's cultural pluralism and feared that it would isolate them and destroy earlier advances toward assimilation. Rabid advocates of assimilation indeed charged Collier with attempting to carry out communistic or socialistic principles.[24]

Despite the many objections, the congresses were generally successful. Collier and his advisors gained a better awareness of Indian fears of losing their allotments and Indian support for self-government. Educational benefits, the revolving credit fund, and the new courts engendered less discussion at the meetings because they promised benefits or were deemed unimportant. Although the congresses did not win over strong opponents, Collier gained the support of moderate leaders. The congresses, in short, were not a complete success, but they improved the bill's chances.

Before the congresses concluded, Collier returned to Washington. The bill he presented to the Senate Indian Affairs Committee in late April contained some thirty amendments based on suggestions at recent meetings. Despite his earlier cooperation with Collier, Senator Wheeler denounced statements in the bill as propaganda inappropriate in a legislative proposal. He rejected Collier's reply that the passages defined policy. Later in the hearings, Senator Elmer Thomas of Oklahoma attacked Collier's statement at the Anadarko congress that the Roosevelt administration could have railroaded the reorganization bill through Congress. Thomas interpreted the statement to mean that it made no difference what Congress thought about the measure. Collier's response that he was merely telling the Indians why they were being consulted did not satisfy the Oklahoma leader.

As the committee took up the more substantive provisions, members voiced objections raised during the House hearings. Both Wheeler and Thomas, for example, argued that self-government would isolate Indians and be retrogressive. They also questioned Indian competence, and Wheeler warned emphatically that Congress would never appropriate funds unless the Interior Department administered their expenditure. When Ward Shepard attempted to show the problems of allotment by displaying elaborate charts and maps, Wheeler brusquely dismissed the graphics as a waste of the committee's time and claimed that policy changes could achieve what was needed. The committee questioned authorizing the secretary of interior to purchase land for landless Indians. With considerable prescience, Thomas warned that white communities would resist removing property from the tax rolls.[25]

Physically worn down by the legislative struggle, especially the Senate hearings, Collier turned to the White House to break a legislative impasse. Roosevelt on April 28 sent letters to Howard and Wheeler urging them to pass the reorganization bill. Collier and Zimmerman subsequently met informally with both committees in an attempt to save the most important parts of the legislation. The resulting compromises dropped the Indian courts and made land consolidation voluntary. The extensive powers assigned to tribal governments were reduced to a single paragraph. Senator Wheeler reconvened his committee and began deliberations on the virtually new bill that now bore his strong personal imprint. When questions arose, he forcefully dictated the answers and proceeded without delay. The House committee meanwhile produced a bill that differed little from Wheeler's.

The floor debates produced few changes. Wheeler stressed that compulsory features had been removed and Indian participation in self-government and other provisions were now entirely voluntary. Senator Patrick McCarran of Nevada requested the portion of a tribe required to petition for a charter of incorporation be raised from one-fourth to one-third of adult population. Responding to mining interests, Senator Henry F. Ashurst won approval of an amendment which rescinded Secretary Wilbur's 1932 order withdrawing the Papago Reservation from mining entry.[26] McCarran also added an amendment guaranteeing that nothing in the proposed legislation would alter the present water laws on lands allocated or acquired by the Indians. The Senate approved the bill by voice vote.

The House debate took a more philosophical turn with opponents claiming that the bill would destroy treaty rights, perpetuate BIA control, and segregate Indians. These objections reflected complaints by Protestant missionary groups and right-wing Indian spokesmen. But defenders maintained that the objections applied to the original bill and that revisions had corrected earlier problems. The House approved the measure 258 to 88, a conference committee agreed to minor revisions, and President Roosevelt signed it on June 18.

What remained of the carefully drafted provisions of the original bill? In format and length, the changes were drastic. The forty-eight-page proposal organized in four titles was reduced to some five pages divided into nineteen sections. The special courts were entirely gone, and the other major sections—education, self-government, and land—were highly abbreviated. Alaska and Oklahoma were excluded from most provisions.

Nevertheless, the act was not inconsequential. Tribes could still constitute themselves as federal municipalities by drafting a constitution and by-laws. Some of the powers assigned to the tribal governments exceeded those in the original bill because the latter required the approval of the secretary of interior for nearly every power granted. The new governments, for example, could unilaterally negotiate with federal, state, and local governments, veto tribal property transactions, and review BIA budgets. A potential source of additional authority was contained in the statement that tribal governments could exercise "all powers vested in any Indian tribe or tribal council by existing law. . . ." Interior Solicitor Nathan Margold soon rendered an opinion that defined many of these powers; he theorized that the tribal governments under the act became "domestic dependent nations," reviving Chief Justice John Marshall's doctrine of the 1830s.[27]

The provisions for tribal business corporations also conveyed authority to the Indians. IRA tribes could receive a charter and form a business corporation. If the charter was then approved by referendum, the corporation could borrow money from the revolving credit fund; make loans to individuals; acquire, manage, and dispose of property; issue shares; and exercise other functions. The authorization of a $10,000,000 loan fund was a vital part of corporations' success. The loans were available only to tribes that came under the Indian Reorganization Act.

Collier's plans for Indian land use were, however, decimated in the final enactment. The repeal of the General Allotment Act, the extension of federal trust over allotted land, the return of surplus land to tribes, and the authorization of funds to acquire new land were helpful but could not consolidate the checkerboarded and fractionalized holdings of allotted reservations. Voluntary transfer was unworkable. Since 1934 a few tribes have consolidated land, but only after expensive and diligent efforts.

Despite its flaws, the Indian Reorganization Act became central to New Deal administration, partly because the legislation permitted tribal governments to exercise authority, partly because Collier forcefully applied his ideas as if the original bill survived. The commissioner, indeed, implemented his policies even among tribes that rejected the act. The importance of the legislation can be found by the repeated efforts of Indian and white opponents' to repeal it.

The act gave the tribes one year to hold the referenda to decide whether they wished to come under its provisions. Conducting the campaigns and elections was an enormous task. Although Collier claimed that the campaigns were purely educational, they were pursued aggressively to secure favorable decisions. Collier, moreover, sought to concentrate initially on key reservations where victories would likely create a "band wagon" effect. Superintendents, tribal leaders, and Washington office representatives, including Collier, became involved.

The strategy succeeded rather well in the Northern Plains and the Great Lakes areas where the BIA conducted the first elections. Several significant groups, however, rejected the act, including Klamath, Crow, Fort Peck, Sisseton, and Turtle Mountain. By far the worst defeat, however, occurred in June 1935, when the Navajos rejected participation by a narrow margin. As was probably true of other reservations, the outcome was determined by various factors. With well over 90 percent of the Navajos illiterate in English, probably only a small minority understood the legislation, and even the more educated did not fully comprehend the many changes made in the original bill. Most traders and missionaries opposed acceptance. The traders feared that self-government might lead to their ouster from the reservation, and the missionaries wanted the Indian saved by "Christian assimilation into American life. . . ." J. C. Morgan, a fiery bilingual Navajo leader, missionary worker, and dedicated assimilationist, led the opposition campaign. Morgan detested Collier's cultural pluralism, but the real basis for his success was Navajo hostility toward recent livestock reductions. His ability to associate the act with the reductions caused the government to postpone the election from March to mid-June 1935. Collier pulled out all stops as the election drew close by sending in top aides, winning over the prestigious Chee Dodge, and personally appearing for a last-minute appeal. The Navajo margin of defeat—only 518 votes out of 15,876 cast—was a shocking blow.[28]

Morgan's campaign was part of a broader Indian opposition to the Collier administration. Joseph Bruner, a well-to-do Oklahoma Creek and strong assimilationist, had opposed the reorganization bill in 1934. Although Bruner and other anti-Collier leaders were not always in full accord, they wanted Collier removed from office, reorganization repealed, and the BIA abolished. In August 1934, the dissidents met at Gallup, New Mexico, and formed the American Indian Federation (AIF), with Bruner as president and Morgan as first vice president. Alice Lee Jemison, a Seneca journalist and the "brains" of the organization, served as the AIF's main lobbyist in Washington until 1940.[29]

Largely through AIF lobbying, Congress made two major revisions in the reorganization act. The legislation had stated that it would "not apply to any reservation wherein a majority of Indians . . . shall vote against its application." Collier interpreted this to mean that a majority of eligible voters had to disapprove the act, or, in other words, those failing to vote were considered as approving the act. This interpretation became one of the major causes of the AIF's attacks on Collier, and in 1935 Congress changed the requirement to a simple majority of those voting. The same act also extended ratification for an additional year.[30]

The passage of the Oklahoma Indian Welfare Act in 1936 reversed Senator Thomas's decision to exclude Indians of his state from the act. Oklahoma Indians expressed misgivings about their exclusion once they understood its potential benefits. Sensing the shift, Thomas toured the state with Collier and met with Indian groups in October 1934. They concluded that the act would have to be revised to fit Oklahoma conditions; legislation was needed for Indian land purchases and credit; and additional safeguards were demanded for present land holdings. The Thomas-Rogers bill separated Oklahoma Indians into two classes based on blood quantum. Those with more than one-half blood came under federal trust protections. Other provisions allowed both tribes and communities to incorporate and receive loans from the revolving credit fund, as well as to enjoy several other benefits. Attorneys from northeastern Oklahoma, especially those who benefited from state control over Indian probate matters in the oil-rich Osage area, strongly opposed the new measure. Nevertheless, Thomas pushed the bill through the Senate Indian Affairs Committee without major change, but Representative Wesley E. Disney, whose district included Osage County, blocked it in the House committee. The following summer, Congress passed a weakened version that essentially left state jurisdiction undisturbed but allowed groups to incorporate and receive credit.[31]

Once Indian groups voted to accept reorganization, Collier pressed them to write constitutions and bylaws. By mid-1937 sixty-five tribes had adopted constitutions, and thirty-two had ratified corporate charters. Nathan Margold and Felix Cohen early on devised a model constitution that contained all the powers that they believed inherent in tribal authority. BIA personnel and attorneys conferred with local drafting committees and agency personnel to decide which provisions to include and to draft others that the Indians wanted. Three basic and interrelated criticisms have arisen about the new constitutions. First, the form of the governments was not Indian but patterned after Anglo-American institutions. Second, the new constitutions, because of the model, were too similar and not always well adapted to local conditions. And finally, mixed bloods gained an unfair advantage over full bloods in the new governments because of superior linguistic skills and political manipulations. These criticisms, especially the use of Anglo-American forms, often resulted from hindsight and were not commonly expressed at the time.

In evaluating the performance of tribal governments, the most important single factor was the reaction of the local superintendent. Collier's official line was that the BIA assumed an advisory role after 1934, but agency heads retained significant authority. Strong superintendents used job patronage, credit and budget decisions, and a host of informal pressures to dominate the tribal councils. At other agencies, they genuinely respected tribal self-government and cooperated whenever possible. In other cases, superintendents allowed tribal governments freedom in some areas, usually domestic relations such as marriage, divorce, and membership in the tribe, and jealously guarded their authority over key matters. In addition, Washington sometimes intervened in council operations to insure conformity with federal statutes, to protect against infringements of religious or civil rights, or to preserve the authority of agency officials.[32] Inevitably, officials found themselves called upon to resolve disputes between superintendents and tribal governments. Their typical reaction was simply to ignore making any decision.

The experiences of the Oglala Sioux Council at Pine Ridge offer a case study of one of the trouble spots of tribal self-government. Bitter factionalism between full bloods and mixed bloods had divided the reservation long before the New Deal. Social and cultural factors more than simply blood quantum largely determined membership in the factions. Mixed bloods generally were apt to be more educated, bilingual, and acculturated, and to enjoy success in agriculture or employment. Full bloods tended to be less schooled, more traditional, and still in possession of their allotments.[33] Divisions between the two escalated in 1931 after disputes over a new council. Younger mixed bloods accepted existing forms of "rational bureaucratic public administration," but older full bloods disdained all elections and modern bureaucracy and claimed authority based on the three-quarters requirement of the Treaty of 1868.[34]

Typical of many allotted reservations, the two Oglala factions responded differently to the Indian reorganization bill. Mixed bloods favored the measure because it promised to provide them with land, but the full bloods strongly feared that they would lose their allotments to improvident landless tribesmen. Despite Collier's promises at the Rapid City congress that allotments would be respected as well as the voluntary nature of land provisions in the final act, the full bloods remained suspicious. In 1934, Pine Ridge approved the reorganization by a vote of 1,169 to 1,095 out of 4,075 eligible voters. Critics even today claim that non-voters mistakenly thought that boycotting the election would defeat the act's application.[35]

The subsequent operations of the Oglala Council were marked by severe strife. While mixed-blood councilmen increased between 1936 and 1944, most members held trust patented allotments, and the full bloods won majorities in every election except in 1936. Despite this, the mixed bloods usually became officers of the council. This included one president elected to three terms starting in 1936. This individual attacked Lakota traditions, clashed with agency personnel openly, favored mixed bloods in patronage matters, publicly scorned full bloods, and frequently exceeded his authority. A shrewd and effective politician, he won office in 1936 with a whirlwind campaign in which he spent money freely and "accused everyone from the [U.S.] President down, and fooled the Indian that he was the only man who could save them."[36] Relations between the Indian leader and agency personnel remained hostile until the president was impeached in 1941 because of financial irregularities.[37]

In the meantime, a separatist full-blood group known as the "Old Dealers" developed a rival political organization at Pine Ridge and Rosebud. The "Old Dealers" formed during the referendum campaign and most were former chairmen or members of pre-New Deal councils. Some "Old Dealers," however, first entered politics after 1936. They never sought to control the new councils on the two reservations. Instead, they regarded them as alien and illegitimate institutions forced upon the Sioux by the BIA and dominated by mixed bloods. The "Old Dealers" also viewed simple majority decisions as a violation of the Treaty of 1868 that required consent by a three-fourths majority. The protesters preferred the old council that had no real legislative powers but discussed reservation questions and then negotiated with agency personnel directly. They regarded the new councils as a barrier between themselves and the government. The fact that their logic was somewhat shaky did not hamper them from becoming a considerable political force when they fought to gain federal recognition of the treaty council.[38]

The Pine Ridge experience highlighted several problems with the reorganization program. The political turmoil was not simple internal factionalism but a political free-for-all involving the BIA, rival groups within the council, and two competing bodies that both claimed legitimacy. Collier's belief that Indian dissension was an aberration caused by white disruption of earlier political traditions and that selfless civic leadership would restore harmony proved remarkably naive. If anything, reorganization increased friction on many reservations.

The Navajo experience with tribal government offers both parallels and variations from the Pine Ridge example. Following the stunning rejection of reorganization in 1935, the Navajo council was inactive after Chairman Thomas Dodge resigned and became an assistant to Superintendent E. R. Fryer. When Collier indicated that he wanted the council reorganized, the group met in November 1936 and approved the formation of a new tribal government.[39] In an attempt to identify and involve the tribe's grassroots leaders, Father Berard Haile, a noted linguist and longtime missionary, headed a canvassing committee that toured Navajo country to identify some 250 authentic local spokesmen. Afterward, Haile reconvened his committee to pare the list to seventy delegates to a constitutional convention and to decide on apportionment and other key questions. Despite their earlier consent to all this, the committee members developed strong misgivings and tried to evade making decisions. Ironically, a Franciscan priest had to browbeat them into acting.[40]

The meeting of the "Headmen's Council" in April 1937 took place in a tense atmosphere. Although some delegates were educated, the bulk were headmen or traditional community leaders. J. C. Morgan served as a delegate, and several of his followers appeared in the audience. The testy Navajo had been fighting against council reorganization, and he objected when a resolution was introduced to make the assembly a provisional council. When Morgan declared that "there is no authority to dissolve this [old] council," Superintendent Fryer asked: "Mr. Morgan, the Navajo Tribal Council was created by the Secretary of Interior, was it not?" When Morgan conceded the point, Fryer declared that Secretary Ickes could dissolve the previous council and create a new one. The exchange cowed Morgan, but the next day he and his followers bolted the convention when a resolution was introduced to draft a constitution.[41]

Morgan's tactics in defeating the government's plans for reorganizing the Navajo council partially resemble those of the "Old Dealers." He rather skillfully manipulated important tribal symbols in a not always logical pattern. He charged, for example, that reorganization and recently instituted range management districts violated the treaty of 1868 and general constitutional rights. Morgan and his followers visited Washington to testify against the Collier administration, and Morgan formed an alliance with Senator Dennis Chavez of New Mexico, who opposed Collier. Morgan also helped organize the Navajo Progressive League in 1937. The group sought to defeat reorganization and all other Collier changes since 1933. But Morgan was personally ambitious and willing to compromise. When Collier abandoned plans for a new constitution and ordered new council elections in 1938, Morgan easily won the chairmanship.

Morgan's tenure as chairman was marked by compromise. Initially suspicious of agency personnel, he gradually became more cooperative. In part, his new attitude grew out of his awareness of the broader problems facing his tribe and a better appreciation of the government's efforts to relieve them, but he also relished the prestige of office. By 1940, Morgan and Superintendent Fryer reached an unspoken truce. The chairman was free to shape council proceedings to fit his puritanical values by outlawing peyote, regulating marriages and divorces, and endorsing national defense; Fryer maintained control over the controversial grazing program.[42]

Collier's attempts to implement reorganization came during a period of retrenchment. Regular BIA appropriations peaked in 1932 with $27,030,046.73 and declined to $16,275,185 in 1935. Reduced tribal funds for administrative purposes added to the decreases. Because of western congressmen, funding always fell well below the amounts authorized in the 1934 reorganization act. Money appropriated for revolving credit amounted to only $5,600,000 between 1935 and 1944 rather than

$10,000,000. The act called for $2,000,000 annually to buy more land, but actual funding between 1935 and 1941 totaled less than half that amount.[43] Cuts in the $250,000 authorized for carrying out the organization of tribal governments were less dramatic but significant.

The reduced funding for both regular BIA activities and reorganization may have had less impact than might have been expected. The figures in the IRA were based on the assumption that virtually all Indians would come under the legislation, but less than half did so.[44] More importantly, Collier's ability to tap emergency funds in the first years offset cuts in the regular budget. During his first two years, for example, he secured $45,000,000 from emergency programs. The outside money was particularly useful for reorganization activities. The Resettlement Administration and its successor, the Farm Security Administration, supplied some $2,400,000 before 1940 to purchase over 900,000 acres of land. Other emergency programs gave the BIA credit funds that nearly matched those appropriated under the act.[45]

The outside money created both advantages and disadvantages. The long delays and frequent disappointments of getting appropriations from regular channels were avoided, and the westerners who dominated the Indian committees were sometimes circumvented. In addition, interagency cooperation brought much needed expertise to the BIA, especially for economic rehabilitation and conservation. In some instances, however, cooperative programs caused severe interagency frictions. The Indian CCC faced a minimum of discord because the parent organization kept a fairly loose rein, but a bitter feud developed between BIA employees and the Soil Conservation Service (SCS) on the Navajo Reservation in late 1935. The strife grew so intense and divisive that in early 1936 Collier replaced a highly respected veteran superintendent with the more forceful E. R. Fryer, who ended the squabbling by a thorough shakeup of Navajo administration.[46]

The Technical Cooperation-Bureau of Indian Affairs (TC-BIA), like the Navajo program, attempted to incorporate the SCS into BIA administration. Organized in late 1935, TC-BIA surveyed reservations with the twin goals of economic rehabilitation and the conservation of soil and natural resources. Teams of BIA and SCS personnel began their work in Arizona, and by the end of 1938 they had completed surveys of thirty-four reservations in eight western states. An additional sixteen would be studied by 1942. Even though TC-BIA avoided the intense strife of the Navajo Reservation, the interagency group was not trouble free.

For two years after reorganization, Collier avoided serious problems with Congress, but by 1936 legislators' criticism became formidable. Clearly, the opposition rested on philosophical and practical grounds. Senator Wheeler of Montana is an example of someone who disliked Collier's policy philosophy. Despite several differences with President Roosevelt, the irascible Wheeler remained a New Deal loyalist until the Supreme

Court fight in 1937.[47] Wheeler's attempt to repeal the IRA the same year may reflect his general disillusionment with the Roosevelt administration. But the paternalistic Wheeler also doubtlessly now recognized that Collier policies violated assimilationist ideals. In any case, Wheeler's failure to secure repeal was more than slightly ironic because he had tailored the legislation so carefully to his own tastes.[48]

Senator Dennis Chavez of New Mexico opposed Collier for practical reasons. Chavez never soured on the New Deal, but he acted against Collier because of economic and political forces within New Mexico. After serving two terms in the House, Chavez in 1936 challenged incumbent Senator Bronson Cutting, a progressive Republican and Roosevelt loyalist. Many of the senator's supporters were furious when Roosevelt failed to endorse Cutting. The contest between the Spanish-American leader and the former Long Island aristocrat was bitter even by New Mexico standards. Chavez supporters charged that Ickes and Collier permitted government personnel to work in Cutting's behalf.[49] Following the election, the *Albuquerque Journal* reprinted an Ickes's telegram warmly congratulating Cutting on his narrow victory. Chavez attempted to contest the election, and his appeal was still pending in the Senate when Cutting was killed in an airplane crash in May 1935. Governor Clyde Tingley immediately named Chavez to the vacancy.

Chavez entered the Senate an enemy of Collier and the Interior Department. His first act in office was to recall a bill that would have finally settled the long-standing controversy over the eastern Navajo checkerboard by extending the reservation eastward. Later angered over Ickes's unwillingness to cooperate on PWA patronage, Chavez repeatedly blocked passage of the measure. Finally in 1939, Ickes abandoned the fight and placed the checkerboard under the Taylor Grazing Act. In the meantime, Chavez formed an alliance with the Resettlement Administration to insure that impoverished Spanish-Americans shared in the land acquisitions in the Rio Grande Valley.[50] Chavez also joined in general harassment of the Collier administration. He supported the several unsuccessful attempts to repeal the IRA and sponsored an act excluding New Mexico from future IRA land purchases.[51]

Chavez's shrewd tactics enhanced his political position in New Mexico. By blocking the Navajo extension, he pleased the powerful livestock lobby; at the same time, he maintained his reputation as a friend of the little man. He even posed as a benefactor of Indians by endorsing J. C. Morgan's agitation. Chavez's criticisms of the BIA, especially its attempts to secure more land, sold well in a state which traditionally despised that agency and resented the presence of untaxable reservations. But Chavez's tactics had a philosophical basis too. As a self-made member of a minority, he strongly disagreed with Collier's cultural pluralism.[52]

Collier's problems with western congressional leaders provided an opening for the American Indian Federation and other critics. Jemison and her allies frequently appeared before congressional committees and denounced BIA programs. The criticisms had some nuisance value, and they also kept Collier on the defensive in the late 1930s. But the AIF failed to achieve any of its basic goals such as ousting Collier and repealing the Indian Reorganization Act. Indeed, AIF's only major victory was the 1935 revision in tallying votes for reorganization.

The AIF's tenuous unity shattered completely after the introduction of the "settlement bill" in 1939. The bill essentially promised $3,000 to any individual who renounced his or her Indian legal status and future claims against the federal government. Although 4,664 members endorsed the measure, it alienated a sizeable portion of AIF adherents. Jemison soon left the organization, and extremists further discredited it with their red-baiting and dalliances with Nazi groups.[53]

The fight over the Supreme Court plan in 1937 and its aftermath had a far greater impact on the Indian New Deal than the AIF. The controversy alienated many western progressive senators and prompted conservatives of both parties to criticize Roosevelt's dictatorial methods. Collier unwisely played into the hands of Roosevelt's critics in March by penning an editorial in *Indians at Work*, a house organ, defending the court plan. Senator Bennett Champ Clark of Missouri charged that Collier had illegally used public funds in publishing the editorial and demanded his removal. Wheeler used the opportunity for another attack on reorganization.[54] The vehemence of the criticisms seemed out of proportion to Collier's indiscretion, suggesting that he became a scapegoat during the court fight.

Diminished budgets and a growing concern with foreign affairs in the late 1930s further handicapped the Collier administration. Roosevelt's decision in 1937 to reduce expenditures for emergency programs placed new restrictions on Indian CCC operations.[55] The Indian CCC in fiscal 1939 was cut approximately 12 percent. Other retrenchments affected interagency cooperation. The SCS allocated only $28,000 to Pueblo projects in 1938 compared to $212,000 in 1936. On the Navajo Reservation, SCS funding dropped from $830,000 in fiscal 1937 to $300,000 in 1940. These drastic reductions incensed Collier, who saw the SCS reneging on its commitments after the Indians had made major sacrifices. When conservation work on all reservations was transferred to the Interior Department the same year, Ickes complained bitterly that he received far less funding than SCS had enjoyed.[56]

If any bright spots appeared in the closing years of the Indian New Deal, they came in 1940 with the revival of the national economy and Indians' increased employment opportunities. A report in mid-1940 estimated that 2,000 former enrollees had left the CCC the previous year and 600 of this number found private employment. Through cooperative arrangements between states and the United States Department of Education, job training for Indian CCC enrollees started in 1941. The classes included radio operation and repair, welding, auto mechanics, sheet metal work, and other subjects. Nearly all who passed proficiency tests secured outside jobs immediately. Navajos and other Indians found jobs when the army started an $11,000,000 ordnance depot near Gallup, New Mexico, in 1941. Many had learned their skills in the CCC program.[57] The increased employment opportunities of 1940 and 1941 were only a prelude to the mass exodus of Indians after Pearl Harbor.

In assessing the impact of the depression and the New Deal on Indians, clearly regionalism was important. The depression provided a respite from white efforts to secure Indian resources. Demand for Indian oil and timber, for example, virtually disappeared after 1929, and business interests, if anything, retreated from existing contractual arrangements. The West's economic woes ended Indians' off-reservation employment opportunities for both seasonal and permanent jobs and forced many to return to reservations. Clearly, the New Deal strengthened the role of the federal government in the West. This grew out of both the emergency work programs and the existing agencies such as the Forest Service and Bureau of Reclamation. In addition, new permanent agencies created during the 1930s, such as the SCS and the Grazing Service, further increased federal influence. Although the trend toward greater national control had little immediate impact on Indians, it laid the groundwork for later clashes between Indians and increasingly powerful federal agencies.

Despite the attention the Collier administration has received, no clear consensus has yet developed about its overall impact. In the short term, Collier was reasonably successful because emergency programs brought new jobs and funds to reservations. Indeed, many Indians remembered the 1930s not as a time of economic destitution but as a fairly prosperous era. In terms of making Indians self-sufficient, the New Deal presents a less clear record. Some reservations benefited from increased funding, more credit, additional land, and improved expertise and made some progress toward self-support. On poorer reservations, fractionalized allotments, aridity, lack of natural resources, and overpopulation posed obstacles too great to solve. Perhaps the Indian New Deal defies generalization but must be studied reservation by reservation and even program by program.

Unfortunately, the Indian New Deal aroused considerable opposition. Collier's Indian opponents, despite their fierce complaints, were not a major threat until men like Wheeler and Chavez gave them a vehicle for criticism. Congressional opposition did not drive Collier from office or overturn his policies, but this opposition, along with budgets cuts, kept his administration on the defensive and hampered his attempts to implement reforms after 1937.

7.

World War II

The Exodus

World War II brought major changes to the West and established new conditions for Native Americans which fundamentally affected their lives. The region made notable strides to escape its traditional dependence on export production and developed a permanent industrial base. Indians adjusted to the changed regional environment by leaving their reservations in large numbers to take wartime jobs or enter the military. The policy debate between John Collier and his western critics continued after 1941, but it became secondary to the wartime changes.

If any factor can be singled out for the transformation of the West from a colonial status to a more mature economic stage, it was wartime spending. Federal expenditures in the region between 1933 and 1939 amounted to $7,582,434,000.[1] Wartime spending, however, has been conservatively estimated at over $40 billion as the federal government established new factories and numerous military bases, training camps, and supply depots in the West. Important side effects of such expenditures included new jobs, improved markets for natural resources, and a general economic revival. West Coast urban centers experienced the most industrial development, and the interior, although affected, underwent much less change.[2]

The most significant wartime change for Indians involved the increased demand for labor after 1939. Indians joined in the massive migration of workers from rural areas to industrial centers in the West. But new opportunities also developed in agriculture, lumbering, construction, railroad maintenance, and other fields that afforded unskilled or semi-skilled Indians with jobs. The first Indians to benefit from the new demand for labor were former enrollees in the Civilian Conservation Corps-Indian Division (CCC-ID) or students completing vocational training at major boarding schools. Even before Pearl Harbor, *Indians at Work,* a CCC-ID publication, reported that Indian welders, machinists, and other skilled workers were winning jobs in war industries. Collier ordered that CCC-ID enrollees would receive most of the benefits from the National Defense Training Act of 1941. Graduates from the job training readily found jobs.[3]

This initial trickle of private employment became a tide after Pearl Harbor.

The Indians' wartime job experiences were varied. The migrants, for example, ranged from Indians who worked for local white ranchers and farmers to individuals who assumed skilled positions in remote industrial centers. BIA publicity, moreover, tended to emphasize the more positive aspects of Indian employment and ignored what were often very serious problems.

One basic characteristic of the Indians' exodus was that tribes tended to specialize in certain types of employment based on such factors as proximity of jobs, recruitment by certain industries, and previous employment experiences. The Sioux, for example, helped build military depots and air training centers in the northern Plains and worked as seasonal farm laborers near their reservations. Most Pueblos took local jobs, but some worked at the Clearfield Naval Depot in Utah during the off-season of farming.[4] Navajos secured employment at army ammunition depots located near the southern edge of their reservation. Northwestern groups worked in shipyards, lumbering, and fish canneries. The Pima and Papagos expanded previous employment in copper mining and cotton picking near their Arizona reservations. Most Indians who took defense jobs on the West Coast were either local residents or migrants with specialized skills.[5]

According to a BIA survey of 1944, wartime employment was split almost equally between agriculture and industry. Superintendents reported that over 46,000 Indians found outside employment in 1943 with 22,192 in agricultural work and 24,422 in non-agricultural pursuits. Their combined income totaled over $40,000,000. The farm workers spent an average of only four and a half months away from their homes, indicating that their jobs were seasonal. Many still engaged in some farming and ranching and refused to take outside jobs for long periods. Non-agricultural workers stayed away for eight and a half months during the year. Despite the high rate of employment and the absence of many Indians in the armed services, an estimated 31,389 able-bodied men remained unemployed on the reservations. This high figure may be attributed to fear of leaving home or to the lack of resources to pay for transportation to jobs and to live until their first paycheck.[6]

The experiences of the Rosebud Sioux may not be typical of those encountered by all Indians, but they show that wartime employment required adjustments. In the 1930s federal emergency programs on the Rosebud largely provided jobs, but several hundred families annually harvested corn and potatoes in Nebraska. Expanded sugar beet production in the Platte River Valley and western South Dakota opened new employment for the Rosebud Sioux. The work was done by gangs under contract to accomplish a specific task. Thinning beets demanded skills, speed, and physical endurance that the Indians found taxing. Frictions developed because white farmers disliked the Indians' unhurried tempo, their refusal to work over eight hours per day, and their frequent requests for wage advances. Mexicans, who normally thinned and harvested, were more skilled, faster, shrewder bargainers, and more responsive to employers' pressures. The Sioux worked slowly but were thorough.

Somewhat similar clashes developed among the Rosebud Sioux who helped construct military depots or air training stations. Most worked as unskilled laborers in crews, although a considerable number secured skilled or semi-skilled jobs. Young men with training and experience, usually derived from CCC-ID, adjusted more easily. Some white employers regarded the Sioux as superior to non-Indians, while other employers, angered by the Sioux's constant complaints and drinking sprees, fired entire crews and refused to hire any Indians. As was true of beet workers, the Rosebud Sioux were not time-oriented and expected a slower tempo of work and toleration for absences or tardiness. They gravitated to employers willing to accommodate such behavior and refused to work for those who demanded absolute compliance with rules.

The study also revealed striking class differences among the Rosebud Sioux who moved to urban centers. In Rapid City, South Dakota, for example, middle-class Sioux had maintained residence for ten to twenty years. Most lived in modern houses and held skilled or semi-skilled jobs. In economic standing, education, and participation in community activities, they had achieved integration, including intermarriage. Virtually all these established residents were mixed bloods with only slight Indian physical characteristics. In sharp contrast, a second group had resided in the city an average of only two years, lived in the worst housing, and worked irregularly. Delinquency, truancy, public intoxication, and frequent encounters with police and relief agencies typified the second group.

A similar dichotomy appeared among Rosebud Sioux who came to the city during wartime. Some found good jobs and integrated into the community with little problem except for occasional drinking sprees. Others, however, came without funds or skills and, in effect, recreated reservation poverty by residing in slums or camping in tents on the outskirts of the city. Those in substandard housing suffered from poor health and sanitation, irregular work, and alcoholism. Local officials who dealt with the Sioux's frequent crises had no idea about Indians' legal status except that they were the responsibility of the BIA. The universal solution for all problems was to return Indians to the reservation.[7]

Indian experiences at ordnance depots at Fort Wingate, New Mexico, and Bellemont, Arizona, illustrate both the difficulties and achievements of wartime employment. Construction of the $11,000,000 depot at Fort Wingate began in 1941, and some 1,500 Navajos and 1,000 other Indians worked at the year-long project. Many of the Navajos were traditionalists who resisted having their pictures taken for identification badges and giving their "real" names for the payroll. They were, however, good workers and skilled at tying steel and pouring concrete. Like the Sioux, the Navajos disliked abusive bosses, and during each day workers slipped away from unpopular foremen and joined work crews headed by tolerant supervisors.[8] After finishing Fort Wingate, 1,500 Navajos helped build the Bellemont depot near Flagstaff, Arizona. The army later hired Navajos and other Indians to load and unload ammunition and explosives at the two depots.[9]

Besides cultural adjustments, the Navajos employed at the depots faced other difficulties. They originally lived in temporary housing without adequate sanitation, which created serious health problems. By 1943 absenteeism after pay days and weekends reached alarming levels at Fort Wingate and Bellemont. The Navajo tribal council and the BIA initiated a publicity campaign against drinking and absenteeism, and over 100 bootlegging cases were tried. Responding to pressures from the BIA, the army constructed modern living quarters inside the depots, permitted workers' families to join them, built schools, and provided day care. Although one Navajo woman who had worked in personnel at Bellemont relished the new living accommodations and high wages, she disliked her second job as a gate guard because it involved searching Indians who entered the depot. She and her husband returned to the reservation immediately after VE day even though they could have remained on the payroll.[10]

Evidence indicates that Indian women used the war as a means of achieving lasting employment advances. Approximately 800 served in the military. A much larger number of Indian women, estimated at 12,000 in 1943, worked in war industries. The Sherman Institute at Riverside, California, recruited women for vocational training because the draft could not interfere with women's finishing courses or holding jobs. Like their white counterparts, many Indian women worked at industrial tasks formerly monopolized by males. Women also assumed many agency jobs. Because of the shortage of teachers, Indian classroom assistants frequently became instructors. Several Navajo and Zuni women became silversmiths, traditionally a male occupation, and at the Gallup Intertribal Ceremonial in 1942, they won seven prizes. Indian women's traditional skills at handwork perhaps were well-suited for certain types of tedious assembly work. Indian women were, like their white counterparts, reluctant to relinquish wartime employment advances and to resume housekeeping.[11]

The degree of racial prejudice that Indians experienced in off-reservation jobs was largely governed by distance. The Rosebud Sioux who moved to nearby urban centers encountered prejudices common to bordertowns. Although not much data exists, the younger and more skilled workers, who took jobs in West Coast war industries, apparently experienced few if any problems. Katherine Archibald's autobiographic account of life in an Oakland shipyard suggests that Indians escaped the seething racial and class hostilities that arose between native Californians and recently arrived blacks and "Okies." "The few full-blooded Indians who worked in the yards," Archibald notes, "were respected, liked, and even admired by their white brethren." One enterprising Navajo developed a profitable sideline selling jewelry that he made in his spare time. The "Okies," who loudly proclaimed their hatred for blacks and Japanese, "were invariably proud of any trace of Cherokee blood which they might claim."[12]

In contrast to the BIA's emphasis on the positive side of wartime employment, the jobs that Indians gained were often a mixed blessing. Some Indians managed to improve their economic standing and smoothly blended into urban life, but others found the adjustments overwhelming. They became transients drifting back and forth between reservations and outside jobs. Frustrated and confused, they often suffered from alcoholism and other social and economic problems. Nevertheless, the Indians' wartime exodus marked an important change. By the end of the war, an estimated 7 percent lived in urban areas, and this number increased to 14 percent by 1950. In other words, many wartime migrants stayed in the cities, and veterans and others joined them. The exodus continues to the present.[13]

Indians' military contributions to the war were impressive. According to the BIA, 24,521 men served. A 1944 survey revealed that about 32 percent of able-bodied males between the ages of eighteen and fifty years were under arms. This group comprised about 7 percent of the total Indian population.[14] The Indians' military experiences often paralleled those of Indians in World War I because both groups came from various backgrounds and levels of acculturation and performed diverse duties. But contrasts were also evident. The exposure to non-reservation life and acculturation influences had a greater impact during World War II simply because the war lasted much longer, and, as a global conflict, it exposed participants to a greater variety of conditions.

One of the major changes for Indians in World War II was that the Indian Citizenship Act of 1924 made all subject to selective service. When the first draft registration took place in late 1940, the BIA handled the responsibility on most reservations because individuals living in remote areas were often confused or suspicious about reporting.[15] Agency officials on several reservations established special registration stations and allowed three days instead of only one to complete the task. BIA interpreters on the Rosebud Reservation explained registration in Lakota. Much to Collier's dissatisfaction, regular selective service workers handled subsequent registrations.

Failures to register and to report for service were much more widespread than BIA publicity indicated. Resisters typically complained about the unfairness of being drafted because they were not allowed to vote or drink and because Indian land had been stolen by whites. Some complained that military service violated their religious beliefs. In the eastern Navajo checkerboard, a group refused to register because of a rumor that they would be hauled away in big trucks, but they changed their minds after Navajo Chairman J. C. Morgan spoke to them. At a registration station near Flagstaff, Arizona, no one appeared because the local headman claimed that Navajos should not fight unless Hitler invaded the United States and that the treaty of 1868 prohibited them from fighting.[16]

The most prominent example of organized resistance against the draft involved Pia Machita, an elderly Papago headman who presided over several villages in the Hickiwan district. Machita refused to recognize the Gadsden Purchase and regarded himself as a Mexican citizen. He and the local superintendent had previously clashed over various agency matters. When Machita adamantly rejected registration in 1940, three law officers tried to arrest him, but villagers roughed them up and forced them to leave.[17] After unsuccessful attempts to negotiate with Machita, a federal posse captured him and several followers in May 1941.

The arrest and trial created local support for Machita. An editorial in a Tucson paper pointed out that he had only wished to be left alone and that what happened to him was another in the many episodes of Indians being forced to give way to a superior force. A letter to the editor in the same paper suggested that American society would be on trial just as much as Machita. At the trial, the federal marshal urged leniency because of the headman's recent cooperation, but the district judge, citing the seriousness of the crimes, rejected probation and sentenced the elderly Papago and a companion to eighteen months.[18]

The only other organized resistance to the draft among western tribes involved Hopis at Hotevilla Village. Collier had Oliver LaFarge, a well-known author who earlier had helped devise the tribe's constitution, prepare a statement about the Hopis' religious traditions to convince the Justice Department that the dissidents were pacifists. Six Hopis, however, were arrested in April 1941 and taken to Phoenix where a federal judge ruled that religious traditions did not have any bearing on registration. The Hopi superintendent conferred with the judge after the verdict and persuaded him to forgo sentencing if the Hopis agreed to register. But all refused, and five were sentenced to a year and a day in a prison camp.[19] A good deal of confusion seemed to surround the dissidents' motives, and the superintendent suggested that no white person would ever persuade the men to explain their reasons for rejecting registration.[20] In reporting new draft resistance in 1942, the superintendent commented that the ex-prisoners were all back, and they were "the envy of nearly all." Their new clothes and positive comments about the food and accommodations at the prison camp, he added, had prompted inquiries about getting into the institution.[21]

The vast majority of Indians who did not register were those who had no religious or philosophical grounds for their resistance. In many cases, they lived in remote areas, held migratory jobs, or did not know about registration. In still other instances, they reported to regular draft boards rather than to agencies.

The issue of separate Indian military units reappeared in 1940. In a memo to Ickes in June 1940, Collier proposed the formation of an all-Indian division administered by the BIA. He argued that Indians wanted such a unit and that it would allow them to retain their own identities and to have their contributions recognized fully. Shortly after the Selective Service Act of 1940, J. C. Morgan, Navajo chairman, wrote Collier requesting the creation of an all-Navajo regiment. Their motives differed entirely. Collier's proposal may have been partly inspired by the success of a separate CCC-ID, but he wanted primarily to strengthen the BIA's role and to preserve Indian culture. Morgan, a patriotic advocate of integration, hoped to induct as many Navajos as possible, and he knew that many would be rejected because of illiteracy unless they received special consideration. Secretary of War Henry L. Stimson totally rejected any sort of separate Indian units.[22]

As a result, Indians performed all sorts of military duties. The highest ranking was Major General Clarence L. Tinker, who assumed command of army air force units in Hawaii after Pearl Harbor. A one-eighth Osage, Tinker attended boarding schools and graduated from a private military academy before becoming a career officer in 1908.[23] He died in 1942 when his Liberator bomber went down en route to a bombing strike against Wake Island.[24] The War Department later named a new airfield outside Oklahoma City after Tinker. His experiences were exceptional. Most Indians, given their limited education and the "sociology" of the military, served in combat units as enlisted men, and few entered the officer corps.

Although Indians served in integrated units, they won some special recognition. The most publicized example was the Navajo code talkers. Philip Johnston, an engineer from Los Angeles, originated the idea of code talkers. The son of a missionary who lived among the Navajos several years, Johnston became fluent in the language as a child. Early in the war, he learned that Indian languages were employed during army maneuvers in Louisiana. His idea, however, was not merely to translate messages, but to develop a code of Navajo words for radio transmissions. The code then would be memorized and mutually understood by Navajo radio operators. Such an approach guaranteed that dispatches could not be deciphered, and eliminated counterfeit messages sent by the enemy because of the difficulties of Navajo grammar and pronunciation.[25]

Johnston received a favorable reception when he presented his scheme shortly after Pearl Harbor. Two weeks later Johnston and several Navajos, demonstrating his technique to Marine Corps brass, transmitted six typical military messages without error. Soon afterward, Washington authorized the recruitment of a platoon of twenty-nine Navajos as a pilot project. Following boot camp, they received communications training and, with Johnston, devised the code vocabulary.[26] Many of the words were descriptive and taken from nature. The Navajo word for *chicken hawk* designated a dive bomber, *whale* described a battleship, and *two stars* meant a major general. Code words for the English alphabet permitted the radio operators to spell out terms not included in the vocabulary.[27] The Marine Corps was sufficiently impressed by the speed and effectiveness of the original code talkers to authorize the recruitment of 200 more Navajos. Eventually 420 served.

The Marine Corps assigned the code talkers in pairs to units involved in the island-hopping campaign from Guadalcanal to Okinawa. Commanders had discretion in using the Navajos, and some employed them extensively;

others virtually ignored them. Code talkers' popularity increased as the war progressed. The original code was improved in 1943 to include new types of weapons and to correct omissions. The code talkers, seldom sheltered in combat, participated in assaults on beachheads and served as forward observers. In several episodes they were threatened by other marines because of their physical resemblance to Japanese. The code talkers, and Navajos in general, developed a special sense of pride in their wartime achievements, a pride that continues to the present.

Because of enlistment in the national guard and assignments based on residence, some Indians tended to be placed in special units. Many southwestern Indians, for example, served in the 200th Coastal Artillery Regiment, a national guard unit sent to the Philippines in September 1941, for duty at Clark Field north of Manila. Members of the 200th who surrendered in April 1942 experienced the Bataan death march and remained in prison camps until the end of the war. Indians made up about 20 percent of the 45th Infantry Division, a national guard unit from Oklahoma and New Mexico which logged 511 days of combat in eight battle campaigns in North Africa, Italy, and southern France. Two Indian members of the 45th, Lieutenants Ernest Childer, Creek, and Jack C. Montgomery, Cherokee, won Congressional Medals of Honor for heroism during the Italian campaign.[28]

The impact of the war on Indians clearly fostered their acculturation. Whites, as in World War I, invariably nicknamed their Indian companions "Chief," but without pejorative connotation. Indians freely socialized with white comrades and found themselves able to drink without the threat of arrest. They seized opportunities to visit major cities and historical sites throughout the world. Their letters reveal attitudes similar to those of young white servicemen. They too expressed their hatred of the enemy, especially the Japanese, and they complained about the insects, rain, cold, heat, and sleepless nights of front-line duty. Like whites, they disliked their officers, tardy promotions, long separations from their families, and the boredom of lonely overseas stations. They relished the "pinups" of movie stars, and one Taos Indian expressed his delight at seeing "American women" for the first time in thirty-four months when a Red Cross contingent arrived. A Cochiti Pueblo described a "swell party" in England during which he "had a cute British lassy on one hand and a glass of beer on the other." Military life clearly was not all bad.[29]

But if the war acculturated, it also intensified racial identity and revitalized Indian traditions. Servicemen's letters often mentioned looking up fellow tribesmen, former schoolmates, or individuals from other reservations. Keats Begay, a survivor of the Bataan death march, noted that the Navajos stayed together during the ordeal and helped one another. When he became ill during the march, a fellow Navajo carried him. Yet Claude Hatch, another Navajo who endured the death march, emphatically declared that "the long days of starving, suffering, and seeing our buddies and companions die binds us together with bonds of steel."[30]

Typical of Americans in general, many Indians, both in and out of service, became more religious during the war. Indian servicemen often practiced both their native religion and Christianity because they believed both followed the same general principles. Compared to World War I, native religious activities at home perhaps were less prominent, but the Sioux composed new war songs and held numerous ceremonies. A white archaeologist who attended a 1947 dance by Hunkpapas in South Dakota described a mock battle in which Indian and white veterans attacked a "German" position! After forcing the enemy to surrender, the victors counted coup on the "Germans," and veterans of old tribal conflicts and the two world wars then performed a scalp dance and a victory dance.[31]

Probably no tribe had maintained its religious traditions more than the Navajos, and this was strongly reflected in their wartime experiences. Virtually no Navajo serviceman left home without a ceremony to protect him against misfortune. Cozy Stanley Brown, a code talker, described killing a Japanese by cutting off his head and then pulling out a bunch of his sideburns as instructed by the medicine man who had performed a sing before Brown left for overseas. Like nearly all Navajo veterans, he received an Enemy Way Ceremony after his return. Brown found that the sing allowed his "mind to function well again."[32]

Perhaps the most important result of Indian servicemen's experiences was the development of new attitudes that remained strong after the war. The most pervasive of these was unquestionably their almost universal support for education, both for themselves and the younger generation. This doubtlessly grew out of the broadening experiences of off-reservation life and the realization that educational deficiencies handicapped Indians. Many also recognized that their military service gave them job skills useful in civilian life. Servicemen also demanded greater equality. As one Navajo put it, "I know that I'm educated and [a] grown up man." He added that his four years of risking his life entitled him to the right to drink and vote once he returned to Arizona. Since veterans readily achieved postwar leadership roles, they often translated new ideals and beliefs into action.[33]

Without question the war reshaped BIA activities. Collier's New Deal policies lost much of their relevance. His attempts to develop reservation resources to make Indians self-sufficient, for example, became pointless for the many who left their homes for wage work or the military. The long-standing debate over cultural pluralism vs. assimilation seemed somewhat hollow when thousands of Indians worked side by side with non-Indians. Those who left home gained a new independence from BIA services. Even those who remained on reservations found themselves preoccupied by the war, loved ones in service, and the success of American arms. The BIA became secondary.[34]

Collier saw the war as a time of enormous threat but great opportunities. His editorial in *Indians at Work*, soon after Pearl Harbor, branded the Axis nations as representing "a planned, organized degradation of human nature, carried out at all the age-levels and progressively over many years with the object of so modifying the soul of whole populations that they will lust for war. . . ." Civilization and all it involved were in jeopardy. Americans must adhere to such values as "self-respect, justice, truth, freedom, respect and reverence for other personalities, love for man [and] belief in the reality of the spirit" and translate these into action. Collier also noted the "intellectual and moral faithlessness" that occurred after 1918. Similar dangers, however, could be avoided if Americans, "in our action and our thought, . . . are true to the light within us."[35]

Collier found his own spirit taxed by the 1942 removal of the BIA from Washington to Chicago. He resisted the move by first arguing that his agency was needed for mobilization, but the Bureau of the Budget ruled that the BIA held the lowest priority for space. Collier next claimed that the BIA participation in Japanese relocation was important to the war effort, but this too proved unsuccessful. The physical side of the move was enormous, involving fifty-four tons of files, 2,000 typewriters, and twenty-two boxcars of furniture. Morale suffered as employees gave up their homes and friends and reestablished themselves in a new city. The BIA was also handicapped because it no longer could monitor legislation or work with other agencies on a daily basis. Collier maintained a small office in Washington, but he found the weekly shuttles to and from the capital taxing.[36]

Budget cuts and shortages of personnel created additional problems. The BIA appropriation dropped from $33,000,000 in 1942 to $28,000,000 in 1943 and remained at that level the rest of the war. Collier also lost the funds from various New Deal emergency programs. Hundreds of key BIA personnel resigned to take better jobs or to join the military. Virtually all expenditures for land, roads, irrigation, and buildings stopped, and even maintenance of existing facilities proved difficult. Education was especially hard hit. School buses were transferred for war work. Many schools closed, plants and equipment deteriorated, teachers became scarce, and students came and went as parents found outside jobs. Only heroic efforts kept part of the schools open. Some Navajo assistants received special permission to become instructors, and they and a few regular teachers remained on duty. Parents volunteered their labor to build temporary quarters at some of the Navajo day schools and served as unpaid matrons.[37] Medical services also suffered as numerous doctors and nurses joined the military or entered the private sector. By 1944 the Indian health service had 73 vacancies for full-time physicians and 27 for part-time, and 183 nursing positions remained unfilled.[38]

Despite these problems, reservations prospered during the war. Part of this resulted from the general economic recovery, but Indians also increased their farming and ranching activities. In 1940 Indians sold $9,124,000 worth of agricultural products and their home consumption was valued at $4,770,000. Sales in 1945 rose to $22,619,000, and home consumption increased to $9,288,000. Net income was estimated at $21,898,000.

Livestock sales in 1945 totaled $16,376,000.[39] Timber revenues also increased sharply. In 1940 the cut of 531,965,000 board feet sold for $1,390,000, and even though the cut fell to 475,662,000 board feet in 1945, revenues rose to $2,113,884. Timber sales, incidentally, continued to rise in the postwar period because of the high demand for new home construction.[40] Despite such dramatic increases, Indians remained impoverished compared to non-Indians. The BIA in 1945 estimated that one-third of reservation families had annual incomes of under $500, and nearly all of the remainder earned under $1,000.[41]

New Deal policies played some role in economic gains that Indians made during the war. Acquiring more land, securing relief cattle, acquiring new sources of credit, and upgrading livestock breeding were helpful. Much the same was true of Collier's conservation policies, which had restored rangelands, reduced overgrazing, and protected against forest fires. In a sense, the New Deal programs provided a seed time that permitted a harvest during the war.

One fundamental issue of wartime was how well the Collier administration protected those resources against non-Indian exploitation. Put another way, were sharp increases in reservation income after 1940 attributable to short-range gains that reduced capital and resources as had happened after World War I? Certainly the general economic conditions and emotional patriotism after 1940 differed little from those of the earlier conflict. In fact, Collier faced some pressures that did not exist in 1917 and 1918.

The government's record in protecting Indian resources was mixed. There is little evidence that Indians succumbed to either government or white pressures to sell off large quantities of livestock breeding animals. In fact, their holdings reportedly increased during the war years.[42] The most intense pressures came from white farmers who wanted to exploit high wartime wheat and flax prices by leasing land on Great Plains Reservations. Such holdings were grazing lands still in virgin sod. Although Collier resisted a second great "plow-up," he approved leasing some 900,000 additional acres, but only if soil surveys and land classification studies indicated that the land would not suffer permanent damage. The government required lessees to reseed the plots when their contracts expired. On the Nez Perce and Coeur d'Alene Reservations, the BIA demanded that wheat farmers sow sweet clover on summer fallow land to protect uncropped areas against erosion and to increase fertility.[43]

The most questionable type of exploitation involved large appropriations of Indian land by the War Department. Although the statistics on the subject are not entirely clear, an estimated 839,000 acres in Alaska and sixteen western reservations were taken over for air bases, gunnery and bombing ranges, and other military purposes. Some of the land was leased or taken under a permit system and evidently returned, but a sizeable portion was permanently lost.[44] By far the largest plot was 400,000 acres on the Pine Ridge Reservation selected by the army in 1942 as a gunnery range. Authorities purchased approximately 300,000 acres from individual Indians, sometimes paying only 75 cents per acre and allowing the 128 families only thirty days to leave their homes. The rest was leased from the tribal council. The Sioux owners went quietly but later developed understandably hostile feelings when they learned that they could not buy comparable land in a rapidly rising market. Only after twelve years of legislative struggle was each family rewarded $3,500.[45]

The Collier administration proved more than cooperative in granting leases for oil, gas, and mining on reservations. In fiscal 1944, for example, the BIA held forty-five auctions for oil and gas and let over 1,000 leases. During the same period, lead and zinc mining on restricted Quapaw lands in Oklahoma produced 415,000 tons of concentrates worth over $38,000,000. Reservations supplied copper, helium, vanadium, asbestos, and coal in small quantities as the BIA issued prospecting permits freely. Apparently because of war needs, Collier seemed oblivious to maintaining future reserves.[46]

Much like the New Deal days, Collier repeatedly attempted to cooperate with other government agencies so as to enhance his agency and help Indians. The operation of Japanese relocation camps on Indian reservations was his only major cooperative venture, and it proved far less than a total success. Collier dispatched several of his "best and brightest" to assist in the original assembly of the Japanese. After Milton Eisenhower organized the War Relocation Authority (WRA) in 1942, Collier hastened to involve the BIA by establishing relocation camps on Indian reservations in the Southwest. He argued that the BIA was uniquely qualified to deal with minorities.

On paper, Collier's arrangements with Eisenhower seemed to justify his excitement over the WRA camps. A recently completed diversion dam opened a potential 100,000 acres of new irrigated land on the Colorado River Reservation, far more than the 1,200 resident Mojaves and Chemehuevis would ever need. By bringing in 20,000 Japanese, Collier hoped to subjugate 25,000 acres. On the Gila River Reservation, the WRA leased some 7,000 acres of irrigated land from the Pima, and the original plans called for the resettlement of 15,000 Japanese to farm this area and to subjugate an additional 8,000 acres. On both reservations, the War Department would build the camps which, like the subjugated lands, would revert to the Indians in the postwar. Irrigable land on the Colorado River Reservation was deemed especially important for the future. The BIA had already decided to relocate Navajos, Papagos, Hopis, and other groups to the area after the war. The WRA arrangement, moreover, appealed to Collier's idealistic impulses. The camps were to "develop functioning local democracies" much like the governments formed under the Indian Reorganization Act.[47]

Relocation, however, created more headaches than benefits. The Indians, intensely hostile toward the Japanese, objected strongly to the camps, and only a combination of browbeating and appeals to patriotism quieted the protestors. Eisenhower resigned in mid-1942, and Dillon S. Myer, a longtime administrator, assumed control. That both Myer and Collier possessed sizeable egos and held completely different social philosophies made frictions inevitable. The strong-willed Myer from the first wanted to disband the camps and resettle the Japanese in the interior West. He claimed that when he announced this goal in a speech on the Colorado River Reservation in late 1942, he learned that Collier "had been there just . . . before and had painted pretty pictures about how they [the inmates] would probably be there for forty years, . . . develop land, and they would have a fine new community, etc., etc."[48] The two men clashed repeatedly. The Gila River camp was transferred from the BIA to the army in 1942, and Myer reneged on Eisenhower's earlier promises. At Colorado River, Collier protested when Myer decided to subjugate only 5,000 acres instead of the promised 25,000 acres. As a kind of final frustration, the barracks at Colorado River were torn down after the war instead of being given to the BIA.[49]

Collier's difficulties with western congressional leaders continued throughout the war. His critics charged that the BIA treated reservations as states or nations within the nation and discouraged assimilation. They also believed that the lack of a clear legal definition of Indians allowed the BIA to provide them with unneeded services. But new issues also appeared. Indians of Arizona in 1941 pressed state officials for Social Security benefits such as old age assistance and aid to the blind. Collier tried to quiet the critics in hopes that new legislation would allow the BIA to dispense the benefits, but the Indians continued their agitation.[50] Perhaps more important, wartime prosperity demonstrated that Indians did not need BIA services, a view that coincided with Collier opponents' desire to abolish the agency.[51]

The greatest challenge came in June 1943, when the Senate Indian Affairs Committee issued Partial Report 310. Although its strident statements purported to summarize the Senate subcommittee's investigation since 1928, it actually blasted Collier's recent written justification for funds before the House Appropriations Committee and, in an almost sentence-by-sentence analysis, accused him of serious distortions. The report attacked Collier's claim that his agency served 400,000 Indians when in reality no more than half that number received benefits. In rejecting his plea that the BIA was financially unable to meet its legal and moral obligations, the report asserted that he had made a "pitiable showing" in expending some $500,000,000 since 1933. Virtually every BIA service, the statement charged, was ineffective, too costly, or unneeded. Collier's agency was keeping Indians from being incorporated into the American mainstream. The states were unfairly providing valuable services to many Indians even though their land and property were not taxable. The report, in short, embodied the West's traditional complaints against the BIA.

The final section of the report listed thirty-three recommendations that would solve existing problems and save $15,000,000 annually. These were hardly new. They included the transfer of education, health, forestry, and irrigation to states or other federal agencies, the immediate distribution of all individual and tribal funds, and the elimination of the BIA within one to three years. The report was signed by Elmer Thomas, chairman, Burton K. Wheeler, Dennis Chavez, and Henrik Shipstead.[52]

Collier's counterattack was polemical but closer to reality. Denying that he had distorted population statistics, underestimated per capita expenditures, or wasted funds, Collier rejected allegations that his administration kept Indians from assimilating and insisted that his main concern had always been their protection. Collier claimed that the senators who signed the report were unaware of its contents and that the real author was Albert A. Grorud, a committee staffer who had broken with Collier earlier.[53] When four hostile bills were introduced to carry out parts of the Senate report, Collier enlisted the support of the American Association on Indian Affairs, which began to publish *The American Indian* in 1943 to defend his administration.[54]

To further offset the Senate report, Collier cooperated with Representative Karl Mundt's House investigation. A moderate assimilationist from South Dakota, Mundt seemed willing to conduct a fair hearing.[55] The investigation centered on questionnaires sent to tribal councils, Indian leaders, and reservation superintendents.[56] The committee also took extensive testimony in the upper Great Plains, Montana, Washington, Minnesota, New Mexico, and Arizona. Indian attitudes ranged from qualified support for current policies to demands that the BIA be abolished immediately. Perhaps the most common Indian demand was for aid to returning veterans, but witnesses often split on whether this should involve "emancipation" from the BIA or rehabilitation programs. One of the interesting sidelights of the hearings was Representative John R. Murdock's opposition to abolishing the BIA. The Arizonian maintained that his state simply could not afford the cost of education and other social services for Indians. The select committee concluded with several sessions in Washington in late 1944.[57]

House Report 2091, issued in December 1944, adopted a moderate position. The goal, the report stressed, was for the Indian "to take his place in the white man's community on the white man's level and with the white man's opportunity and status. . . ." Poor economic and educational services, inferior extension services for adults, pending tribal claims, fractionalized lands, and lack of a procedure to permit Indians to achieve full citizenship were cited as major obstacles to assimilation. Unlike the Senate report, the House Subcommittee ignored radical solutions. Most Indians were not prepared to be "turned loose," nor had the government met its obligations so the BIA could be abolished. The report even complimented the Indian Reorganization Act (IRA) for improving economic conditions and giving Indians experience in self-government. The BIA, however, was severely criticized for its red tape and chronic slowness. The tone and the recommendations often bore a striking resemblance to the Meriam report of 1928.[58]

The formation of the National Congress of American Indians (NCAI) at Denver in November 1944 gave Indians a potential voice in legislation and administration. Several factors helped create the new group. Although organized by Indians, it relied heavily on precedents established by the reorganization constitutions and by-laws. Many of the organizers had gained valuable political experience from IRA tribal governments. The larger number of Indians employed by the BIA since 1933 worked to the same end. Collier supported the new group perhaps because of his many wartime frustrations. Because of their contributions to the war, Indians were more insistent about voting rights, ending the ban on drinking, gaining Social Security benefits, and adjudicating their claims.[59]

The Indian BIA employees, who planned the Denver conference, adroitly anticipated potential pitfalls. In background meetings at Chicago, D'Arcy McNickle, Collier's assistant, and other BIA colleagues met regularly over several months, and they determined that the NCAI should be broad enough to represent both defenders and critics of New Deal reforms. It should also be non-partisan and capable of working within the system. The organizers accepted voluntary acculturation, but they also demanded protection of civil and tribal rights and the preservation of cultural values. They chose Denver for the meeting because it was accessible to the Plains and southwestern tribes. Mark Burns, a veteran BIA staffer, and Archie Phinney, superintendent of the Northern Idaho Agency, drafted the preliminary constitution.[60]

The meeting itself overcame several basic hurdles. Eighty delegates from some forty tribes and twenty-seven states attended, including both supporters and opponents of Collier. Approximately one-fourth had ties with the BIA. Virtually all had achieved success in business, professions, or politics. A majority were affiliated with reorganization governments, although few officially represented tribal councils. To gain the support of reservation Indians and to forestall fears that tribal autonomy might be threatened, Burns told the conference that NCAI decisions were not binding on tribal governments.

A more pressing issue arose when several delegates proposed that no BIA employees could hold office in the organization. The suggestion reflected fears that their first loyalty would be to the government and that the NCAI would become Collier's tool. Although the delegates defeated the proposed amendment, none of the initial officers were BIA officials. N. B. Johnson, the president, served on the Oklahoma supreme court; Edward L. Rogers, vice president, was a Chippewa attorney from Minnesota; and Dan Madrano, secretary, held a seat in the Oklahoma legislature. The eight-member executive council represented a broader constituency. Five members resided on western reservations. Arthur Parker, a museum curator and major figure in the much earlier Society of American Indians, served as an elder statesman. McNickle and Phinney were the only two BIA personnel named to the council.[61]

The NCAI plunged into a variety of activities. The organization requested a conference of Indian leaders, the two congressional Indian Affairs Committees, and officials from the BIA and Interior Department. A legal division filed lawsuits and drafted a claims bill. NCAI officers appeared before congressional committees in support of tribal autonomy, claims legislation, veterans benefits, and civil rights.[62] The NCAI's moderate and pragmatic approach followed the spirit of traditional Indian government.

Changes in Collier's personal life and his growing frustrations as commissioner led to his resignation on January 19, 1945. He had long been interested in the broader questions of colonial administration of ethnic groups outside the United States. The war intensified this interest, and when it became clear that the United States would inherit "the administration of occupied and liberated areas," he envisioned forming an institute within the Interior Department to train persons in governing "pre-literate and pre-industrial people." His association with Laura Thompson, a noted anthropologist, in a wartime research project, resulted in a Nevada divorce from his wife and his marriage to Thompson in 1943. Doubtlessly, Collier felt frustrated by congressional hostility, the strain of weekly commutes between Chicago and Washington, and his failure to win more BIA funding.[63] Finally, Collier believed that his successor, William A. Brophy, would maintain his policies.[64]

Probably no event since the creation of reservations altered Indian life as much as World War II. Approximately one-fourth of all Indians gained a broader exposure at national and even international levels. Many also developed a new sensitivity about legal and social issues as well as a commitment to correct abuses. It was no accident that the stances taken by the NCAI so closely paralleled Indian veterans' determination to attack voting discrimination, the ban on drinking, and poor educational opportunities. Because of the high wages of war jobs, the increased income on reservations, and dependents' allotment checks, many Indians for the first time enjoyed a standard of living which approximated that of non-Indians, and they were no longer willing to submit to the grinding poverty of the past.

Although these changes were important, what seems even more significant were the many uncertainties which Indians faced when the war ended. Would wartime prosperity and jobs end in an economic collapse as many predicted? What would happen when Indian veterans and war workers returned to reservations that could not support existing populations? Would Indian leaders resolve to gain a fuller measure of economic benefits and civil rights and would they be frustrated by a conservative reaction? Would new legislation end the BIA and negate long-standing treaty and statutory obligations? In short, had Indians helped in a war fought abroad to achieve freedom only to lose rights and privileges at home that many regarded as valuable?

8.
The Postwar Era, 1945-61

The postwar years, 1945 to 1961, brought changes to the West and presented serious threats to Indians. A conservative reaction characterized much of the Indian legislation as Congress tried to reverse New Deal policies and "free" the Indians from federal control. Although land losses increased after the war, Indians' more basic problems dealt with the construction of dams and other projects that reflected white interests. Postwar opportunities, both in the West and nationally, caused thousands of Indians to move to cities. The reservations, because of improved transportation and greater access to media, lost much of their isolation. Finally, trends started during the New Deal and World War II accelerated.

Although pockets of the West's traditional economy remained, two basic changes occurred in the region during the postwar era. First, the areas of greatest population increase, California and the Southwest, significantly increased their political influence at the national level, and, second, economic growth in the more populous states broke many earlier restraints. Federal spending was central to both changes. Highway construction after 1945, for example, brought money into the West and eased severe transportation problems. On the Columbia, Snake, and Missouri Rivers, the Corps of Engineers and the Bureau of Reclamation built numerous multipurpose dams aimed at electric power generation, flood control, irrigation, and navigation. The completion of the massive irrigation works in central Washington with water from the Grand Coulee Dam in the mid-1950s was particularly important.[1] Federal spending associated with the cold war and the Korean conflict fueled growth in aerospace and electronics. Military installations continued to enrich many communities. Federal expenditures in the West between 1945 and 1960 have been estimated at $150 billion.[2]

The economic successes of the West proved to be a double-edged sword for Indians. While many welcomed the off-reservation employment and lessened isolation, they often found adjustment to the postwar environment difficult. Agricultural mechanization reduced seasonal employment Indians formerly enjoyed, and regional development projects sometimes jeopardized their rights and economic prospects.

The BIA entered a period of drift. The new commissioner, William A. Brophy, continued cultural pluralism but with less zeal. During Brophy's confirmation hearings in March 1945, for example, he promised to follow congressional dictates.[3]

Postwar shifts in liberalism also affected Indian affairs. Collier's administration had pursued the "community ideal" of ethnic identity, collective land management, and tribal self-government, but postwar liberals favored the assimilation of minorities and, in the case of Indians, a reduced federal role. Such goals obviously endangered existing policies.[4]

Personnel changes had a similar effect. Secretary Harold L. Ickes's resignation in early 1946 removed a stalwart defender of Collier's policies.[5] Ickes's successor, Julius Krug, was less committed to liberal ideals. Brophy's bout with tuberculosis removed him from his duties from late 1946 until his resignation in mid-1948. William Zimmerman, assistant commissioner since 1933, acted in Brophy's place, but he had little success in fending off congressional critics.

Virtually all the attacks on the BIA came from westerners. In 1946 Senators Burton K. Wheeler of Montana, Elmer Thomas of Oklahoma, and Harlan J. Bushfield of South Dakota renewed attempts to repeal the Indian Reorganization Act. Several western congressmen introduced legislation to remove trust restrictions from Indian veterans. Others sponsored bills to end federal controls over the Klamaths and other tribes. Although Secretary Krug supported individualizing funds and property, he successfully resisted blanket releases and warned that repeal of reorganization would seriously disrupt the political and economic development of the participating groups.[6]

Indian applications to remove individual trust restrictions rose sharply in the postwar era. Ickes had liberalized the guidelines, and higher postwar land prices and veterans' requests swamped the land division with a flood of new applications. Prominent Indian assimilationists O. K. Chandler of Oklahoma and Wade and Ida Crawford of the Klamath Reservation demanded an end to all trust restrictions, charging that reorganization was communistic. In a cold-war atmosphere, such charges could no longer be taken lightly.[7]

Congressional opponents also attacked the BIA budget. Brophy's first budget request of $30,000,000 enraged the House appropriations subcommittee who pared it to $26,000,000 by reducing relief, rehabilitation, and credit, but the Senate restored half the cuts. The following year the House Subcommittee demanded a reduction to the pre-1938 level and ignored the Bureau of the Budget's recommendation of $44,000,000. The Senate's restoration of half the cuts created another marginal budget.[8]

The BIA adopted tactics of accommodation. Brophy's 1946 plan to decentralize BIA administration attempted to meet congressional demands but retain the tribal governments. The reorganization also involved the establishment of a date when federal controls would end on each reservation.[9]

Acting Commissioner Zimmerman's appearance before the Senate Committee on Civil Service in February 1947 gave Congress a ready-made formula for reducing responsibilities over Indian affairs. Testifying under subpoena, Zimmerman responded to the committee's demands for cutting BIA expenditures with a plan that divided reservations into three categories. The first group (Flatheads, Klamaths, Menominees, Osages, Iroquois of New York, Potawatomis of Kansas, several California groups, and, conditionally, Turtle Mountain), Zimmerman suggested, were ready for immediate withdrawal of federal services. The second group of reservations would require an additional ten years of BIA supervision, and a third group should remain under federal control indefinitely. Zimmerman outlined several criteria for withdrawal: degree of acculturation, economic condition, willingness to assume independence, and states' ability to provide needed services. Zimmerman even presented three draft bills for Klamath, Osage, and Menominee withdrawal.[10]

Unwittingly, Zimmerman had presented conservatives with a rationale for a "staged approach" to withdrawal. He recognized his mistake, but his later retraction before a House committee antagonized several members. Conservatives were more concerned about achieving withdrawal than meeting Zimmerman's criteria.[11] What emerged after 1947 was a legislative consensus that rejected a blanket end of trust restrictions in favor of selective withdrawal for individual tribes. The "staged approach" became a central feature of the termination policies of the Eisenhower administration.

Meanwhile, the problem facing Indians was the reintegration of individuals who returned to reservations from war jobs or the military. A comparative study of Navajo and Zuni veterans indicated that these tribes reacted quite differently. Zuni leaders had resisted young men entering the armed services and deferred some by claiming that they were preparing for the priesthood. Fearful of a threat to traditions, elders insisted that returning veterans undergo a cleansing rite. The Zuni veterans' excessive drinking and refusals to meet family responsibilities upset conservatives. Tribal members also regarded the veterans as outspoken and "stuck up." The veterans complained of the constant gossiping about their behavior, and resented those awarded deferments. Community pressures eventually forced most to conform, but some 10 percent had left the village by mid-1947, apparently unwilling to adjust.[12] The reception of Navajo veterans in the nearby Ramah, New Mexico, area contrasted significantly. The community had supported selective service calls, and it did not demand that veterans undergo a cleansing ceremony. Even traditionalists tolerated innovations that ex-servicemen introduced, and no one attempted to force conformity.[13]

Ira Hayes's tragic fate offers a dramatic example of failed reintegration. A full-blood Pima, Hayes had enlisted in the Marine Corps in 1942 and fought in the Solomon Islands with an elite paratrooper unit. At Iwo Jima in early 1945, a photographer took a picture of Hayes and five other marines raising an American flag on Mount Suribachi. The dramatic photograph and Hayes's Indian identity made him an instant hero and led to his return to the United States to help promote a new war bond drive. Troubled by unwanted publicity and local racism, the quiet Pima became an alcoholic. His much publicized relocation to Chicago in 1953 ended on skid row, and a brief stay in Los Angeles proved equally unsuccessful. An Arizona newspaper later reported on his repeated arrests for public intoxication. His death from exposure while intoxicated two years later made Hayes a symbol of the castdown hero.[14] Postwar readjustment for most Indian veterans was neither trouble free nor tragic. As happened with rural whites, some Indian veterans easily found outside employment immediately, and others confronted overwhelming economic obstacles that forced them to relocate.

Many Indian veterans became politically active. This doubtlessly rankled many existing leaders, but veterans' status normally led to toleration of their assertiveness. Even the conservative Pueblos, for example, began to select younger and more dynamic governors dedicated to greater tribal authority.[15] Accustomed to equal treatment in the service, the veterans opposed racial discrimination, especially federal liquor controls and denial of voting rights.

The issue of voting rights in New Mexico and Arizona was the first of several clashes between Indians and state authorities after 1945. Even after the Indian Citizenship Act of 1924, New Mexico denied the vote to "Indians not taxed." Although the solicitor of the Interior Department in 1938 had declared New Mexico in violation of the Fifteenth Amendment, the state continued to deny Indians the franchise. Arizona's rationale rested on the state constitution, which excluded "persons under guardianship" from voting.

Strong pressures from Indian veterans and white reformers broke the barriers in both states in 1948. When Arizona officials refused to register two Mohave Apaches that year, the Indians brought suit, and the state supreme court ruled that "persons under guardianship" applied only to wards of the courts and not Indians. In New Mexico, an Isleta Indian filed a suit in 1948 after election officials rejected his ballot. A special panel of federal judges ruled that the state's voting ban was unconstitutional.[16] The immediate impact of the decisions was slight, but during the 1960s Indians gained a surprising influence in several western states.

The Indian Claims Commission Act in 1946 best reflected postwar Indian affairs. The legislation largely dealt with land cessions before 1894.[17] Although Congress had approved numerous jurisdictional acts that allowed tribes to sue before the Court of Claims, passage was always complicated and time-consuming for Indians, their attorneys, and Congress. Before 1930, the time lapse from a jurisdictional act until a trial started averaged ten years, and adjudication required another five years.[18]

The 1946 legislation represented disparate viewpoints about Indian affairs. For liberals, it fulfilled their idealism. Ironically, conservatives saw a resolution of Indian claims as a step toward "getting out of the Indian business." To pragmatic legislators, the legislation avoided the endless deliberations over individual jurisdictional bills. Undoubtedly, the most pervasive attitude was that the claims act represented a reward for Indians' wartime contributions.

The new law gave tribes five years to file claims and permitted suits based on either law, equity, or "fair and honorable dealings that are not recognized by any existing rule of law or equity." It further noted that treaties, contracts, or agreements with the government that involved "fraud, duress, unconscionable consideration, [or] mutual or unilateral mistake" constituted grounds for suits. Commission decisions could be appealed by either side to the Court of Claims and then to the Supreme Court.[19]

The three-man commission's early years established precedents that influenced its subsequent operations. In 1947 the commissioners notified Indian groups about filing claims.[20] Their adoption of Court of Claims procedures satisfied the government's fears about a raid on the treasury, responded to lawyers' unwillingness to lose their role, and pleased Indians who wanted an adversarial relationship rather than decisions from a commission immune from outside pressures.[21]

A large majority of the 852 claims dealt with land cessions and the government's failures to offer adequate compensation, to recognize fully the territory a tribe occupied, or to fulfill treaty obligations. Such cases involved three stages of litigation. In the first, Indian attorneys tried to establish the tribe's title to a territory. If successful in this, the commission next determined the value of the land at the time of cession. If the value exceeded the amount paid, the difference became the government's liability. The commission then held hearings on offsets or gratuitous expenditures by the government for the benefit of the claimants that could be deducted from the award. Finally, Congress appropriated the net award.[22]

Approximately fifty accounting cases made up a second category of suits filed. The issue in such cases was whether the government had met its trust or fiduciary responsibilities. Because accounting cases dealt with administrative actions and financial transactions over long periods, they were more complex and contentious than land suits.[23]

The commission adopted very liberal rules about admissible evidence. In attempting to establish title and determine value-liability, both sides used historians, anthropologists, foresters, land appraisers, and other experts. Since little primary evidence existed, expert witnesses presented not only "facts" but also interpretations and theories based on the evidence. Thus, opposing expert witnesses often reached very different conclusions from the same data.[24]

In the years between 1946 and 1978 the commission underwent numerous changes. The 852 suits, even though consolidated into 370 dockets, far exceeded expectations. During its initial decade, the commission completed eighty claims, but only fifteen involved awards. Congress reauthorized the commission four times, simplified procedures, added two commissioners in 1967, and increased the budget several times. When disbanded in 1978, sixty-eight remaining dockets were transferred to the Court of Claims.[25]

Certainly the commission's work "was a mixture of positive results and substantial failure."[26] Its achievements included giving the Indians "their day in court," allowing them to base their suits on generous grounds, and awarding $800,000,000 to the Indians. No doubt the claims litigation sensitized Indians to legal issues and prompted many to become lawyers. Unquestionably, the cases unearthed an enormous amount of information on Indians and fostered the development of ethnohistory.

On the negative side, the Claims Commission did not fulfill the hopes that it would fully resolve past differences. Indians resented awards based on land values at the time of cessions and the government's failure to pay interest.[27] The awards also were not adjusted to the value of the dollar at the time of land cessions. If a claim originating in 1830, for example, produced an award of $1,000,000 in 1962, the Indians received only $386,500 in 1830 dollars. The per capita payments awarded most groups did not contribute to long-range development of reservations. Indians regarded the offsets as unfair. Finally, Indians bore the burden of proof even though they were the victims of fraud and misrepresentation.[28]

The issue of Indian eligibility for Social Security benefits in Arizona and New Mexico also led to conflict. The problem did not involve retirement benefits but public assistance payments for the elderly, dependent children, and the blind. Although federal grants in aid paid for 75 percent of the costs of such benefits, states administered the programs and determined eligibility. Both Arizona and New Mexico refused to include Indians. In 1947, Felix Cohen, acting on behalf of the All-Pueblo Council, persuaded a federal court to order Arizona and New Mexico to include Indians in public assistance programs.[29] The two states claimed they could not afford the payments to Indians and that the BIA had the responsibility for public assistance. Critics, however, dismissed these arguments as racial discrimination. The Department of Interior agreed to assume the states' share of the cost.[30]

The legislative battle over the Navajo-Hopi rehabilitation bill in 1949 placed a new twist on the clash over Social Security benefits. The legislation grew out of a serious crisis on the two reservations during the winter of 1947-1948. Postwar unemployment and overpopulation became critical when blizzards repeatedly lashed the Southwest. Reports of Indian suffering led to private and federal relief efforts and intense pressures on the Department of Interior to formulate a long-range rehabilitation program.

Secretary Krug issued a report that became the basis of the Navajo-Hopi rehabilitation bill. Companion bills in 1949 outlined a ten-year program—costing $88,000,000—aimed at eliminating poverty and eventually transferring administrative responsibilities to the tribes. After the main hearings, an amendment by Representative Antonio M. Fernandez of New Mexico placed the two reservations under state jurisdiction.[31] Although later modified to continue tax exemptions, federal control of education, and maintenance of treaty and statutory rights, the Fernandez amendment was, in effect, legislative blackmail aimed at extending state authority.

When a conference committee met in late summer, Senate members called for the federal government to reimburse Arizona and New Mexico for 80 percent of their normal share of public assistance payments to the Indians.[32] The Senate conferees wanted the Fernandez amendment dropped for fear it "would obligate the States to make available the benefits of the State social-security laws to reservation Indians. . . ." But House members refused to back down, and both state jurisdiction and the 80 percent formula remained in the bill presented to President Truman in October 1949.[33]

The brief period between passage and Truman's veto produced extraordinary controversy. Collier published an editorial in the *New York Herald Tribune* scoring Arizona and New Mexico for their failure to offer Social Security benefits to Indians and warned that the bill would inspire similar discrimination by other states. He also noted that Arizona had recently canceled its property taxes and returned $421,389 in Social Security funds to the state treasury. Collier further warned that state jurisdiction could destroy basic legal immunities, especially those dealing with water rights.[34]

Reactions within the executive branch varied. The attorney general's office warned that additional legislation would be required to clarify jurisdiction. Secretary Krug supported the bill but acknowledged that state jurisdiction presented serious problems.[35] Truman's veto message of October 17 ignored the Social Security issue but strongly condemned state jurisdiction.[36] Without the Fernandez amendment, the measure passed in 1950, and the resulting programs did improve economic conditions among the Hopis and Navajos.[37]

Federal construction of high dams also threatened Indian security. Postwar plans to build eight dams on the Columbia River and four to six on the Snake drew strong public support because of a growing need for electricity. Eastern Washington and western Idaho residents believed that navigation made possible by the new dams would significantly reduce transportation costs. The dam at The Dalles, however, would flood Celilo Falls, the only major Indian fishing site remaining on the Columbia.

The BIA enlisted several allies in its attempts to forestall the construction. Conservation groups in the Northwest, the Fish and Wildlife Service, and the National Park Service joined with the BIA in condemning the dams as a threat to Columbia salmon fisheries. The Corps of Engineers and, to a lesser extent, the Bureau of Reclamation supported the dams. By early 1947, recognizing the futility of blocking all construction, the BIA and its allies switched tactics. They claimed that electricity needs could be met by increasing the generating capacity of existing facilities and by building new dams on the headwaters and called for a ten-year moratorium on main stream dams until the Fish and Wildlife Service could explore ways of preserving the salmon runs.

Regional development forces won the "fish versus power" conflict, but the Indians received substantial compensation for the loss of their fishing rights. After Congress authorized The Dalles Dam in 1950, the Corps of Engineers calculated the value of fishing rights at $23,000,000. Over the next few years, the corps negotiated settlements with the Warm Springs, Umatillas, Yakimas, Nez Perces, and Celilos that totaled nearly $27,000,000. Despite this, those who fished at Celilo Falls realized that monetary rewards would never adequately replace an important part of their lives.[38]

The Northwest dams did not involve major relocations of Indians, but those built on the upper Missouri River had a devastating impact on six reservations.[39] A system of multipurpose dams on the Missouri had been discussed since 1934 when Senator George Norris proposed a Missouri valley authority (MVA). Patterned after Norris's famous Tennessee Valley Authority, the MVA attracted considerable public support, but it never gained congressional authorization.[40]

After severe flooding on the Missouri in April-May 1943, Colonel Lewis A. Pick of the Corps of Engineers prepared a plan for flood prevention and other purposes. He proposed building 1,500 miles of levees below Sioux City, eighteen tributary dams, and five main stream dams above Sioux City. His plan promised the flood control and navigation that downstream interests wanted but largely ignored the irrigation needs of upper-basin residents.[41] The Bureau of Reclamation quickly released its own proposal, emphasizing smaller tributary dams better suited to irrigation and hydroelectric power.[42] Amidst heated public discussion, Pick met with William Glenn Sloan of Reclamation, and after only two days of negotiations, the two concluded the famous Pick-Sloan plan. Under the agreement, the corps would construct the levees, five major dams, and several tributary dams needed for flood control and navigation, and Reclamation would build numerous smaller dams in the upper basin. Clearly, the two agencies wanted to kill the MVA, which both feared more than they hated each other. Their hastily drawn agreement consisted of a one-page statement without detailed cost estimates or engineering data. Essentially, the two agencies accepted each other's earlier plans. James S. Patton, president of the National Farmers Union, accurately denounced the Pick-Sloan agreement as "a shameless, loveless shotgun wedding."[43] From an Indian perspective, the description was mild. Nevertheless, Congress approved the Pick-Sloan plan in 1944.

Although twenty-three Indian reservations would be affected by the Pick-Sloan plan, five main stream dams would have a devastating impact. These included the Garrison Dam in North Dakota and the Oahe, Big

Bend, Fort Randall, and Gavins Point Dams in South Dakota. The Garrison Dam flooded part of the Fort Berthold Reservation. Among the Sioux to the south, the Standing Rock and Cheyenne River Reservations lost land to the Oahe Dam; the Yankton was affected by the Fort Randall Dam; and the Crow Creek and Lower Brule lands were flooded by Fort Randall and Big Bend Dams. The dams inundated some 550 square miles of tribal land and displaced 900 families.[44]

Even though the Indians negotiated settlements with the Corps of Engineers, the contests were always uneven. The Indians were handicapped by factionalism, and the BIA lacked the expertise, incentive, and political clout to protect them. Congressional leaders gave lip service to Indian needs, but they were more responsive to white constituents. The corps, in short, ran rough-shod over the Indians.[45]

The Indians at Fort Berthold—the first to deal with the corps—fared the worst. Although Congress had stipulated that the Indians were entitled to lieu lands "comparable in quality and sufficient in area" before construction, the corps went ahead with preliminary work at Fort Berthold. After the tribal council rejected two proposals for lieu lands, the only option left by 1947 was a cash settlement for land flooded by the reservoir. Fort Berthold eventually received $7,500,000. The corps also dominated later negotiations with the five Sioux Reservations, but tribal leaders had learned from Fort Berthold's experiences and secured more lucrative settlements.[46]

The relocations of residents caused by the reservoirs severely disrupted life on all the Missouri River reservations. The percentage of Indian land flooded was not large, but it contained most of the areas used for subsistence. Only 6 percent of the Sioux's land, for example, was flooded, but approximately one-third of the residents underwent relocation. In addition, resettlement disrupted long-standing communal and kinship ties and deeply felt attachments to the land. Factionalism intensified during the prolonged disputes. At Fort Berthold, for example, dissension developed over whether relocation awards should be spent for long-term development or per capita payments. The reservation economy hit bottom in 1957 when the final per capita payment was made.[47]

The period of drift ended in 1950 with the appointment of Dillon S. Myer as Indian commissioner.[48] A professional bureaucrat, Myer earlier directed the War Relocation Authority (WRA). In recalling the challenges involved, he characteristically commented, "I never have been bothered when it comes to carrying on a job that I feel that I am responsible for."[49] Myer approached his BIA assignment with the same attitude. If national leadership wanted a reduced BIA role, Myer would provide the policies, directives, and personnel for "an orderly progression from initiation to conclusion."[50] Myer, however, rejected radical plans to abolish the BIA and force instant assimilation on Indians. He recognized, in short, that improvements in education, health care, employment opportunities, and reservation development were required before the federal government could relinquish its trust responsibilities.[51]

Myer's actions illustrate how an experienced administrator consolidates power. When Secretary of Interior Oscar Chapman, an old friend, asked Myer to become commissioner, Myer insisted that he report directly to Chapman. He also won Chapman's permission to replace Zimmerman with H. Rex Lee as associate commissioner. Erwin Utz and John Province became assistant commissioners in charge, respectively, of land and resources and of health, education, and social services. All three had worked for Myer during the war, and their appointments signaled a cleaning out of Collier holdovers. Myer's completion of earlier decentralization efforts further consolidated his control. Essentially, he strengthened the positions held by himself, Lee, Utz, and Province while converting the branch directors in the Washington office into staff positions. His reorganization seemingly strengthened the area offices, but decentralization was illusionary because Myer rigidly controlled the area directors.[52]

The new administration enjoyed strong ties with western congressional leadership. Myer already knew Senator Clinton P. Anderson of New Mexico, former secretary of agriculture and an influential member of the Interior and Insular Affairs Committee, whom Myer had known since the New Deal. Immediately after Myer's appointment, Anderson warned him about betrayal by Collier holdovers.[53] Associate Commissioner Lee had grown up in Utah and was close to Senator Watkins of that state. Watkins cooperated with Lee during the remaining Truman years and throughout the Eisenhower administration.

Myer undertook the relocation of Indians from reservations to outside jobs as a first step in his withdrawal policies. The BIA merely needed to determine where employment existed, upgrade vocational training, and cooperate with state employment agencies. The goal was to rescue Indians from reservation poverty by incorporating them into the postwar economy. Unfortunately, Myer's 26,000 placements were in low-paying and seasonal jobs, and only 3,000 Indians found "permanent" jobs.[54] Without improved social services, relocation could not relieve Indian poverty.

Another important facet of withdrawal involved the transfer of BIA services to other federal agencies and state governments. Existing legislation, especially the Johnson-O'Malley Act, permitted cooperative arrangements with states for education and welfare but not other services. Myer, hence, moved most decisively by placing more mixed-blood youngsters in public schools and maintaining boarding schools for full bloods. In both instances, instruction about Indian cultures was abandoned. Myer and Lee also turned over extension programs on several reservations to states.[55]

Congressional support for Myer's withdrawal policies was evident from the moment he took office. In June 1950, Representative Reva Beck Bosone of Utah introduced a joint resolution that called for a study of all Indian groups by the secretary of interior to determine their readiness for withdrawal. By January 1, 1951, he was to specify which groups should be released from federal control, and a year later he was to report on existing efforts to end federal jurisdiction and to propose new programs for the same purpose. At the same time, the secretary would present legislation to end federal controls of those groups currently unprepared for withdrawal. The resolution authorized up to $250,000 to pay for the studies. When the measure came to the House floor, Francis Case of South Dakota reduced funding to $50,000, and the House approved the measure.[56] Senator Watkins, claiming earlier studies had already established which Indian groups were prepared for release, killed the resolution.[57]

Despite its defeat, the Bosone resolution demonstrated how little support New Deal policies commanded after 1948. Both Collier and Ickes had charged that it would destroy earlier reforms and invite a plundering of Indians' resources. But neither their efforts nor Indian criticisms had any real impact. Indeed, the official climate had shifted so drastically that the resolution could actually be viewed as a shield against the kind of instant termination conservatives demanded. Moreover, the defeat of the resolution only delayed matters. The House in July 1952 ordered an investigation similar to the Bosone resolution.[58]

Myer in late 1951 had anticipated congressional action by establishing a "division of program" within the BIA. Various specialists in the unit sought to formulate a systematic sequence of steps leading to withdrawal. By June 1952, they completed compiling elaborate data on the social, political, and economic makeup of all reservations. In August, Myer ordered BIA personnel to devise withdrawal plans for all groups and institutions. He encouraged cooperation with Indians and local and state governments but directed field workers to proceed even if Indian support was lacking. To spur cooperation, Myer noted that future appropriations would be targeted to those groups directly involved in withdrawal. He ordered field workers to report by September 15 on the status of their plans.[59]

States with Indian populations initially welcomed the opportunity to assume withdrawn BIA services. The governor of Minnesota in early 1950 convened a preliminary meeting of representatives from "Indian states" at St. Paul. Formal organization of the Governors' Interstate Indian Council (GIIC) followed at Salt Lake City in May, with representatives from sixteen states. Kansas, Texas, and Colorado were the only western states not represented. Both Minnesota and Wisconsin sent delegates. Governor Dan E. Garvey of Arizona denounced the BIA, and Governor George T. Michelson of South Dakota added that "the Indian will never become an American until we get him off the reservation." The GIIC established study committees on education; employment; health; housing; law and order; state-federal relations; treaties, claims, and lands; and welfare. Committee recommendations would be forwarded to Congress.[60]

The makeup of the GIIC committees proved important. State officials invariably came from education or social agencies already involved with Indian services. Among the Indian appointees, Sam Akeah, Navajo chairman, served on the education committee, and Vine Deloria, Episcopal clergyman, chaired the study group on employment. Edward Rogers, a Chippewa and longtime county attorney in Minnesota, served on two committees. N. B. Johnson, an Oklahoma supreme court justice and first president of the National Congress of the American Indians (NCAI), chaired the committee on law and order. Frank George, a Nez Perce from the Colville Reservation, who served as the NCAI vice president and executive secretary, became vice president of the GIIC. Both Johnson and George's reelection at the NCAI convention in 1951 seemingly indicated considerable Indian support for state assumption.[61]

The impact of the GIIC remains unclear. Certainly the group's withdrawal activities received strong support from the states. A national meeting of governors a month after the Salt Lake City meeting approved resolutions calling for a settlement of treaties, the assimilation of Indians, and "an early end to federal wardship, with adequate federal aid in the interim."[62] It was equally clear that friction developed within the GIIC. One observer characterized the meeting in late 1951 at Helena, Montana, as the "latest battle of the Little Big Horn."[63]

Western state governments in the same period began to study Indian affairs. In Oregon, for example, Governor Douglas McKay appointed an advisory committee that included representatives from tribal councils, state and federal agencies, and the general public. North Dakota established a commission with an executive secretary and a $20,000 budget. The Montana legislature authorized a coordinator for Indian affairs but failed to appropriate salary funds. Other states conducted studies and made inquiries about what others were doing.[64] Eventually every western state would create a commission or agency devoted to Indian affairs.[65]

By late 1952, the withdrawal controversy reached a climax. Eisenhower's victory in November meant a major shakeup in top interior personnel although probably not a basic shift in Indian policy. Myer tried to use his ties with conservative western leaders to continue as commissioner. Appalled at this prospect, Collier intensified his propaganda against the commissioner. Some Indian leaders also attacked Myer because of their fears of state jurisdiction and Myer's withdrawal policies.

Myer's speech before the Western Governors Conference in Phoenix on December 9, 1952, carefully designed to win his reappointment, repeatedly stressed his determination to transfer BIA services to state and local governments. He noted a need for "careful planning and programming" and for full cooperation between the Indians and all levels of government. In discussing reservation poverty, Myer warned that maximizing Indian land use offered limited hope, and endorsed education, job training, and industrial jobs.[66] Although Myer was not reappointed, the data compiled by the division of program remained for the Eisenhower administration.[67]

The Eisenhower campaign in 1952 was calculated to win the support of western whites and Indians. His speeches denounced federal tyranny over the West, promised freedom from eastern business interests, declared that arid lands would someday become green fields and thriving cities, and applauded western traits such as courage, vision, and heart. Eisenhower's equally shrewd address at the Intertribal Indian Ceremonial in Gallup, New Mexico, denounced previous mistreatment of Indians and praised their participation in World War II. At Gallup he pledged that Indians would be consulted about future policy changes. This promise would become a major source of controversy once he took office.[68]

Eisenhower's delay in naming an Indian commissioner did not slow the termination policy. A crucial meeting between Senator Watkins, Representative William Harrison of Wyoming, and Assistant Secretary of Interior Orme Lewis on February 27, 1953, outlined termination and a legislative strategy.[69] Watkins, chairman of the Senate Subcommittee on Indian Affairs, dominated the meeting. Lewis soon informed Watkins that Interior Secretary Douglas McKay had approved termination. In June all area offices and agencies received formal notification of the new guidelines. Significantly, Lewis never contacted Indian leaders.

Termination meant that the federal government would end its administrative responsibilities as soon as each tribe's circumstances permitted, transfer these to state and local governments, and distribute tribal assets either to tribes or individual members. Federal trust over Indian land would be relinquished to either individuals or tribes, and any tribal income would be distributed on a per capita basis. General rehabilitation legislation to effect termination would be enacted, but individual tribes might receive additional aid.[70] Termination differed little from withdrawal except that withdrawal had never gained legislative backing, while two major enactments in 1953 underwrote termination.

Watkins's dominant role behind termination seems clear, but interpreting his motives presents interesting problems. The senator had grown up near a Ute Reservation and, like many westerners, considered himself an expert on Indian affairs. After college, he spent two years as a Mormon missionary and attended law school. His legal practice largely dealt with irrigation, but he also published newspapers, wrote articles on reclamation, and promoted irrigation generally. Reclamation became his major concern after he entered the Senate in 1947. He initially supported Robert Taft in 1952 and switched to Eisenhower only after assurances that upper Colorado basin states would gain a share of the Colorado River water.[71]

Like other conservatives, Watkins sought to revamp Indian policies, but his interest was unusually intense. One Eisenhower official noted that Watkins "was the only one I know of who insisted on being on the Indian Affairs Committee. . . ." The same official suggested a link between Watkins's interest in Indians and his strong Mormon background. Watkins, according to the official, "thought he was paying off a debt which the Mormons owed the Indians."[72] Although Mormons have always felt a special obligation to convert Indians or Lamanites to the true faith, Watkins's own religious motives, if any, present an intriguing but elusive puzzle.[73]

In a 1957 article, Watkins defended termination with assimilationist arguments. He maintained that Indians throughout American history had been "accorded a status apart." Termination led to equal opportunity and freedom "from special federal restrictions on the property and the person of the tribes and their members."[74] In a 1968 interview, however, Watkins virtually ignored termination and sounded like a pork-barrel politician with do-gooder overtones: "I put over a lot of projects for the Indians along with my Western associates. We worked together very well, both Democrat and Republican." He especially relished converting a former military hospital at Brigham City, Utah, into a major Indian boarding school. The project was, he enthused, "my pride and joy," and a greater achievement than even his reclamation victories.[75]

Watkins wasted no time in securing termination legislation. House Concurrent Resolution 108, signed on August 1, 1953, declared that Indians should be subject to the same laws and entitled to the same privileges, rights, and responsibilities as other citizens. It further recommended ending federal supervision over all Indians of California, Florida, New York, and Texas as well as specific tribes in other states (Flatheads of Montana, Klamaths of Oregon, Menominees of Wisconsin, Potawatomis of Kansas and Nebraska, and the Chippewas of North Dakota). The resolution ordered the secretary of interior to examine all existing statutes and treaties and by January 1, 1954, to recommend legislation to end federal responsibility.[76]

A companion measure, Public Law 280, dealt with extending state laws over Indian reservations. The act permitted California, Minnesota, Nebraska, Oregon, and Wisconsin to exercise both criminal and civil jurisdiction over reservations.[77] The act, however, noted that state jurisdiction did not affect existing trust restrictions and obligations secured by treaties or statutes. Sections 6 and 7, however, aroused severe criticism because they permitted other states unilaterally to assume jurisdiction over Indian reservations.[78] The original bill had not contained the two provisions, but Senator Butler of Nebraska had added them to the bill.[79]

John Collier, the NCAI, and other reform groups lodged strong protests against P.L. 280. One veteran tribal attorney wrote Eisenhower that it caused an unprecedented furor.[80] Criticisms of the government's failure to consult with Indians and the coercive nature of sections 6 and 7 caused the administration to hesitate. Acknowledging that the bill violated the consultation pledge, Lewis promised that he would consult with Indians and states before implementation, and he falsely claimed that both supported the measure. In a press release in mid-August, Eisenhower stated that he had given his signature despite his misgivings about the failure of P.L. 280 to require "full consultation." He naively called for amendatory legislation in the next session to rectify this omission.[81] Watkins made sure that none of the bills passed in 1954.[82]

The long delay in appointing a new Indian commissioner ended in August with the naming of Glenn L. Emmons, a Gallup, New Mexico, banker. The appointment had been marked by unusual competition for the post. Indians' demands that one of their own be named centered largely on Henry J. W. Belvin, an educator and principal chief of the Oklahoma Choctaws. By June, however, the race narrowed to Alva A. Simpson, Jr. and Emmons.[83] Simpson, who chaired the GIIC and directed the New Mexico public welfare department, later withdrew, allegedly because of Senator Anderson's opposition.[84] Emmons's strongest qualification was the support of Navajo leaders whom he had frequently advised.

The "Emmons plan," which focused on Indian health, education, and economic conditions, did not conflict with termination, but he seemed to view termination as a long-range goal. He left the passage of termination bills to Watkins and his allies, and seemed content to deal with social and economic problems.[85]

Congressional deliberations on termination bills for individual tribes started on February 15, 1954, when the Senate and House Subcommittees on Indian Affairs opened joint hearings.[86] Senator Watkins, somewhat defensively, explained that the joint hearings would save time. HCR 108, approved the previous August, allowed the BIA only until January 1, 1954, to consult with field workers and Indian leaders and to draft termination bills. Pressured by the absurd deadline, the BIA engaged in various shortcuts, including the use of data and plans compiled by Myers. Associate Commissioner Lee, who attended all of the hearings, repeatedly admitted that the bills might need revisions.

Although Watkins usually presided, E. Y. Berry, chairman of the House subcommittee, actively assisted. Like Watkins, Berry was a conservative Republican who believed that his residence in Indian country qualified him as an expert. He had practiced law at McLaughlin, South Dakota, on the Standing Rock Reservation, since 1927. He had concluded that local Indians were progressing satisfactorily toward assimilation until the Collier era. Berry denounced Collier's programs as wasteful and retrogressive communist experiments.[87]

Berry and Watkins dominated throughout the hearings. If Watkins was absent, Berry presided and vice versa. Other terminationists, such as Representatives Wesley D'Ewart of Montana and William Harrison of Wyoming, sometimes attended, but neither they nor anyone else participated regularly. Watkins was probably correct when he stated that "if it was not for my good friend, Mr. Berry, we would not have been able to keep the hearings going."[88]

Watkins frequently interrupted testimony to state his own beliefs. One theme he often reiterated was the failure of federal guardianship. Indians, he declared, "have not been permitted to grow and develop as they should."[89] Similarly, Watkins denounced reservations because they kept Indians "from doing things [for] themselves that would really help."[90] Watkins repeatedly attacked the validity of treaties. He initially argued that Indian treaties were "like the treaties with Europe. They can be renounced at any time." Later he shifted to the equally specious argument that the Indian Citizenship Act of 1924 had eliminated treaty rights because the United States did not recognize dual citizenship.[91] Watkins frequently condemned mixed bloods because they evaded their civil responsibilities.

As the hearings proceeded, it became clear that the theory of "staged termination" of tribes according to education, acculturation, and business acumen was an illusion. Indeed, it was difficult to find any rational basis for the selection process. The frequent charges that termination was a thinly disguised land grab might have some validity for the Klamaths, Menominees, and Flatheads, but other groups had little worth grabbing. The Turtle Mountain Reservation, for example, was so impoverished that a per capita division of tribal assets amounted to only $37.[92]

Certainly leadership and tribal unity helped determine whether a group successfully resisted termination. The intense factionalism of the Klamaths made that reservation vulnerable to termination, but the hearings on the Flatheads offered a strong counter example. Montana's Senator James Murray appeared at the opening session and denounced Watkins because the room was too small for the large audience. Senator Mike Mansfield cautioned against any violation of the Flatheads' treaty rights.[93] Representative Lee Metcalf filed a long statement objecting to the Flathead bill.[94] The well-connected Klamath attorney warned that termination would destroy Flathead treaty rights.[95] D'Arcy McNickle, former BIA employee and later distinguished historian, questioned whether his tribe had received adequate consultation. After Watkins declared that "this matter of consultation, of course, can be overdone," McNickle quickly countered, "it can be underdone too."[96] When Tribal Chairman Walter McDonald testified, he brought with him a panel of Flathead leaders, including a hereditary chief, who presented a united front against termination.[97] The solid opposition handily defeated Flathead termination.

The hearings revealed that some western leaders had developed strong misgivings about termination. Although Utah Governor J. Bracken Lee endorsed termination as "a step in the right direction," others recognized that termination offered a Pandora's box of burdens that they hesitated to assume, at least without federal subsidies.[98] Essentially the states' only compensation for control over Indian affairs was the ability to tax former trust land. John B. Hart, executive director of the North Dakota Indian Affairs Commission, frankly admitted that his state had created the commission to get more federal funds. He added that Indians deserved the same social services as whites, but public assistance expenses for Indians were fifty-five times higher in Rollette County than for non-Indians. Hart blasted the idea that additional taxes from Indian land would meet the added financial burdens and flatly demanded federal compensation. "Any other course," he declared, "means bankruptcy to the local governments concerned or probably the complete abandonment of the Indians. . . ."[99]

After the hearings, Congress approved six termination acts. These included the Menominees, the Klamaths, the sixty-one bands and tribes of western Oregon, the Alabama-Coushattas, and the Mixed-Blood Utes and Southern Paiutes of Utah. Legislation in 1956 terminated the Wyandottes, Peorias, and Ottawas of Oklahoma. Two years later Congress acted on the California Rancherias, and in 1959 it released the Catawbas of South Carolina. The final act in 1964 dealt with the Poncas of Nebraska. In all, termination involved 13,263 Indians and 1,365,801 acres of trust land.

Of all the western tribes that underwent termination, the Klamaths were not necessarily typical, but their experiences provide insights into non-Indian reactions to economic and ecological threats. Proposals for a sale of Klamath timber and per capita distribution had been advocated since at least 1945 by Wade Crawford, veteran tribal politician.[100] Largely because of Crawford's insistence that Klamaths were prosperous and acculturated, the tribe had been picked for early termination. Other leaders strongly opposed termination. Klamath factionalism was intense even by reservation standards.

Public Law 587 unsuccessfully attempted to satisfy both groups. The central feature of the act allowed individuals to withdraw from the tribe and accept a cash payment for their share of tribal assets or to remain tribal members with a claim to the unsold portion of the reservation. Three "management specialists" would appraise the timber, determine what proportion must be sold to make per capita payments, and select a private trustee for the remainder. The law also authorized educational programs that would permit Klamaths "to assume their responsibilities as citizens without special services because of their status as Indians." The act specified full implementation within four years.[101]

Implementation revealed serious problems. Surveys by the Stanford Research Associates revealed that 39 percent of those interviewed possessed only a grammar school education, and nearly half of those over eighteen had only sporadic employment experience. Klamaths had little understanding about termination, but about 70 percent indicated that they wanted to withdraw. One management specialist flatly warned that the tribe was unprepared for termination, but such misgivings did not deter Washington officials.[102]

The government responded, however, when the prospective sale of Klamath timber created consternation among white interests. Conservationists, fearful of clear cutting the timber, insisted that sales carry a sustained-yield proviso. Possible ecological damage to the Klamath Marsh, a major area for migratory waterfowl, produced demands that the federal government purchase the marsh. Oregon businessmen and lumbermen became worried about a drop in prices if all Klamath timber was sold at once. Many Oregon citizens feared that the Klamaths would become a public burden once they exhausted their per capita payments.[103]

By late 1956 Interior Secretary Fred A. Seaton, who had replaced McKay, instructed the BIA to prepare an amendment which would impose a sustained-yield requirement and guarantee the highest prices possible for Klamath timber. Senator Richard L. Neuberger of Oregon, chairman of the Indian affairs subcommittee, proposed that the federal government purchase the Klamath timber and sell it with a sustained-yield proviso to either large or small buyers, including the Klamaths. When this failed, Neuberger accepted an amendment delaying Klamath termination until 1960.[104] In 1958 Congress approved a measure that required timber sales by competitive bids equal to or above the appraised value. The act also stipulated sustained-yield cutting and other conservation practices. Unsold lots would be purchased by the government and placed in a national forest. The government would acquire the Klamath Marsh as a wildlife refuge. The act extended the deadline to April 1, 1961.[105]

Claims that termination offered a simple solution to Indians' problems were hardly borne out by later events. In 1958, 1,659 Klamaths (77 percent) elected to withdraw from the tribe and accept a per capita payment of $43,700. The remaining 474 members (23 percent) continued their tribal status, but numerous withdrawing members were ruled legally incompetent, and a total of 48.9 percent came under private trust. Another 13.6 percent, although legally competent, opted to join those under trust. For 62.5 percent of Klamaths, termination meant a shift in trust from the BIA to a Portland bank. The Klamaths reportedly became as unhappy with this arrangement as they had been with the BIA. The disposal of the tribe's 997,925 acres was equally complex. Slightly over half failed to receive a bid and was purchased by the Forest Service. Tribal members acquired only 79,107 acres, and Crown Zellerback Corporation purchased 91,539 acres. Land retained for non-withdrawing members totaled 144,960 acres. The rest of the former reservation consisted of unrestricted allotments and "fringe" lots sold to private bidders.[106]

An economic analysis of Klamath termination reached several important conclusions. Tribal members had been receiving $800 annually in per capita payments, and the value of BIA services probably equaled this figure. After termination, Klamaths under private trust earned $1,500 or about the same.[107] Termination apparently had no decisive social or economic impacts among the non-trust Indians. Many moved from remote reservation locations to border towns, and Klamath employment rose but remained lower than white rates. Income seemed skewed toward moderately high and low levels, probably because older Klamaths possessed job skills and younger ones did not.[108] Despite numerous stories about whites duping terminated Klamaths out of their money, this was not typical. But they generally spent their money on homes, home improvements, and cars, rather than investments that produced future income.[109] Although Indian welfare rates were high, termination did not produce the feared raid on state funds.[110]

The great loser from Klamath termination was clearly the federal government. The administrative costs of termination was $3,400,000 and the purchase of timber reached $69,000,000. The timber sales from the land acquired by the government brought in $1,600,000 annually, a 2.25 percent investment return, but this does not include intangibles such as conservation benefits. Before termination Klamath timber sales had paid all BIA administrative expenses except for $200,000 spent on roads, soil and moisture conservation, and irrigation.[111] Freedom for the Klamaths was clearly no bargain.

Opposition to termination was not clear-cut. Critics of Myers transferred their hostility to the Eisenhower administration when it reneged on consultation. After the furor over P.L. 280 subsided, white reformers and Indians' attitudes seemed uncertain. Many Indians still distrusted the BIA, doubted its competence, and saw termination as a possible solution. This tentativeness seemed clear when the Watkins-Berry hearings opened. Joseph R. Garry, president of the NCAI, testified that his appearance "is not to oppose or favor this particular legislation. . . ." A stronger statement by Helen L. Peterson, NCAI executive director, accepted the goal of assimilation but warned "there remains much unfinished work which the States are not prepared to assume. . . ." Peterson wanted improved education, medical care, and relocation services as well as full consultation before tribes were terminated.[112]

What had been tentative criticism hardened as termination proceeded. Indians who still hated the BIA began to see termination as a greater menace. During the termination hearings, the NCAI held an emergency meeting to consolidate its opposition. Peterson afterward appeared at the Turtle Mountain sessions and declared that "tribal existence, tribal life, [and] pride in Indian culture" were moral responsibilities that were being ignored by the government.[113]

The most important shift, however, occurred in Congress. In 1955 the Democrats gained control of both houses, and in 1957 they increased their majority. Western Democrats controlled the Interior and Insular Affairs Committees and the subcommittees on Indian affairs. Representative Lee Metcalf and Senator James Murray of Montana led the anti-terminationists, and their allies included Senators Mike Mansfield of Montana, Frank Church of Idaho, and Joseph O'Mahoney of Wyoming. The seven-man delegation from Oklahoma lent support with issues affecting their state. Senator Anderson of New Mexico, once an advocate of assimilation, recanted in 1955, claiming that Klamath termination had demonstrated a failure to manage tribal assets properly.[114] Although Senator Barry Goldwater defended the administration, he claimed that HCR 108 defined long-range goals.

The anti-terminationists accepted eventual assimilation but believed that reservation conditions must be improved before implementation. Some objected to the heavy-handed application of HCR 108, maintained that treaty and statutory obligations must be fully recognized, and insisted any Indian group must fully understand and consent to termination. Congressional critics seldom expressed concern that termination threatened Indian cultures, but based their objections on such needs as improving relocation, expanding economic development, ending land sales, and upgrading BIA services.[115]

The opposition did not seek a complete reversal of termination. Congress did not repeal P.L. 280, HCR 108, or the individual termination acts. Senator Neuberger, for example, never proposed restoring Klamath tribal status. Instead, he painstakingly molded a series of revisions of the original legislation in response to complaints of interested groups. The anti-terminationists, however, put the administration on the defensive and broke the impetus of termination.[116]

Changes in the Eisenhower administration contributed to stalemating termination. Secretary of Interior Douglas McKay resigned in early 1956 and returned to Oregon to run for the Senate. Embarrassed by the sobriquet "Give-Away McKay," Eisenhower named Fred A. Seaton to fill the post. A former newspaperman, Seaton had been a senator from Nebraska before becoming assistant secretary of defense and administrative assistant to the president. A moderate with broad intellectual interests, Seaton quieted the public outcries of conservationists, abandoned strong support for termination legislation, and concentrated on upgrading BIA social and economic programs.[117] In September 1958, in a radio address in Arizona, Seaton declared that the intent of HCR 108 was to state an objective, not an immediate goal, and he pledged that any group facing termination must fully understand and concur in the plan involved.[118] Coercive termination was dead.

The relocation of Indians from reservations to urban areas was a corollary to termination. Conservatives argued that industrial jobs freed Indians from BIA control, gave them access to improved education and other social services, and provided a means for ending Indian poverty. The Indian work record during World War II was often cited to support relocation. Emmons took the lead in the relocation program. In a sense, "official" relocation was somewhat pointless. Migration to urban areas was a general trend both in the West and nationally during the postwar years and affected every rural community. Pressed by the same economic forces as rural whites, increasing numbers of Indians abandoned reservations for urban jobs. Many first settled in border towns before moving to large cities. Probably 75 percent of the Indians relocated without government assistance.

Government relocation started as part of Navajo-Hopi rehabilitation in 1948 when the BIA began recruiting males for agricultural and railroad work. After Navajo veterans demanded better jobs, the BIA established job placement offices in Denver, Salt Lake City, and Los Angeles. Congress expanded the program in fiscal 1952 by appropriating $579,600 for additional offices in Los Angeles, Denver, and Chicago. By 1970 employment services also existed in Oakland, San Francisco, San Jose, Dallas, and Cleveland.[119] The BIA provided transportation, job placement, subsistence funds until the first paycheck, and some counseling. Emmons intensified the program. In 1953 placements reached 2,600; they peaked in 1957 with 6,964; and by 1960 a total of 33,466 had been relocated.[120]

Public Law 959 in 1956 added vocational training to the relocation program. Primarily aimed at Indians between eighteen and thirty-five years of age, participants could receive a maximum of two years of benefits for either on-the-job experience or classes in recognized vocational schools. The legislation also increased counseling services. In practice, the apprenticeship provisions were reserved for Indians who worked in factories on or near reservations, and individuals who relocated received vocational training. The latter received spartan living expenses, and they were allowed to switch from one trade to another.[121]

The Indian reaction to the relocation program produced some unexpected results. Government officials saw it as a one-way ticket to a city and assumed participants would take up permanent residence. Many, however, briefly took jobs and then returned home. Some repeated the same process several times. The pattern continued even after vocational training started in 1957. In addition, adjustment to urban life was not necessarily related to acculturation levels. One study of Oklahoma Choctaws, Sioux, and Navajos in Dallas indicated that although the Navajos were less acculturated, they adapted better to urban life than the other two groups.[122]

The official relocation program became almost as controversial as termination itself. Critics charged that it forced Indians to leave reservations and assume life in an alien and hostile environment. The program, they added, did not improve living standards but exposed participants to slum housing, alcoholism, and other social problems. The quality of job training and counseling also drew heavy fire. Relocation was, in short, another misguided and cruel attempt to force Indian assimilation. The charges were overdrawn. In many instances, the social problems critics cited were simply carried to cities. For every failure, one could find examples of successful adjustment and increased prosperity and self-esteem. Critics also overlooked the fact that Indians had adapted to changes for centuries, and life in a city was less traumatic than earlier challenges. Finally, official relocation, despite its many detractors, had a long waiting list at many agencies.

The long-range effects of relocation remain unclear, but several tentative conclusions may be ventured. While Navajos and Turtle Mountain Chippewas in San Francisco associated only with members of their own tribes, other Indians intermingled and created a new pan-Indian identity. This was not a final stage before acculturation. Some Indians, indeed, had never attended cultural activities until they moved to San Francisco.[123] The reservation, moreover, remained "home" to most urban Indians, and they returned whenever possible to visit their families, to attend ceremonies, and to enjoy what was familiar. Similarly, many Indians retired from urban jobs to their own people. The reservations, hence, will likely retain an importance greater than white migrants place on their home communities.

Unfortunately, relocation also contributed to divisiveness that often appeared in the postwar years. The "absentee" Klamaths, although comprising some 10 percent of the tribe, acted as an effective minority in securing termination. To these non-residents, the chance to gain per capita payments from tribal assets far outweighed any emotional attachment to their reservation. Urban Indians invariably demanded per capita payments in claims settlements rather than lump sums for reservation development. They also resented the loss of BIA benefits and exclusion from tribal political decisions.

Unlike termination and relocation, the government's industrial development escaped major criticism. Emmons viewed manufacturing, like relocation, as a solution for poorer reservations. He also believed that younger Indians had little interest in agriculture, but they had "a remarkable degree of manual dexterity and proficiency in mechanical processes." Earlier development efforts had encouraged tribal enterprises, but Emmons concentrated on attracting private manufacturers to reservations. Industrial development, like relocation, became Emmons's "baby."[124]

Unfortunately, his industrial development program faced serious obstacles. Despite differences, reservations were typically handicapped by remote markets, weak infrastructures, shortages of capital, and limited credit. Individual income generated on reservations typically came from leases, small-scale agriculture, handicrafts, and limited employment. With few exceptions, tribes did not gain significant wealth from sales of natural resources. Regardless of source, income tended to move off the reservation immediately rather than passing through several hands and creating a multiplier effect. Many Indians lacked basic business expertise. BIA schools stressed office skills but totally ignored managerial training. In one instance, a young Navajo clerk asked her employer for a day off so she could report him for charging more for goods than he paid for them. Profit, to her, violated proper business ethics. Even more damaging was the scarcity of Navajo "entrepreneurs" willing to seek business opportunities, take risks, and make decisions.[125]

Emmons, in late 1954, created a private group known as the American Indian Research Fund, Inc. (AIRF). By raising funds from foundations and hiring research engineering firms to conduct economic surveys of reservations, the AIRF hoped to avoid red tape and insure that the best qualified companies made the surveys. The results proved frustrating. The AIRF raised only $30,000, and the surveys were uneven. Moreover, industrial firms demanded special "inducements" before they would relocate to reservations.[126]

By mid-1955 industrial development moved to a new phase when Emmons and an assistant arranged meetings between business executives, tribal leaders, and local businessmen to establish factories. The two men also appeared before business organizations to explain the program and to solicit support. Their presentations stressed that Indians constituted a new (and presumably cheap) source of labor and a potentially important group of consumers. Emmons hoped to attract only reputable and labor-intensive firms. [127]

By late 1957 Emmons had recruited ten firms, but all had received subsidies. Tribes typically provided the plant building and then leased it to the manufacturer. Under Public Law 959, which provided vocational training, the BIA paid half of the minimum wage for Indian employees. Because of possible legal problems on reservations, companies usually located factories in border towns. [128]

Western congressional leaders soon began to show a surprising interest in reservation development. At the end of 1956, the Defense Department announced the closing of the Turtle Mountain ordnance plant at Rolla, North Dakota, that manufactured jewel bearings and employed numerous Indians. Convinced that jobs would best solve reservation problems, Senator William Langer of North Dakota convened western congressmen in early 1957 to keep the plant open. Langer and several cosponsors shortly introduced a bill authorizing $20,000,000 in loans and grants to encourage manufacturing on reservations. Emmons successfully opposed the bill, but Congress subsequently approved a measure patterned after the "Point Four Program" that President Eisenhower vetoed. [129]

After this defeat, Representative Berry of South Dakota became the major advocate of industrial development. Given Berry's conservatism, his action was little short of startling. Berry, however, was willing to compromise his laissez-faire principles to help business. His district also contained 30,000 Indian voters, and he doubtlessly wanted to offset his earlier support for termination. A visit to Puerto Rico in 1958 convinced him that "Operation Bootstrap" could be tailored to Indian needs. In 1959 he introduced the first of several "Operation Moccasin" bills. Each placed a ten-year moratorium on taxes for businesses established on reservations and subsidized on-the-job training for Indian employees. His bills never won either administration or congressional approval. [130]

By the end of the Eisenhower administration, industrial development lagged. What had started as a simple program had become increasingly involved with government controls. Moreover, only four of Emmons's ten firms survived in 1961, none had flourished, and they employed relatively few Indians. Some of the failures could be attributed to poor management and inadequate financing, but the severe recession of 1957 caused several to close. Perhaps the main contribution of industrial development was that it provided some background for the Kennedy-Johnson administrations' much more ambitious programs. [131]

From the perspective of reservation Indians, the land losses in the 1950s seemed more threatening than anything except termination itself. Emmons's land policies went beyond even Dillon Myer's. After 1953 the BIA not only liberalized land sales, but also, in 1955, Emmons decreed that individuals could sell allotments regardless of the impact on their tribe. Reservation Indians saw the policy as a threat to community life, an abrogation of trust responsibilities, and a check on rehabilitation. Councils demanded the right to buy land offered for sale, especially "key tracts" vital to land management, and they wanted long-term loans. They questioned lavishing money on relocation and industrial development and Emmons's unwillingness to help reservations. The more vocal denounced land sales as another raid on Indian resources and a way of getting rid of Indians in general.[132] Interior spokesmen replied that individual Indians should have a right to sell their land. Emmons repeatedly denied that land sales were linked to relocation and termination.[133]

The transfer of health treatment from the BIA to the Public Health Service (PHS) in 1954 meshed with the terminationists' drive to reduce or eliminate BIA services for Indians. Although BIA health care improved after 1945, it remained subpar. Only a transfer to PHS seemed to offer a solution because it possessed more resources and legislative clout. Despite the apparent advantages, a 1953 bill authorizing a transfer encountered objections from interior officials who wanted Indians integrated into general health care programs. The Department of Health, Education, and Welfare, parent agency of PHS, seemed reluctant to assume the new burdens. In 1954 the Interior Department shifted its position, and Senator Watkins pushed a bill through Congress. The transfer itself took place on July 1, 1955.[134] Indians' responses were mixed. The NCAI supported the shift because it believed that PHS would improve health care. Several Oklahoma tribes, however, worried that PHS would close hospitals and clinics, forcing them to travel long distances for treatment.[135]

Observers agree that PHS has improved Indian health care. PHS budgets rose after 1955, more Indians sought treatment, and morbidity and mortality rates, although well above national averages, gradually declined. The major negative effect was that PHS closed many smaller treatment centers and forced some Indians to travel farther for medical care.

Although Indians are often depicted as strongly opposed to withdrawal and termination, this view distorts the actual situation. The intense problems of reservations and inferior BIA services caused at least some Indians to consider a transfer of BIA services to states. Indian opinion shifted to opposition to termination with the failure to consult over P.L. 280. Such misgivings culminated during the 1954 joint hearings on termination. Indian opponents by then realized that their reservations, treaty rights, and cultural heritage were vital. It is revealing to compare Indians' equivocal statements regarding withdrawal and termination in the early 1950s with their harsh denunciations after Congress terminated several tribes. Clearly, this shift contributed significantly to the militancy of the following decade.

The development of the anti-termination faction led by Representative Metcalf was one of the most remarkable developments of the postwar era. Unlike the almost universal assimilationist outlook of the past, a sizeable portion of western leaders assumed a more tolerant and sympathetic attitude toward Indians. In a 1955 letter, Angie Debo, distinguished Indian historian, commented on the change. She noted that the Oklahoma delegations of the past had cooperated with "a constituency whose major industry was robbing Indians. . . ." And she expressed gratitude that the current delegation seemed responsive to Indian needs. Ever the realist, Debo admitted that the Indians of her state had little left to steal.[136] No doubt Metcalf and other anti-termination leaders may have used their attacks on termination policies for political advantage. Much like the conservatives of the New Deal, western liberals recognized the dangers of attacking the popular Eisenhower, but criticisms of the BIA and termination brought political gains without serious repercussions.

What seems most important about the postwar era is not the controversies over withdrawal and termination, but the general changes at the regional and national levels. The postwar boom in the West, increased urbanization, lessened isolation, and the migration from rural to urban areas affected Indians as much or more than other westerners. Indian migration to cities, for example, had a far greater impact on their daily lives than the relatively few groups affected by termination legislation. Although numerous studies have analyzed the short-term impact of urban life on Indians, the more important results, such as retention of tribal and racial identity, may not be fully understood for several generations.

9.

Self-Determination
and Red Power
1960s and 1970s

After 1960 major changes took place in federal policy and in Indian thought and behavior. Although termination had stalled by the late 1950s, Indians feared the John F. Kennedy administration's shift toward self-determination. Many Indian leaders saw the new and ill-defined national policy as termination in disguise. These misgivings, and Indian protest tactics derived from the civil rights and anti-war movements, produced dramatic confrontations, such as fish-ins in the Pacific Northwest, the seizure of Alcatraz, the occupation and trashing of the BIA building, Wounded Knee II, and a host of lesser protests.

Indians during the 1960s and 1970s became more adamant, vocal, and sophisticated about tribal sovereignty and jurisdiction and their individual legal status. Indian lobbying, meantime, helped produce important legislation on civil rights, religious freedom, health care, and education. Through favorable court decisions and their claims to water rights and energy resources, Indians served notice that they wanted a greater voice in solving economic problems.

As the West emerged from the postwar boom and achieved a more mature economy, residents discovered that it was not entirely divorced from past problems. Many areas, for example, remained dependent on exporting unprocessed or semi-processed goods. Westerners could take comfort in the continued growth of "clean" defense manufacturing and high technology industries, but both old and new enterprises remained subject to boom and bust cycles. Natural resource industries—lumber, mining, and energy—all underwent cycles of growth and depression after 1960. The West was also affected by developments abroad. The oil embargo in the mid-1970s resulted in a boom for western energy resources followed by a dramatic down-turn. Above all, the region remained tied to the federal government, which, in fact, replaced Wall Street as the West's favorite "whipping boy."

The connections between general western development and Indian affairs were far greater after 1960 than at any previous period during the twentieth century. As the West urbanized, Indians continued to leave reservations for cities. In 1960, 30 percent of the Indian population was urban, and by 1970 the figure had risen to 45 percent. Because of federal development programs and new jobs on reservations, the migration slowed after 1970, but by 1980 the figure stood at 49 percent.[1] Large urban centers attracted a majority of Indian migrants. After 1970 Tulsa, Albuquerque, Riverside, San Diego, Anaheim, and Sacramento showed the highest percentages of new Indian population. These more recent arrivals favored long-term residence. According to the 1980 census, 77 percent of urban Indians had resided in the same county for five years or more.[2] While reservation population continued to rise, its growth between 1970 and 1980 was 62 percent compared to an increase of 116 percent in urban centers.[3]

Although historians do not entirely agree on the impact of the Kennedy administration, it definitely shifted away from termination and reflected greater respect for Indian culture. Secretary of Interior Stewart L. Udall, a native of Arizona, had served two terms in the House and carried into office a reputation as a conservationist and a supporter of economic development of reservations.[4] In February 1961, Udall appointed a special task force to study Indian affairs. W. W. Keeler, principal chief of the Cherokees and an executive of Phillips Petroleum Company, chaired the group that also included William Zimmerman, Jr., Philleo Nash, and James Officer. Their report in July 1961 conveyed a mixed message. It seemed to endorse termination by recommending a withdrawal of federal services for Indians competent to look after their own welfare. However, the task force also called for special assistance for other Indians. This included attracting new industries to reservations, additional vocational training and job placement, and improvements in the BIA's existing social programs. Two themes of the report would have special significance in coming years. First, the government would place much greater emphasis on the industrial development of reservations rather than on improving agriculture, and second, Indian self-determination would be accorded more respect.[5]

The task force report came close on the heels of a private study released earlier in the year. The Commission on the Rights, Liberties, and Responsibilities of the American Indian had researched Indian conditions for four years. Its summary report strongly condemned termination and emphasized a need for greater sensitivity for Indian culture and its preservation while preparing Indians for incorporation into the "broader society."[6]

A third watershed event in 1961 was the meeting of some 500 Indians in June at the University of Chicago. Sol Tax, an anthropologist at the university, organized the conference, and members of Udall's task force attended as private individuals. The diverse makeup of the Indian delegates included conservatives and non-conservatives, urban and rural, old and young, and educated and uneducated. Conference planners invited a number of Indian college students to serve as pages, but they insisted on participating in the discussions.[7] The major purpose of the meeting was to establish policy goals for the new Kennedy administration, and D'Arcy Mc-Nickle, a historian and reformer, had drafted a preliminary statement to serve as a basis for discussions. McNickle later noted that the diversity of delegates and long-standing intertribal antagonisms produced such heated debates that the conference repeatedly threatened to dissolve. Somehow the participants always found "an acceptable base for continuing discussion. . . ."[8] The conference's "Declaration of Indian Purpose," among other things, called for an end of termination and a greater recognition of "the inherent powers of Indian tribes."

The failed attempt to exclude college students from the Chicago debates contributed to the formation of the National Indian Youth Council (NIYC) later in 1961. Chartered in New Mexico, the group operated through a loose network of chapters on many western campuses, and it published a newspaper called *Americans before Columbus.* Clearly influenced by the civil rights movement, NIYC leaders adopted radical rhetoric and identified with impoverished reservation Indians. Speakers commonly labeled whites as fascists and racists, but they also denounced the NCAI and existing tribal leaders as "Uncle Tomahawks" or "Apples." The charismatic Clyde Warrior, an Oklahoma Ponca, quickly gained a reputation as the most militant NIYC orator. Before his premature death, however, Warrior resigned from the organization because too many young Indians were getting "sucked into the system."[9]

Shortly after the government released its task force report, Secretary Udall appointed Philleo Nash as Indian commissioner. He brought impressive credentials: a Ph.D. in anthropology, a wealth of experience in federal agencies during and after World War II, and an instrumental role in Truman's 1949 veto of the first Navajo-Hopi rehabilitation bill. Nash's social philosophy represented an updated version of cultural pluralism. His strongest qualification was that he liked Indians and they liked him. During his five-year tenure, the indefatigable commissioner visited virtually every reservation, including the most remote villages of Alaska. The visits and Nash's personal ties with Indian leaders largely overcame what he called the "termination psychosis."[10] James Officer, an anthropologist at the University of Arizona, served as associate commissioner.

Nash never repudiated termination, but he also did not push for legislation to sever ties with more tribes. The plans already underway were completed, and Congress terminated the Nebraska Poncas after Nash took office. The key legislation, HCR 108 and P.L. 280, remained on the books. The basic issues of the Eisenhower administration—jurisdictional disputes between Indians and state governments over law and order and social programs—remained.[11] Nash, however, focused his attention on economic development, educational reform, vocational training, and housing.

The Area Re-development Act of 1961 marked an important step in a new trend in Indian affairs. The measure offered financial and technical assistance to "pockets of poverty," including Indian reservations, and it opened a new source of funds for economic development. Similarly, Indians became eligible for benefits from the Public Housing Administration, the Small Business Administration, and the accelerated Public Works Program of 1962. Much like John Collier, Nash was able to use both regular BIA appropriations and outside agency funds to finance various programs and to add new sources of credit. No doubt, the area of greatest attention was industrial development and tribal enterprises. Nash claimed in 1964 that the BIA had attracted forty new manufacturing plants on or near reservations and opened 1,300 new jobs for Indians. Despite these efforts, the rate of failure was quite high, and the contributions of the plants was equally low.[12]

When President Lyndon B. Johnson's "Great Society" got under way in 1964, Indian reservations received a flow of funds exceeding even the New Deal. The Job Corps, Head Start, Upward Bound, and VISTA all operated on reservations. The Community Action Program allowed tribal governments and private organizations to receive grants directly from the Office of Economic Opportunity (OEO) and to administer the programs independent of the BIA. The program corrected several shortcomings of the Area Re-development Act and drastically changed the dynamics of reservation power.[13] Several cabinet departments added "Indian desks" in recognition of the unique legal and cultural conditions of reservations. In a relative sense, the BIA found itself weakened as it assumed an advisory and intermediary role between tribal governments and these federal agencies. In other words, federal trust responsibilities did not stop with the BIA.

Tribal leaders sometimes clashed with personnel from the new federal programs. On the Navajo Reservation, Chairman Raymond Nakai attempted to oust a young white attorney who headed a legal services program, but a federal court blocked the removal. Unfortunately, the War on Poverty often worsened factionalism. When the BIA monopolized local administration, tribal leadership meant a modicum of prestige and access to jobs, but the OEO raised the stakes decisively. On the Sioux Reservations, for example, bitter charges arose that tribal housing authorities had enriched themselves in corrupt deals with white contractors who threw together substandard housing units. One Sioux leader denounced the Johnson years as a "tidal wave of theft, embezzlement, graft, and corruption."[14]

Despite his popularity with Indians, Nash's relationship with Udall deteriorated, apparently because the interior secretary wanted faster results. Senator Henry Jackson, chairman of the Senate Interior and Insular Affairs Committee, also became disenchanted when Nash resisted termination of the Colville Reservation.[15] In March 1966, Udall replaced Nash with Robert Bennett, the first Indian to hold the post since Ely S. Parker during Grant's administration. A Wisconsin Oneida and Haskell graduate, Bennett had joined the BIA in 1933 and worked his way up the ranks. A skilled administrator who knew many Indian leaders, Bennett had little taste for dramatic policy shifts but preferred quietly manipulating the federal bureaucracy and congressional committees. Given the hectic nature of the War on Poverty programs and rising Indian militancy, his moderate approach was probably wise.[16]

President Johnson's special message to Congress in March 1968 reflected the public's growing awareness of Indian problems. It was, indeed, the first special message devoted to the subject. Johnson emphasized that the goal of self-determination would end the debate over termination and erase "old attitudes of paternalism." To coordinate the several agencies now offering Indians services, Johnson created the National Council on Indian Opportunity (NCIO). Vice President Hubert Humphrey chaired the group, which consisted of the secretaries of agriculture, commerce, labor, health, education and welfare, and housing and urban development and the director of OEO as well as eight Indian representatives. A small staff ran day-to-day operations.[17]

The self-determination policies of the Kennedy-Johnson era continued when Richard M. Nixon assumed office in 1969. During his campaign, Nixon had carefully responded to Indian fears about a return to termination by sending a message to the NCAI strongly endorsing self-determination. As president-elect, he commissioned Alvin M. Josephy, Jr., a historian sympathetic to Indians, to study past policies and to suggest needed changes.[18] The administration searched diligently for a commissioner who was Indian, a Republican and "safe," and after much difficulty appointed Louis R. Bruce, a Sioux-Mohawk. Nixon not only met earlier promises to retain the NCIO, but also in 1970 the agency received legislative authorization and its own funding. The new NCIO director, Robert Robertson, reported to C. D. Ward, an assistant to Vice President Spiro Agnew. Robertson also had ties with Bradley Patterson, an assistant to Leonard Garment, a White House advisor on domestic affairs and the administration's "house liberal."

Nixon's special message to Congress on July 8, 1970, like Johnson's statement, marked a major step in self-determination. Nixon reiterated his opposition to termination and called for a repeal of HCR 108. Nixon asked for new legislation which would permit tribal governments to contract for all existing services provided by the BIA and other agencies. He promised also to upgrade education, economic development, and health programs. The message noted the growing number of urban Indians and proposed greater support for Indian community centers as a means of linking urban residents with federal, state, and local social services. To provide more protection for land and water resources, the message asked Congress to establish an Indian trust council to represent Indians in legal suits. Finally, Nixon called for a new post, an assistant secretary for Indian and territorial affairs. To avoid long-standing criticism about conflicts of interests in the Interior

Department, the sole responsibility of the post would be the welfare and protection of resources of Indians and territorial residents.[19]

Although many Indians and whites hailed the special message as a major advance, the administration's legalistic outlook soon produced problems. Its willingness to meet trust responsibilities did not include urban Indians who were to receive only normal public services. The administration willingly cooperated with existing tribal authorities, but it rebuffed the demands of various dissident factions who demanded a restructuring of reservation governments. Most importantly, every major proposal required getting legislation through a Congress controlled by the opposition party. Finally, Indians used the Nixon promises as a measuring stick and viewed failures as evidence of insincerity.

The Nixon administration first sought to use a settlement of the Indian occupation at Alcatraz as a symbol of its liberal outlook on race relations, and when that failed, it turned to Blue Lake and Taos Pueblo. The latter controversy reflected many of the regional problems western Indians faced in the twentieth century. The Taos Indians had suffered considerable encroachment on their land during the Spanish-Mexican period, and the problems worsened after 1848 when the United States assumed control of New Mexico. Blue Lake, located east of the pueblo, was important to the Indians because it provided irrigation water, and it also served as a shrine for annual pilgrimages and other religious activities. When white ranchers, hunters, prospectors, and lumbermen intruded around 1900, Indian complaints went unheeded. In 1906 Theodore Roosevelt incorporated the Blue Lake area into the Carson National Forest, but this did not end Indians' complaints, and it meant, in fact, that the Forest Service controlled the land. In 1965 the Indian Claims Commission awarded Taos Pueblo damages for another grievance, but village leaders rejected the money and demanded a return of Blue Lake. Prior to the 1960s the Indians refused to discuss religious reasons for wanting the land returned for fear of revealing their beliefs to outsiders. When called to testify on legislation to restore Blue Lake in the mid-1960s, Taos leaders cautiously mentioned religion, but committee members seemed completely insensitive to the Indians' spiritual outlook.

By 1970 the parties were polarized. Opposition to the return included the Forest Service and conservationists who argued the Indians would not protect the area, and Senator Clinton P. Anderson of New Mexico, who claimed that restoring title would serve as a dangerous precedent. On the other side were the Taos Indians, white allies such as church groups and reformers, and the Nixon administration. Despite Anderson's alleged threat to block funding of Nixon's anti-ballistic missile program, the administration pushed the restoration bill through Congress in late 1970.[20]

The return of Blue Lake did little to counter the rise of Indian militancy. A major catalyst for the new mood were clashes in the mid-1960s between Washington State and Indian fishermen at Frank's Landing on the Nis-

154 Indians and the American West in the Twentieth Century

qually River. Disputes over Indian treaty fishing rights and state regulatory agencies dated back to the late nineteenth century. Several earlier Supreme Court rulings had not fully resolved the issues. Sport fishing organizations and commercial fishing interests had for decades falsely blamed Indians for declining salmon and steelhead runs, and state game officials who caught Indians violating fishing regulations habitually arrested them and confiscated their boats and gear.[21]

Unlike the past when Indians endured such treatment, the Nisquallies formed an organization, issued a newsletter, sought legal aid from the National Association for the Advancement of Colored People, and called in the media to cover arrests at Frank's Landing and other locations. The publicity attracted the support of the NIYC, Marlon Brando, and other white liberals. Neighboring tribes joined in the fish-ins and legal suits in the late 1960s.[22]

The organization of the American Indian Movement (AIM) in Minneapolis in 1968 reflected urban complaints. The Chippewa founders, Dennis Banks and George Mitchell, wanted to deal with the unemployment, alienation, and poverty of Indians living in the Twin Cities. AIM patterned itself after the Black Panthers and adopted confrontational tactics. Upset by police arrests in an Indian ghetto in Minneapolis known as the "reservation," AIM developed "red patrols" that took drunks home and broke up fights. Many AIM members experienced a cultural conversion that resulted in a new sense of identity and pride in their "Indianness." Virtually all assumed a traditional Indian appearance with braids, jeans, jewelry, and feathers. Unlike the NIYC which saw tribes and reservations as essential to preserving Indian heritage, AIM opted for more of a pan-Indian or supratribal outlook which subordinated tribalism. Inspired by Tecumseh, Crazy Horse, and Geronimo, AIM leaders saw themselves as latter-day warriors fighting white oppression. Although the personalities and outlooks of AIM members varied widely, white and Indian critics early on characterized them as criminals, ex-convicts, money-hungry opportunists, and publicity-seeking egomaniacs.[23] Despite this, AIM enjoyed widespread support, especially among urban Indian groups, dissident factions on reservations, and, initially, by congregations in the Twin Cities.[24]

Indian activism became widespread at all levels. LaDonna Harris, enrolled Comanche, wife of Senator Fred Harris of Oklahoma, and an original appointee to the NCIO, had presided over that agency's public hearings in 1968 and 1969. Incensed at the government's refusal to offer special services to urban Indians, she formed Americans for Indian Opportunity, which became a leading lobbying organization. Even the NCAI took a radical turn when its 1971 convention elected Leon Cook as president. The handsome Cook had recently resigned from the BIA, charging that Nixon's policies were disguised termination. He unsuccessfully attempted to use the NCAI post to coordinate other Indian organizations. Both the fish-ins and occupation of Alcatraz continued.

Indian militancy began to attract more media attention when AIM expanded its activities beyond Minneapolis–St. Paul to other major cities and to reservations. Street tough, AIM figures knew that their colorful appearance and angry denunciations appealed to the media, especially television. They specialized in audacious tactics. In July 1970, AIM seized a building during a conference at Augustana College and demanded $750,000 from the Lutheran Church, USA. On Thanksgiving they seized *Mayflower II*, and the following month at a government conference on urban problems, they vandalized the plush Airlie House at Warrenton, Virginia. AIM and its allies briefly seized Mt. Rushmore the following June, and three months later Russell Means and several others unsuccessfully attempted to enter the BIA and place Wilma Victor, special assistant to the secretary of interior, and John Crow, deputy BIA commissioner, under citizen's arrest. Early in 1972 an AIM demonstration at Gordon, Nebraska, protested the murder of a Sioux.[25]

The Nixon administration's response to such activism was essentially moderate. The mild and likeable Bruce had pledged to allow Indians decision-making power, and he had added a dozen or so young Indians, who disdained the guarded attitude of older bureaucrats and Nixon appointees, to the BIA. "Bruce's Braves" demanded immediate contracting with tribes, stronger protection of economic resources, and more employment preference for Indians. They criticized Victor and Crow and condemned Harrison Loesch, assistant secretary of interior for public land management, who served as Bruce's superior.

Nixon officials clearly preferred legitimate leadership over activists. Frustrated by the lack of stable leadership at Alcatraz, for example, NCIO Director Robertson encouraged the formation of a confederation of Indian organizations in the San Francisco area so the negotiations could proceed, but his tactic failed. The Nixon administration did not organize the National Tribal Chairmen's Association (NTCA) in 1971, as critics frequently charged, but Nixon subordinates obviously saw advantages in dealing with the generally cooperative tribal leaders and offered them free office space in Washington and expenses for meetings. Such perks predictably incensed other Indian organizations.

The "Trail of Broken Treaties" and the occupation of the BIA building in November 1972 symbolized the administration's failure to defuse activism. The idea for the famous protest march first developed at the Rosebud Sun Dance the previous summer. Several AIM leaders attended. The organization seemed in decline. It had suffered a serious setback in the spring when it tried to intervene in a dispute at Cass Lake, Minnesota, and local Indians demanded that AIM withdraw. Robert Burnette, former Rosebud chairman, suggested a march of 200 Indians to Washington. He envisioned the event as a spiritual journey with participants avoiding drugs and liquor as they sought to educate and enlist the support of the public and government leaders.[26] Two months later, the march organizers completed plans at

Denver. Eight groups were to participate, and caravans from several starting points would meet at Minneapolis–St. Paul before proceeding to Washington.[27]

AIM leaders dominated the meetings when the caravans converged at the Twin Cities. According to one source, participants scrapped an earlier moderate set of fifteen proposals and approved a more radical document known as the "Twenty Points." The purpose of the march changed too. Burnette's concept of well-behaved Indians engaged in a spiritual and educational sojourn turned into a defiant protest. AIM's actions, plus its brief occupation of the local BIA area office, infuriated Burnette who was in Washington negotiating arrangements with interior officials.[28] Tactically, the substitution of new demands was probably unwise because the administration had little time to prepare a response.

The "Twenty Points" contained both conventional and radical proposals. The more moderate items included repeal of the 1953 termination legislation, restoration of terminated tribes to a trust relationship, abolition of the BIA, and its replacement by the creation of a three-man commission attached to the White House. The radical demands centered on a reordering of the relationships between tribes and the federal government. The Indians insisted on a restoration of treaties as the sole basis for future Indian affairs and full recognition of tribal sovereignty. Tribes, for example, would exercise complete legal jurisdiction over non-Indians on reservations. The "Twenty Points" also demanded an increase in the Indian land base to 110 million acres and the cancellation of most existing leases held by non-Indians.[29]

The marchers lost whatever slight chance the "Twenty Points" had as a basis for serious negotiation on November 2, when they seized the BIA building. The demands got lost in the shuffle as the Indians and federal officials exchanged charges over whether the occupation was premeditated or caused by the government's failure to provide living accommodations, whether the occupiers were legitimate representatives of "real" Indians or merely urban toughs, or whether the extensive damage to the building represented wanton actions or resulted when frightened Indians prepared to barricade themselves against a threatened attack by police.

The government itself was badly divided. Commissioner Bruce showed his sympathy with the protestors by staying overnight in the building. Assistant Secretary Loesch and others favored clearing out the militants by force. With the election pending on November 9 and the Kent State tragedy fresh in minds, John Ehrlichman and other White House aides wanted to avoid bloodshed. On November 6 Leonard Garment and John Carlucci took over negotiations, and two days later they reached an agreement with Hank Adams, a veteran of the fish-ins and the most responsible caravan leader. Garment and Carlucci promised to recommend against prosecution of the occupiers and to review the "Twenty "Points." The distribution of $66,000 to defray Indian travel expenses became an interesting controversy within a controversy. Some claimed that AIM leaders seized the funds and used them to buy weapons for Wounded Knee II.[30] Others believed that several AIM figures stole most of the money. Regardless, many rank and filers were stranded in Washington. AIM co-founder George Mitchell, upset at the distribution, quit the organization.[31]

After the march, AIM's attention shifted to the Pine Ridge Reservation and southwestern South Dakota. The impoverished reservation had one of the lowest per capita income levels in the nation. Unemployment normally ran 50 percent and during recessions rose to 70 percent. Statistics on health, life expectancy, education, and related categories were equally dismal.[32] Political turmoil was endemic. Conservatives, who had never accepted the tribal government instituted during the New Deal, demanded that the only legitimate basis for political authority was the Treaty of 1868. They saw the council as dominated by mixed bloods who discriminated against full bloods. But there were also factions within factions based on communities and kinship ties. Pine Ridge chairman, Dick Wilson, a pugnacious and outspoken foe of AIM, delighted in denouncing the militants as deadbeats preying on the already impoverished Oglalas.[33]

AIM's return in force to South Dakota increased tensions both at Pine Ridge and nearby. In November, the council passed a resolution banning AIM members from the reservation, and BIA police arrested Russell Means who had been invited to speak to an anti-Wilson group. Means had not been among the founders of AIM, but he had gained prominence as an associate of Dennis Banks. An Oglala, he had spent most of his life in cities prior to joining AIM. After the protest at Gordon, Nebraska, Means had settled at Porcupine, a traditional community near Wounded Knee, and expressed a desire to become tribal chairman. Once released on bond, Means denounced Wilson for violating his civil rights. After several off-reservation protests, Means and other AIM leaders staged a demonstration on February 20, during a court hearing at Custer, South Dakota. The hearing involved the death of a young Sioux during a fight outside a bar. A full riot developed, the court house was set on fire, and twenty-seven Indians were arrested. On February 22 Wilson's foes unsuccessfully tried to impeach him for the fourth time in eleven months.

The latest failure prompted AIM's occupation of Wounded Knee. AIM claimed that it took the action at the request of the Oglala Sioux Civil Rights Organization (OSCRO), an anti-Wilson group led by Pedro Bissonette. While this appears true, the additional claim that the occupation was unanimously supported by traditional chiefs, medicine men, and headmen seems debatable.[34] The AIM and OSCRO demands included a convening of the Senate Foreign Relations Committee to review treaties and full investigations of the BIA at all levels and at all of the Sioux Reservations. Additionally, the occupiers demanded Wilson's removal and replacement of the Pine Ridge tribal government with traditional political forms. Government representatives, although willing to compromise on secondary issues, rejected concessions on substantial matters, including immunity from arrests.

Something close to the surreal characterized the seventy-one-day occupation of Wounded Knee. Both sides established roadblocks on the four roads entering the hamlet, but people came and went freely. AIM leaders readily made outside speaking and fund-raising appearances, and FBI records show that agents closely shadowed AIM figures and knew to the penny how much money they raised. Indeed, the FBI seemed to know more about what transpired inside Wounded Knee than did the occupiers. Although the White House obviously did not want to be connected with the episode, it also feared bloodshed. The force of over 200 FBI agents and federal marshals constituted a small army with armored personnel carriers, airplanes, helicopters, and other equipment. Furious fire fights erupted repeatedly, but somehow only two occupiers were killed; one marshal was seriously wounded. Both sides suffered from internal dissensions. The status conscious FBI agents regarded the marshals as inferiors, and both had little use for the BIA or tribal officials except to validate decisions already made. AIM and OSCRO reportedly disagreed over the latter's desire to end the occupation. Agreements to end the affair appeared certain several times, but AIM leaders always added another stipulation to block a settlement.

AIM's most serious mistake was letting the occupation run too long. It started with several major advantages: the symbolic value of Wounded Knee, abundant and positive media coverage, and wide support from young white and Indian radicals, church groups, and liberal organizations. These were lost, especially in the last month. Media coverage dwindled because the story became too old and too repetitive. Government negotiators refused to compromise on AIM's basic demands. The only item in the final agreement that came close to AIM's agenda was the creation of a presidential commission to review the Treaty of 1868. The other terms merely defined the mechanics of ending the occupation.

South Dakota newspaper coverage on Wounded Knee offers insights on local reactions to the occupation. The state's few large dailies normally used national wire service stories that favored the Indians, but the editorials, letters from readers, and cartoons accurately reflected public opinion. The editorials expressed a surprisingly mild hostility toward the activists, but vigorously criticized outside media and federal officials. Several editorials, blaming the federal government, demanded that it solve the problem. Another concern was the creation of a negative image of South Dakota and possible damage to the tourist industry. The editorial writers reserved their strongest condemnation for the National Council of Churches and member denominations that supported the activists and tried to mediate a settlement. The papers gave especially thorough coverage to amounts of money spent by such religious groups, and local congregations condemned their own denominations for such support.[35]

A Harris poll taken shortly after the occupation showed a very different reaction toward Wounded Knee II. Over 90 percent of those polled had heard or read about it. People from higher income and educational levels were more apt to know about the episode. In response to a question about the past treatment of Indians, 84 percent of easterners were critical, followed by 77 percent of midwesterners and 75 percent of westerners. Only 61 percent of southerners, however, were critical of Indians' treatment. Individuals from higher income and educational levels believed that Indians had been mistreated and sympathized more with militants at Wounded Knee than with the federal government. Despite AIM's confrontational tactics, a sizeable majority of Americans supported their cause.[36]

AIM's decline, which probably had started during Wounded Knee and was apparent in 1974, can be attributed to several factors. Many of the activists faced criminal charges, and those found guilty were, of course, imprisoned. Those who avoided conviction faced legal expenses and investment of their time and energy. A media backlash also hurt. A series of articles in national periodicals in 1973 and 1974 criticized AIM for bamboozling the public. AIM's reputation suffered another setback when Carter Camp, a national co-chairman, shot and seriously wounded Clyde Bellecourt during a personal dispute on the Rosebud Reservation. Finally, AIM's support from white groups diminished. Some Indians complained that AIM's bravado was not matched by its actions.

The impact of AIM and other activists is problematic. The immediate results appear meager. Neither the Alcatraz seizure, the BIA occupation, or Wounded Knee II produced significant, long-term, and direct gains. Government promises to investigate grievances offered a face-saving device but little else. The fish-ins, however, contributed to the complex legal battles that led to the famous 1974 Boldt decision confirming Indian treaty fishing rights. Activism also brought about some important intangible changes. Younger Indians doubtlessly gained a sense of self-respect and cultural identity. The widespread media coverage also sensitized the general public to Indian conditions and problems.

Ironically, the chief beneficiaries of Indian militancy were the moderate NCAI and NTCA. As happened in the black civil rights crusade, radical demands prompted the government to cooperate with moderates as a means of isolating the militants. Knowing this, the NCAI and NTCA in 1973 rejected AIM's overtures about forming a national coalition.[37] The strategy of avoiding an open alliance obviously worked. During the 1970s, Indian moderates and Congress cooperated in numerous investigations and hearings that resulted in over a dozen major legislative acts.

A key example of the moderates' success was the creation of the American Indian Policy Review Commission (AIPRC). Senator James G. Abourezk from South Dakota introduced a joint resolution authorizing the commission in 1973, and the Senate passed it in December. Representative Lloyd Meeds of Washington secured House approval of an amended resolution the following year, and in 1975 the Senate accepted the changes.[38]

Three senators and three representatives on the commission met in

March and elected Abourezk chairman and Meeds vice chairman. The same meeting appointed the five Indian commissioners. Of these, Ada Deer, who led the fight to restore the Menominees to federal recognition, and former Commissioner Louis R. Bruce were national figures. Jake Whitecrow, former Quapaw chairman, John Borbridge, Tlingit-Haida leader, and Adolph Dial, a Lumbee scholar, were known more at the tribal or regional levels. Ernest L. Stevens, a Wisconsin Oneida and former BIA administrator, became staff director. Kirk Kickingbird, a young Kiowa attorney and author, served as general counsel.

Although observers often compared the AIPRC to the Meriam Commission, the two investigations differed. The AIPRC was much more elaborately staffed and richly endowed, and it also reflected an Indian perspective. Indians made up thirty-one out of the thirty-three individuals on the eleven task forces. The latter's areas of investigation included trust responsibilities, tribal government, federal administration, federal, state, and tribal jurisdiction, education, health, resource development and protection, urban Indians, codification of Indian law, terminated and non-recognized Indians, and alcohol and drug abuse. Two special task force reports dealt with Alaska Natives and BIA management. While Meriam's group had concentrated on field conditions, the task forces worked through conventional research, hearings, and questionnaires. Finally, the Meriam investigation had no official standing, while the AIPRC conferred over task force reports and consolidated them into a final report.

Perhaps the most important difference, however, was Senator Abourezk's support for the AIPRC. Abourezk had grown up at Wood, South Dakota, in what had been the Rosebud Reservation until it was opened to white settlement in 1911. His Lebanese father moved to Wood about that time and started a general store that catered to both whites and Indians. James, born in 1931, witnessed the chronic poverty, wretched housing, and alcoholism that devastated local Sioux, but he admits in his autobiography that "I grew up believing it was permissible, even heroic, to ridicule the Indians of Wood."[39]

Two experiences reshaped his attitudes. While working as a bartender at Winner, Abourezk converted to political liberalism through his friendship with a local physician. His racial views changed when a friend in college showed him "how destructive my attitudes were."[40] Later, as an attorney in Rapid City, he often provided free legal services to Indians. In 1970, he ran successfully for the Second Congressional District seat that E. Y. Berry had held for twenty years before his retirement. Two years later Abourezk won a Senate seat. An iconoclast with a sympathy for the underdog, Abourezk became chairman of the Indian Affairs Subcommittee in 1973 and later headed the Select Committee on Indian Affairs that visited many reservations. Unlike most western members of Congress, who gave lip service to Indian causes but retreated under white pressures, Abourezk's support for Indians reached legendary proportions.

By March 1977, the AIPRC completed a rough draft which summarized major findings and conclusions of the individual task forces. Copies of the document went out to tribal leaders, government officials, and private individuals for comments. The AIPRC then filed the *Final Report* in May.[41] The 206 recommendations included a request that all existing programs in Interior and other departments be consolidated into a single agency headed by an assistant secretary.[42] The commission also recommended that the new agency relinquish management duties and concentrate solely on services.[43] The report argued that urban Indians were entitled to the same services as the general public as well as trust services and protections.[44] Throughout the report and in a variety of contexts, recommendations stressed that Indians must be able to deal with the federal government as equals and that "their sovereign rights are of the highest legal standing, established through solemn treaties, and by layers of legislative actions."[45] Tribes, in short, should exercise the same legal powers as states and territories, including the authority to enact and enforce laws and to receive federal funds.[46]

This emphasis on Indian sovereignty produced a major clash between Meeds and Abourezk. Meeds filed a lengthy legal brief against the recommendations, complaining that they were one-sided and influenced by what AIPRC "members wanted the law to be" rather than what it was.[47] According to Meeds, "fundamental errors" existed in the claims of Indian sovereignty. He argued that all tribal authority was derived from the federal government and that tribes could not exercise jurisdiction over non-Indians in taxation or law enforcement matters. He also attacked the 1974 Boldt decision upholding Indian fishing rights as an illegal extension of tribal authority beyond reservation lines.[48] Abourezk's rebuttal noted that Meeds's slanted views could not match the AIPRC's "meticulous, thorough, and dispassionate analysis . . . [and] the wisdom and fairness of the conclusions it reaches." Meeds's views seemed ironic, Abourezk added, since he had sponsored the legislation authorizing the study in the House and accepted the commission's composition but now charged it with "one-sided advocacy." Abourezk concluded that Meeds's ideas amounted to effective termination and threatened Indians more than anything since allotment.[49]

Meeds's stance makes sense only if one examines his political situation. He had served in the House since 1964, and as chairman of the Subcommittee on Indian Affairs he had supported several key reform measures. In fact, the NCAI gave its 1974 "Congressional Award" to Meeds for his work on the Menominee Restoration Act. Unfortunately, the Boldt decision the same year unleashed a great deal of anti-Indian hostility in Washington state, and in 1976 Meeds barely won re-election. Public opposition to the Boldt decision prompted Meeds to shy away from championing Indian causes, and in 1978 he introduced a bill that would have abrogated virtually all Indian jurisdictional rights and a second measure that would have effectively destroyed Indian water rights. His anti-Indian actions, however, evidently failed, for Meeds refused to seek re-election in 1978. Abourezk, in contrast, decided during his first year in the Senate that he would not seek re-election, and this permitted him to follow his liberal inclinations freely.[50]

The Indian reaction to the AIPRC was guarded from the start. Mark Thompson, an aide to Abourezk, later maintained that the South Dakota senator originally envisioned a major investigation by Congress and Indians that would suggest a basic restructuring of Indian affairs. Meeds and conservative opponents, however, restricted Abourezk's plans with amendments to limit the size of the commission, to reduce the budget, to tone down the preamble, and to shorten the duration of the investigation. Frictions over appointments to the commission and the task forces caused more problems. Ernest L. Stevens's selection as executive director, for example, upset supporters of Sam Deloria, director of the Indian Law Center at the University of New Mexico, but this was only one of many clashes.[51]

While the AIPRC may have fostered the passage of some subsequent reform legislation, it did not achieve an overhaul of Indian affairs. In part the failure may be attributed to the flawed nature of the AIPRC itself, especially the split between Abourezk and Meeds. Another factor was the growing conservative mood of the nation, which the Carter and the Reagan administrations both represented. The most important factor, however, was the absence of a single, dynamic leader who had the knowledge and will to secure basic legislative revision. Such a figure never emerged.

The "Longest Walk" in July 1978 indicated that the time for militant protests had passed. The marchers' main goal was to protest against pending anti-Indian bills and corporate interests that wanted access to Indian water and mineral resources. Hoping to counter white backlash, the march organizers emphasized their peaceful intentions. Much like the original goals for the "Trail of Broken Treaties," the 1978 protestors sought to awaken the public conscience through educational and spiritual means. Some 1,500 Indian marchers arrived in Washington on July 15 and, joined by a sizeable party of non-Indians, proceeded to the Washington Monument for a rally. A *New York Times* reporter described the rhetoric as militant but the mood as peaceful.[52]

The week of marches and rallies produced no gains. Worried about another takeover of the BIA building, the Carter administration rushed to supply equipment for the Indians' camp outside the city. On Tuesday a delegation kept Vice President Walter Mondale waiting an hour and then spent most of their meeting unsuccessfully demanding a meeting with President Jimmy Carter. The same day, Senator Edward Kennedy, upset with charges that one of his bills jeopardized treaty rights, waded into a rally, grabbed the microphone, and demanded that the Indians read the bill's contents.[53] Wilcomb Washburn, a historian with strong sympathies for Indians, lashed the "radical Indian minority" in the *New York Times*. Washburn charged that AIM's tactics and not greedy corporations had produced the recent backlash. He added that the government's kowtowing to activists undermined the sovereignty that legitimate leaders had fought for since the Indian Reorganization Act.[54] The most telling weakness of the "Longest Walk" was its lack of purpose. None of the anti-Indian bills had any chance of passage, and one activist admitted this during a news conference, but he lamely justified the protest as a means of countering white backlash.[55]

While the results of Indian militancy were uncertain and indirect, Indians since the early 1960s won unprecedented court victories. Prior to 1960, the U.S. Supreme Court seldom ruled on Indian questions, but during that decade it heard twelve cases. The figure rose to thirty-five in the 1970s, and during the first seven terms of the 1980s, the court ruled on thirty-two cases. Despite occasional setbacks, federal court rulings favored a surprising degree of tribal authority over civil and criminal matters.[56]

Williams v. Lee (1959) "opened the modern era of Indian law." The case dealt with a non-Indian who sued in a state court to collect money from Navajos who had entered a debt contract on their reservation. The court ruled that the case must be heard exclusively within tribal courts "to promote and protect tribal self-government."[57] The decision strengthened the view, dating back to John Marshall's famous trilogy, *Johnson v. McIntosh* (1823), *Cherokee Nation v. Georgia* (1831), and *Worcester v. Georgia* (1832), that tribes were largely autonomous bodies subject to federal but not state control. American political theorists since the American Revolution had debated over the division of sovereignty or supreme power between the federal government and the states, but this had left the status of tribal governments in doubt. Proponents of Indian rights had claimed that tribes retained all the powers not specifically relinquished to the federal government by treaties, agreements, statutes, or the constitution. These "reserved rights" (or residual powers), whether exercised or dominant, provided the basis for tribal governance of reservations, including partial jurisdiction over non-Indians. An even stronger view held that tribal authority was extra-constitutional. Tribes, in other words, held powers that existed independent of Congress.

Since this stronger vision of tribal autonomy rested largely on case law, opponents readily constructed an opposing position. They often took the view that Congress exercised plenary powers over Indian affairs and concluded that tribes possessed only delegated authority. Congress thus could unilaterally restrict tribal governments, legislate on property, and alter treaties and agreements. Several precedent cases supported these views. In *United States v. Kagama* (1886), *McBratney v. United States* (1882), and *Lone Wolf v. Hitchcock* (1903) the Supreme Court had ignored tribal authority in favor of unlimited congressional power. *Lone Wolf* proved especially useful because it upheld a statute that violated a treaty and specific property rights and, in effect, suggested that Congress never acted in bad faith.

While the legal battles over tribal authority were interesting in the abstract, they assumed more importance on western reservations after the 1960s. Tribes that possessed valuable natural resources demanded control of their development both as a matter of principle and because Indian leaders feared that their interests would not be protected if, as had often happened in the past, the Interior Department negotiated leases with private firms. Many checkerboarded reservations contained non-Indian populations and private businesses that tribes wanted to govern even though the non-Indians occupied fee simple property. Tribes also hoped to protect themselves from various state controls. While these trends were certainly discernible by the mid-1970s, the quest for greater tribal authority really hit stride the following decade.

Several cases illustrate the federal courts' acceptance of increased tribal authority. *Menominee Tribe* v. *United States* (1968) dealt with whether Wisconsin hunting and fishing laws applied to the Menominees after Congress had terminated the tribe. The basic issue was "implied repeal" or whether the 1954 statute had legally ended the Menominee tribe and its treaty rights to hunt and fish free of state control. The Supreme Court ruled that Wisconsin laws did not apply because this would have abrogated a treaty and forced Congress to compensate Menominees for their losses. The decision was an extraordinary defense of tribal authority because the Menominee termination act had stated that state laws would apply to tribal members.[58]

United States v. *Washington* (1974), better known as the Boldt decision, established no major new legal precedents in behalf of tribal rights, but it assumed a special importance in Washington and Oregon. A series of cession treaties in 1854-1855 in the Northwest had guaranteed tribes "the right of taking fish at all usual and accustomed grounds and stations. . . ." Several previous cases had dealt with Indians' rights to fish off reservation and the authority of Washington and Oregon to regulate seasons, catches, and equipment before the fish-ins of the 1960s. Although Indians won some concessions, they continued to believe that Washington State used its regulatory powers to deny their fishing rights, and in 1973 thirteen tribes sued the state in the Tacoma federal district court. Federal attorneys later joined in the suit.

Judge George Boldt's decision in 1974 "received more public attention in the state of Washington than any other court case in history."[59] Boldt noted that the Indians' fishing rights had been reserved by the cession treaties, while non-Indians held only the privilege of fishing. Even more central was his ruling on the Indians' right to fish at off-reservation sites "in common" with non-Indians. Boldt held that "in common" meant Indians and whites were each entitled a 50 percent share of the "harvestable fish." The decision aroused widespread opposition by state officials and sports and commercial fishing interests. Indians afterward complained about extralegal harassment by both state game officials and private individuals. Between 1974 and 1978, the federal government, state officials, or tribes appeared in court more than thirty-five times. Upset by a lack of compliance, Boldt in

1978 assumed control of the fishery. The Supreme Court, after refusing Washington's appeal in 1976, reviewed the case again in 1979 and upheld Boldt's decision with minor revisions. The state resumed control in 1979 and undertook to enforce the revised decision.[60] Non-Indian resentments continued, but in more recent times the state has reconciled itself to the point that it now deals with Indian tribes on a government-to-government basis.

In *Arizona v. California I* (1963), Indians won a victory in their quest to fulfill the *Winters* decision of 1908, which held that reservations were entitled to sufficient water to meet their irrigation needs. *Arizona* v. *California I* involved the long-standing conflict over division of the Colorado River waters and whether Arizona was entitled to 2.8 million acre-feet of water necessary for the impending Central Arizona Project. The significant case involved the largest documentary record ever presented to the Supreme Court. Almost as an aside, the court ordered that five Indian reservations on the Colorado with small populations and meager water use at present were entitled to the water needed for all their irrigable land. The case not only affirmed the *Winters* decision but upheld the view that executive order reservations possessed the same water rights as treaty reservations.[61]

Despite these victories, perhaps Indians' most important gains were legislative in nature. Congress approved more basic legislation in this period than any comparable time since general allotment. The Indian Civil Rights Act of 1968 attempted to provide legal guarantees to Indians living under tribal governments and courts. In 1961 the Senate Subcommittee on Constitutional Rights, chaired by Sam J. Ervin, Jr., held hearings on Indian rights, and four years later Ervin introduced blanket legislation to guarantee all Indians the same rights enjoyed by non-Indians. Testimony during the committee hearings, however, indicated that imposition of a full bill of rights would create problems. This was especially true of a ban on established religion for tribes governed by "quasi-theocracies."[62] Ervin eventually accepted a specific list of legal guarantees, mostly derived from the Bill of Rights, that did not entirely place Indians in the general constitutional framework.[63] Nevertheless, some Indians viewed the legislation as a continuation of federal paternalism because it limited punishments that tribal courts could render and it ignored bills of rights that several tribes had incorporated into their tribal constitutions.[64]

Protecting Indian civil rights and maintaining tribal authority led to several legal disputes after passage of the act. Indians welcomed provisions that shielded them from state jurisdiction and some federal controls, but several groups, especially the Pueblos, viewed the new law as another misguided imposition of white legal forms that weakened tribal authority. The civil rights legislation also led to legal suits in which individuals claimed that the tribal government had violated their civil rights. In the most famous case, *Santa Clara v. Martinez*, the female plaintiff protested a tribal ordinance that denied tribal citizenship to children of women, like Martinez, who married outside the tribe. Martinez claimed that this constituted both sexual discrimination and a violation of her civil rights. The Supreme Court, however, rejected the plaintiff's grounds and upheld tribal self-government. Controversies of this sort are apt to continue.

Congress seemed especially receptive to improving Indian education in the 1960s and 1970s. In the mid-1960s, the federal government increased its support for remedial education, adult education, and preschool education. The well-known Rough Rock Demonstration School on the Navajo Reservation that started in 1966, for example, featured community control and teaching English as a second language. Two years later the Navajo Community College started as the first tribally controlled institution. In the meantime, Indian school boards were formed for most BIA institutions, although these were advisory in nature.

The most dramatic event in Indian education during the period, however, was the release in 1969 of the report of the Senate Special Subcommittee on Indian Education. The report came after two years of investigation under Chairman Robert F. Kennedy. (After Kennedy's assassination, his brother, Edward M. Kennedy, chaired the subcommittee.) The investigation had covered Indian education at all levels, and it concluded that all had failed when judged by normal standards of quality. The committee's recommendations stressed the need for greater cultural awareness and more control by Indians. Other studies of Indian education also found serious problems, but they adopted a more moderate tone.[65]

Reform legislation on Indian education followed. The Indian Education Act of 1972 called for a policy of meeting the special needs of Indian students in public schools that received federal assistance. The act also demanded that public school officials consult with Indian parents in designing programs and allow them to help evaluate the results of education of Indian students. The law authorized the BIA to make contracts with tribes to develop model programs to provide for Indian student needs, adult education, literacy training, high school equivalency, and research on Indian education. The act also established the National Advisory Council on Indian Education. The members were Indians and Alaskan natives, and they were assigned to monitor educational programs operated by the BIA and the Department of Health, Education, and Welfare (HEW).[66]

The Indian Self-determination and Educational Assistance Act of 1975 repeated many of the same policy goals. It noted that Indian schooling had not achieved adequate results and that "parental and community control . . . is of proper importance to the Indian people." The act provided broad authority for the secretaries of interior and HEW to enter into contracts with tribes for educational programs and also to improve the ability of tribal governments to carry out such programs. Title IV outlined guidelines for public schools that received assistance for educating Indian students. Recipient schools, for example, had to file a plan to show that they would meet the needs of these students, and they were required to consult with Indian parents either on school boards or on special committees.[67]

The Indian Health Care Improvement Act of 1976 attempted to close the gap between the health services for Indians and those enjoyed by the general public. The legislation noted that sizeable improvements had been made in Indian health care, but that Indians still suffered from high rates of tuberculosis, influenza, pneumonia, and infant mortality. Indians living in remote areas also lacked access to treatment facilities. The legislation authorized increased funds for health treatment, improved water supplies, and waste disposal. It also authorized educational grants to encourage more Indians to enter health careers. Title IV ordered HEW to launch studies of health care resources available to urban Indians and to provide or to contract for health services for the urbanites. Indian preference and consultation were incorporated into the act.[68]

In 1978 Congress approved the Tribally Controlled Community College Assistance Act. This relatively short statute authorized the secretary of interior to establish two-year colleges for tribes that met certain guidelines. HEW was to assist in conducting feasibility studies for the applicant tribes. The act authorized $4,000 annually for each full time student, but the colleges could also seek other federal funding.[69] A central goal was to provide training so that tribal members could assume reservation jobs.

A study by the Carnegie Foundation in 1989 revealed that the act had resulted in twenty-four community colleges, mostly located in the Dakotas and Montana, that enrolled the equivalent of 4,400 full-time students.[70] While the report praised the colleges for offering educational opportunities to reservation residents, fostering cultural awareness, and serving as centers for Indian communities, it severely criticized the federal government's lack of support. In 1989 the schools received only $1,900 per full-time student, and many of the facilities were in deplorable physical condition.[71]

The Indian Child Welfare Act of 1978 gave tribes greater control over Indian children taken from their families and placed in foster homes. Indians had long resented what they regarded as insensitive and heavy-handed actions by state courts and social agencies. The act determined that tribes exercised exclusive jurisdiction over custody decisions on reservations. Tribal courts, indeed, could assume jurisdiction over cases involving minors who were not residents of a reservation by simply requesting a transfer from state courts. A provision that would later create national headlines involved the right of an Indian parent to withdraw consent to the adoption of a child at any time. The law also established guidelines for the adoption of Indian children. First preference went to the child's extended family, second to members of the tribe, and third to Indians of other tribes.[72]

Another congressional action in 1978 that demonstrated increased sensitivity to Indian needs was the Joint Resolution on American Indian Religious Freedom. The measure noted that federal laws, regulations, and policies had previously ignored or abridged religious freedom, and it then proclaimed the policy of extending complete religious freedom to all native people. The resolution ordered the president to direct federal agencies to respect Native Americans' religious rights and practices.[73]

Although these legislative enactments were not always fully implemented, they indicate that Indians made significant gains after 1960. Self-determination, often used to describe the era in terms of federal policy, was initially not well defined, and it usually meant whatever a speaker wanted it to mean. But certainly many of the ideas associated with self-determination resembled John Collier's cultural pluralism. Collier's support for Indian culture and his attempts to foster self-government, however, were heavily qualified by limitations on Indian authority in the Indian Reorganization Act and the tribal constitutions and bylaws created under this legislation. Indeed, Collier's outlook would have seemed passe to even the more moderate Indian leaders of the period after 1960. By the early 1970s they had defined self-determination much more specifically as they devised increasingly more sophisticated and precise definitions of tribal autonomy.

A companion development to this was the success of Indian leaders in shaping new legislation and policies at the national level. Tribal leaders in recent times have been judged largely on how many benefits they can get from the federal government, and they have learned how to lobby. Thus, they regularly attend hearings on appropriations or other legislation and visit Washington when important policy decisions are pending. They carefully cultivate the support of their state's congressional delegation and other members of Congress sympathetic to their interests. Like all lobbyists, these same tribal spokesmen have learned how to present information selectively and the importance of personal contacts with federal officials, either by frequent telephone conversations or by face-to-face meetings.[74] Unfortunately, greater tribal participation in federal programs has not reduced their dependency on government but merely shifted it from the BIA to other federal agencies.[75]

Although Indians moved toward self-rule after 1960, they often found themselves locked into a contradiction. On the one hand, they insisted that the federal government maintain its traditional trust responsibilities by providing the full protections and services created by treaties and statutes; on the other, they demanded that tribes be recognized as autonomous bodies with independent powers. Self-rule, however, involved serious risks that some Indian leaders feared. Clearly, the federal trust role and Indian self rule were not always compatible, and the incompatibilities produced a great deal of confusion and friction for both Indians and non-Indians.

10.
The New Indian Wars
Energy, Water, and Autonomy

The energy crisis of the 1970s affected western reservation Indians more than any other event in the recent past. According to a report in 1976, Indians owned about 3 percent of the nation's total reserves of oil and natural gas or approximately 4.2 billion barrels of oil and 17.5 trillion cubic feet of gas. Reservations also contained from 100 to 200 billion tons of coal or from 7 to 13 percent of American reserves and a large proportion of uranium reserves.[1]

As energy prices rose, tribes learned belatedly that their previous contracts were disastrous. Peabody Coal, for example, had negotiated leases with the Navajos and Hopis in 1966 in the Black Mesa area. Company representatives at the time informed the Navajo council that its oil and natural gas reserves were nearly depleted and that nuclear power would soon make coal obsolete. Peabody added that it was doing the Indians a favor by undertaking the massive strip mining project. Neither tribal council understood the environmental damages involved or the impact upon local residents displaced by the operation. John S. Boyden, the Hopi tribal attorney at the negotiations, was listed in a professional directory as a legal representative of Peabody. Although severe criticism of the Black Mesa contracts made them notorious by the early 1970s, they were not invalidated.[2]

Several early coal leases called for flat-rate royalties. Instead of a percentage of the market value of coal mined, eight of the eleven early contracts provided for a set sum (typically 17.5 cents) per ton. The Omnibus Mineral Leasing Act of 1938 allowed contracts to continue unchanged as long as minerals were found in paying quantities. As coal prices soared from $4.40 per ton in the 1950s to $17.00 in 1974, Indian royalty rates rose only 35 percent. Obviously, companies holding flat-rate contracts could afford to pay more, but their response to Indian complaints was to make the best of a bad bargain.[3]

Clearly much of the blame for the inequitable contracts belonged to the Bureau of Indian Affairs (BIA). The agency staff did not understand that regional population growth since World War II had greatly increased the value of coal and reduced such earlier handicaps as transportation costs and weak demand. Indeed, coal producers, well before the energy crisis, had demonstrated increased interest in mining western coal reserves. BIA officials, moreover, did not inform tribal councils about the advantages of percentage royalties over flat rates. One individual confessed that he did not know that the federal government in 1971 had stipulated percentage leases on all public lands. The BIA also lacked geological expertise to provide the reliable data that tribes needed during their negotiations with coal companies. The lack of data was so serious that Indian leaders themselves did not know how bad existing contracts were until they began comparing notes on the moccasin grapevine.[4]

Angry protests against mining companies and the BIA had several repercussions. Tribal leaders found themselves hard pressed to justify earlier contracts, and younger critics used the failures to achieve leadership roles. Energy companies came under pressure as tribes demanded the renegotiation of contracts. The Department of Interior, in 1976, raised the royalty rates to 12.5 percent for coal and required environmental studies. The Northern Cheyennes and other tribes by the late 1970s placed a moratorium on all energy development until they could control energy contracts and receive the revenues they wanted.[5]

Charles Lipton, head of a New York consulting firm and a United Nations advisor, became a prominent critic of Indian energy contracts in the mid-1970s. Lipton's speeches blasted the energy companies, claiming that the Indians got worse deals than third-world countries. He urged tribes to use foreign contracts as guidelines for their negotiations, and he listed eighteen points to include in any oil or gas contract. Ironically, the list helped energy companies because it convinced some tribes to end their moratoriums, but it also frightened off a few firms. Eventually, tribes devised their own formulas for negotiations.[6]

As Indians sought control over their resources and fairer prices, they turned to intertribal cooperation. In 1974 tribes in the northern plains created a natural resources federation that dealt with minerals, water, and agriculture. Some participants believed that a national organization was needed because several important energy tribes—Navajo, Hopi, and Laguna Pueblo—were not included. In 1975 LaDonna Harris, the head of Americans for Indian Opportunity, and Charles Lohah, an Osage then with the Native American Fund, established the Council of Energy Resources Tribes (CERT), which included twenty-five tribes. CERT's original goals were moderate but far-sighted: to improve reservation conditions, to gain reliable inventories of resources, to serve as a clearinghouse, to use resources on reservations rather than exporting them, and to supply impartial information on environmental impact.[7]

CERT's focus changed as its goals and sources of funds shifted. Initially, the Department of Energy provided most of its funding, and the BIA opposed the organization. After claiming that it was conducting its own inventory of Indian energy resources, the BIA relented and began giving

CERT financial support.[8] Meantime, CERT quietly worked as a service organization that supplied information to member tribes and advised them on negotiations. In March 1977, Peter McDonald, Navajo chairman and also chairman of the CERT's directors, announced in Phoenix that the organization would act as a "domestic OPEC." McDonald's reputation for controversy insured media attention when he threatened that tribes would withhold their energy resources to get higher prices. A backlash developed as critics charged CERT with blackmail. Unfortunately, the public also got the mistaken idea that Indians were oil-rich sheiks. In reality, few tribes had energy resources, and lease revenues seldom allowed Indians to escape poverty. The Osages and Jicarilla Apaches were exceptions with annual per capita distributions of over $10,000. Aside from uranium, Indians' energy resources did not permit them to impose an embargo.

One positive effect of McDonald's threat was to win more funding from federal agencies. Later in 1977 CERT installed Ed Gabriel, a former administrator in the federal energy agency and close friend of McDonald's, as executive secretary. Two years later CERT hired Ahmed Kooros, an Iranian economist trained in the United States, as an adviser. Kooros had participated in oil negotiations in Iran, and his background and understanding of Indian needs proved invaluable. CERT also established a headquarters in Denver to provide technical information to member tribes. Its headquarters in Washington handled lobbying efforts.

In 1979 McDonald tried to turn CERT into an energy broker. In a letter to President Carter, he claimed that by obtaining 1 percent of the administration's energy program, CERT tribes could produce the equivalent of two million barrels of oil per year. McDonald's reversal brought charges that he did not speak for member tribes or recognize the disruption to reservation life that would result. CERT, some alleged, had become a front for multinational corporations. A few tribes withdrew from CERT, but most worked on correcting its flaws.[9] By 1980 Indian oil production reached approximately one million barrels, but by 1985 it fell to 365,000 barrels as prices slumped.[10]

Dissatisfaction with CERT led to a major overhaul in 1982. Complaints arose that McDonald and Gabriel had lavished money on the Washington office and that both had acted autocratically with member tribes. Critics also charged that CERT wasted too much time publicizing its achievements and slighted its duties on supplying technical information. In 1982 CERT replaced Gabriel with A. David Lester, an Oklahoma Creek. Wilfred Scott, Nez Perce chairman, supplanted McDonald after the Navajos voted him out as tribal chairman. A year later Lester closed the Washington office. The Denver office remained open to supply technical data. After retrenchment, CERT concentrated on environmental and economic impact studies and relied on the tribes and reform groups for lobbying. Its main financial support meantime shifted to the Environmental Protection Agency.[11]

A crucial element behind the formation of CERT was the tribes' desire to exercise control over leasing terms. Indians objected to the standard leases signed under the Omnibus Leasing Act of 1938 because it excluded tribes from both decision making and higher profits. Based on the experiences of third-world countries, Indian leaders demanded partnerships with energy companies rather than competitive bidding on bonuses and set royalties. Joint ownership, however, always involved a degree of financial risk. Nevertheless, the Navajos in 1972 signed a contract with a joint ownership option, and the Blackfeet and Jicarilla Apaches followed soon afterward. The Department of Interior, which initially opposed partnerships, agreed to such contracts but retained a veto power. Fearful of lawsuits, the Department soon reversed itself and rejected all joint ventures. Although the Indian Mineral Development Act of 1982 authorized joint ventures, reduced energy consumption and dramatic declines in oil and natural gas prices made the provision irrelevant. Demand for uranium fell after utilities canceled plans for nuclear power plants. Clean air legislation and abandonment of the Carter administration's synfuels program caused problems for the coal industry. In an interesting reversal, energy companies in the mid-1980s approached tribal councils asking for relief from contracts negotiated during the energy crisis.[12]

Water rights have remained a vital subject for both Indians and whites. The basic issues changed little after the late 1970s. In the absence of general legislation defining Indian water rights, Indians believed that the *Winters* doctrine and other case law entitled them to sufficient water for their irrigable land and additional quantities for other types of development.

Their hopes have received some serious setbacks in recent years. The weakening of Indian water rights stemmed partly from the McCarran Amendment of 1952 that permitted state adjudication of federal water rights in "general streams." In 1976 in *Colorado River Water Conservation District v. U.S.*, the Supreme Court ruled that "certain states" have control of allocating water to Indians. Although the ruling was not entirely clear, Indians recognized it as a major defeat because state courts and agencies had historically discriminated against their water claims. In 1983 the Supreme Court in *Arizona* v. *San Carlos Apaches* ruled on a consolidated appeal and upheld the 1976 ruling. Both rulings, however, noted that federal courts held concurrent jurisdiction and could hear appeals from the state courts.[13] Nevertheless, the decisions reflected the Supreme Court's swing toward deference to state authority and a major potential reversal of its historical role of protecting Indians in legal matters. In seven water cases since 1970, Indians have lost six decisions, mostly on jurisdictional grounds.[14]

During the past two decades new issues have added to the complexity of water law. Most tribes, for example, do not want their water rights quantified because they fear bias in cost-benefit formulas used for that purpose and also because unquantified water rights give them greater bargaining power.[15] Indians increasingly have considered selling their water rights to off-reservation purchasers. Opponents have claimed that the treaties, statutes, and executive orders that established reservations provide no legal basis for such sales. As water becomes increasingly scarce in the West, converting Indian water into money could become a major source of new revenue.[16] Indian water rights have also become associated with environmental issues. There is a concern about the contamination of reservation water supplies by uranium mining and other types of pollution. Non-Indians are convinced that industries fled to reservations to evade federal and state environmental controls. Since an estimated 1,200 hazardous waste sites are located on or adjacent to reservations, such fears are not entirely groundless.[17]

Resolution of Indian water rights seemingly should be a fairly simple matter, but a congressional stalemate has prevented passage of needed legislation. Supporters of the Indians in Congress regularly introduce bills to define Indian water rights favorably, but a western coalition just as regularly blocks passage. The anti-Indian faction, meantime, has consistently introduced measures calling for state control or condemnation of Indian water rights, and their opponents have managed to defeat such bills. The resolution of water disputes thus has remained largely with the courts and the endless expenses, delays, appeals, and enforcement problems associated with litigation.[18]

The Carter and Reagan administrations strongly advocated that tribes and their opponents negotiate settlements of water rights and other disputes. Theoretically, this would circumvent the congressional stalemate and the problems of litigation. One prominent example of a negotiated settlement involved the Tohono O'odhams, formerly known as the Papagos, and their complaint that Tucson, mining operations, and agriculture were depleting the tribe's ground water supply. Following decisions in 1974 that ground water came under the *Winters* doctrine, the Tohono O'odhams (and later the federal government) filed a suit against the non-Indian water users. During the legal proceedings, the tribal attorney hinted that his clients might accept a negotiated settlement.

Representative Morris Udall took an active role in achieving a settlement. In 1977 the disputing parties formed an advisory board, and Udall assisted them in formulating an agreement. Under its terms, the Tohono O'odhams relinquished their *Winters* rights in return for an annual quota of 40,000 acre feet of water from the Central Arizona Project (CAP). The Interior Department would award damages if the CAP was not completed or other obstacles arose. Udall also established a trust fund to insure payments would be made to the Tohono O'odhams. The tribe could market its water off the reservation but under state control. President Reagan vetoed the $35,000,000 settlement as too expensive, but Udall, with a fine touch of irony, then secured passage by attaching the bill to a measure that allowed large land owners in California to gain access to cheap water.[19]

Although a half dozen or so tribes have agreed to convert their "paper water" into "wet water" in recent years, negotiation of water rights disputes probably has limited potential. In every instance, tribes accepted settlements because additional supplies of water were available, and Indian leaders decided to abandon or limit their *Winters* rights when whites agreed to share the new water.[20] Because little new water is likely, future disputes will probably be settled by either litigation or unilateral action by Congress. Both methods of resolution involve risks for Indians. With the recent tendency of federal courts to uphold state authority, the *Winters* doctrine may become a dead issue if state courts render adverse decisions and quantify the amounts of water that tribes may use. Despite their recent lobbying victories, most tribal leaders still prefer litigation over settlements dictated by Congress. They recognize that, despite their recent lobbying victories, they cannot match the pressures that white interests can exert and, perhaps more importantly, that their opposition could produce punitive legislation.

Despite the importance of Indian water rights in the West, the issue has become secondary in importance to Indians' recent success in gaining political autonomy. This trend has evolved from a variety of diverse factors. Tribal governments became more effective, assertive, and sophisticated after the Johnson administration allowed tribal officials to bypass the BIA, receive funding from other agencies, and administer programs on reservations. The Red Power Movement, although not effective in a direct way, heightened Indians' sense of identity and focused attention on treaty rights and the belief that the federal government and states should deal with tribes as sovereign and equal powers. Court victories that recognized hunting and fishing treaty rights, that blessed tribal authority to levy taxes, to conduct gambling operations, and to sell cigarettes, and that supported independent tribal negotiations with corporations have all bolstered autonomy. Finally, the work of the National Congress of American Indians, CERT, and numerous other groups operating at regional or state levels assisted individual tribes and enlisted the support of non-Indian organizations.[21]

The importance of tribal political resurgence varies among the reservations in the West. Tribes that receive large revenues from natural resources, for example, have enjoyed greater success in their relations with government and private businesses. These tribes have hired experts and law firms capable of defending their interests or established their own legal departments. Another factor relates to whether a reservation has been allotted or remains intact. Councils on unallotted reservations face fewer obstacles in achieving tribal autonomy than those that try to extend authority over checkerboarded reservations containing a high percentage of whites living on fee simple lands. Tribes also differ a great deal in terms of internal unity, ability to overcome factionalism during crises, and, above all else, the quality of leadership. Tribes that seemingly have very little promise have often been quite successful in achieving autonomy because of their unity and knowledgeable and aggressive leaders.[22]

Tribal governments have also won several major victories in extending their authority over reservations. The severance taxes that the Navajos, Crows, and Jicarilla Apaches imposed on energy firms in the late 1970s are an example. Other tribes took similar actions. Worried about what would happen when energy resources were depleted, they hoped to establish trust funds or to foster future economic development. Later they used the taxes to offset the disastrous budget cuts of the Reagan administration. Several oil companies filed suit in federal court, claiming that the taxes were illegal. The Mountain States Legal Foundation filed a brief as a friend of the energy companies. James Watt, later Reagan's controversial secretary of interior, headed the organization. Despite the oil companies' expert legal talent, the Supreme Court in 1982 ruled that tribes possessed "inherent power" to tax and thus endorsed the severance taxes. Recently the courts upheld a utility tax levied by the Fort Peck and Blackfeet tribal councils against the Burlington Northern. Fort Peck's revenues from the railroad totaled $650,000 in 1991.[23]

Tribal autonomy received a boost from a surprising source in early 1983 when President Reagan released his policy statement on Indian affairs. His two key goals involved increased self-government and economic self-sufficiency. What was especially striking was the administration's promise to deal with tribes on a "government to government" basis. Indian affairs, in fact, were subsequently transferred to the White House's Office of Intergovernmental Affairs, the agency which dealt with federal-state relations, instead of being handled by the Office of Public Liaison. Reagan held out the prospect of block grants to the tribes, but he also promised to honor federal trust responsibilities.[24]

Indian reaction to the policy statement ranged from skepticism to opposition. Reagan's budget cuts during his first two years had reduced funding for Indian programs from $3.5 billion to $2.5 billion. The administration's "New Federalism" supposedly provided a "safety net" by which state and local governments would offset federal reductions. Unfortunately, the impact of the cuts for Indians was greater than for non-Indians, and their tribal governments could not provide a safety net.[25] In addition, Indians were enraged over a recent television appearance by Secretary of Interior Watt and his condemnation of reservations: "If you want an example of the failure of socialism. . . ," he demanded, "don't go to Russia, come to America and go to the Indian reservations." Watt then proceeded to blame reservations for drug abuse, alcoholism, unemployment, divorce, and venereal diseases. In a final blast, Watt lashed tribal leaders for keeping Indians on reservations because otherwise "they'd go out and get a job and that guy wouldn't have his handout as a paid government official."[26]

Nevertheless, the Reagan administration seemed to move in the direction of greater empowerment of tribes after his policy statement. Apparently, Kenneth L. Smith, assistant secretary of interior for Indian affairs and a Waso Indian from Oregon, took the "new federalism" seriously and believed that tribes, like states and local governments, needed greater authority.

A particularly important victory for tribes took place in 1988 when Washington State abandoned its long struggle against the Boldt decision of 1974. Some observers, indeed, drew comparisons between Washington State after 1974 and the resistance of southern states to civil rights during the 1960s. Pressured by sports and commercial fishing interests, state officials had obstructed Boldt's decision, and law enforcement officials failed to protect Indians who tried to fish according to the court's ruling.[27] Both Representatives Lloyd Meeds, a Democrat, and John Cunningham, a Republican, had introduced anti-Indian bills during the controversy. In 1984 anti-Indian organizations had secured voters' approval of Initiative 456, a measure that called for an end of Indian treaties. After state officials and tribes had cooperated on fish management for several years, Governor Booth Gardner's "Centennial Accord" in 1988 agreed to deal with Indian tribes as sovereign bodies. Gardener's action infuriated eastern Washington hunters who had no previous experience with treaty rights and resented giving Indians any special concessions.[28] While other western states have not formally announced their willingness to deal with tribes as sovereign bodies, some states now negotiate with tribes almost as a matter of course.

Perhaps the most controversial action by tribal governments was their exercise of local government authority over non-Indians living within reservations. On unallotted reservations, council ordinances normally cause few problems because the handful of traders, businessmen, and missionaries have long accepted tribal authority. On allotted reservations, however, whites often make up a majority of the population, and because they own their property in fee simple, they reject any sort of tribal jurisdiction. The tribal ordinances themselves usually parallel those exercised by local white governments, dealing with such matters as zoning, building permits, law and order, sanitation, business licensing, and hunting and fishing.

The most visible manifestation of tribal sovereignty, at least to the general public, has become Indian gaming. Virtually every major highway in the West (or upper Midwest) displays billboards advertising Indian bingo halls or casinos at area reservations. Indian gaming may not match the glamour or scope of Las Vegas or Atlantic City, but it is not penny ante to the sponsoring tribes. According to one tribal official, gross revenue from gambling has recently risen to $5 billion with net revenues of over $720 million.[29] Some reservations provide charter buses to attract outsiders, the gambling facilities are clean and plush, and tribal leaders frequently consult with Nevada operators on management questions. The employees, usually young and well-groomed Indians in formal garb, could easily fit into a Las Vegas casino. Gambling, moreover, brings two major benefits to the tribes. It reduces the extraordinarily high unemployment rates common to reservations. It also reverses or at least slows the normal flow of dollars from reservations to border towns.[30] The sizeable revenues from gambling have, like the severance taxes, helped offset budget cuts and reduced royalties from energy. Tribes have used the money to supplement often meager federal funds available for health, education, law and order, housing, roads, and utilities. Reservation economies that were moribund a few years ago are now thriving because of the "White Buffalo."

In 1988 Congress approved the Indian Gambling Regulation Act. The measure defined three classes of gaming with class I consisting of traditional Indian low-stakes gambling done as part of ceremonies. Class II dealt with bingo and several similar forms of gaming, and class III involved slot machines, baccarat, blackjack, and other casino games. The latter two classes came under the supervision of a five-member commission that was given authority to investigate and regulate gaming operations. Clearly, the law did not try to override state governments. It prohibited Indian gaming if a state had rejected gambling by criminal law or as a public policy. In addition, a tribe that wanted to start casino gambling could do so only if it concluded a compact with appropriate state officials.[31] Several states, especially Kansas and Arizona, have blocked Indian attempts to start gaming operations, and this has created a major controversy. Indians leaders demand that states should have no control and that gambling operations should come solely under federal jurisdiction.[32]

Opposition to gambling, which led to its regulation, came from two major sources. First, critics claimed that Indians were not competent to manage gaming. Second, others feared that tribes needed protection from corrupt non-Indians. Leonard Prescott, a Shakopee Mdewakanton Sioux and chairman of the National Indian Gaming Commission, strongly denied both charges. Prescott argued that the national media had made charges about Indian gambling scandals but provided little or no evidence to substantiate them. One story, for example, discussed the arrest of Chicago Mafia figures who tried to infiltrate a California Indian casino, but the writer failed to point out until the final paragraph that the attempt failed and that tribal officials had helped block it.[33]

Increased tribal authority has produced a strong anti-Indian backlash in many parts of the West and upper Midwest. Western hostility is hardly new. State officials have always resented the presence of reservations and their tax-free status. Indians faced serious problems gaining voter rights and Social Security benefits from Arizona and New Mexico until after World War II. Western state courts have been notably hostile to Indian hunting, fishing, and water rights. Indians have complained bitterly about police brutality and harsh sentences of local judges. On a personal level, many westerners stereotyped Indians as lazy, stupid, drunken, and untrustworthy. Bars until recent times sometimes displayed racist signs such as "No Indians, No dogs!" White resentment is sometimes fueled by the persistent myth that all Indians receive a monthly government check. Unlike past hostility, the recent anti-Indian backlash is aimed at increased tribal autonomy and treaty rights.[34]

Because of their ephemeral nature, the twenty or so anti-Indian organizations are hard to trace, but they generally date from the mid-1970s. The American Indian Policy Review Commission, for example, encountered a backlash group known as Montanans Opposed to Discrimination (MOD). The organization claimed that it sought "to enforce uniformity in the customs and uses of a nation [sic], State [sic], and local laws which relate to personal and property matters," and "to prevent the unjust and unreasonable discrimination against any citizen . . . regardless of race, creed, or national origin." MOD claimed a membership of 3,000 on or near the Flathead Reservation, and it strongly opposed the tribal council's ordinances that applied to whites on fee simple land.[35] This particular reservation has uncommon friction because the tribal government shares jurisdiction with the state.

Although MOD and other anti-Indian organizations differed considerably in makeup, they shared several traits. The operations of the AIM and similar militant groups apparently had little or nothing to do with the white backlash. The organizations developed from non-Indian complaints against the extension of tribal jurisdiction over non-Indians on reservations or because of federal court rulings that upheld Indians' hunting, fishing, or gathering rights on non-reservation areas.

The anti-Indian organizations have drawn heavily from the ideology and rhetoric of the American Revolution. Backlash groups frequently depict themselves, like the American colonists, as innocent victims of outside tyranny and complain that Indians hold unwarranted legal rights and privileges. More to the point, the backlash leaders insist that they are forced to obey tribal ordinances that they had no voice in creating. References to taxation without representation and similar allusions are commonplace in their statements.

Because the anti-Indian movement and the Sagebrush Rebellion—a conservative protest against recent federal controls over the public domain—developed at approximately the same time and adopted similar rhetorical strategies, links between the two would seem likely, but this does not seem to be the case. James Watt and fellow Sagebrushers may have sympathized with the anti-Indian groups, but no evidence of consistent cooperation exists. The Sagebrush Rebellion enjoyed an abundance of funds for research, legal work, and lobbying, and its publications and press releases were obviously the work of experts in public relations.[36] Anti-Indian propaganda tended to be amateurish and crude. In short, Watt and his colleagues were "high rollers" with little concern for small-time white operators or sportsmen in the anti-Indian movement.

The anti-Indian organizations have proliferated and spread from their early centers, Montana and Washington, and formed umbrella groups. In 1976 at Salt Lake City, Howard Gray, a former outdoor writer and photographer from Seattle, who was identified with several groups opposing the Boldt decision, joined with other anti-Indian leaders to form the Interstate Congress for Equal Rights and Responsibilities (ICERR). The group attempted to link whites opposed to tribal jurisdiction with the protesting sportsmen organizations in Washington state. ICERR's platform included the belief that all state and local laws should apply to reservations, that constitutional rights should supersede treaty rights, and that tribal jurisdiction should not apply to non-Indians.[37] ICERR apparently was not successful in winning the cooperation of MOD and various other groups outside Washington state.

In 1983, ICERR, sportsmen groups, and white property owners in Washington state formed a second umbrella organization, the Salmon Steelhead Preservation Action for Washington Now (S/SPAWN). The group's strategy of interposing state authority against federal actions resembled southern states' early reactions to the civil rights movement. Senator Jack Metcalf, a conservative Republican member of the Washington legislature, introduced a bill that denied Indians any special legal rights. When this failed, Metcalf converted the bill into a public initiative that failed to gain sufficient signatures in 1983 to be placed on the ballot. By softening its language, Metcalf obtained sufficient signatures in 1984, and Washington voters approved Initiative 456. State officials, however, recognized the jurisdictional problems involved and refused to enforce the initiative. S/SPAWN next lobbied for a presidential commission to investigate the impact of Indian policies on non-Indians, but it won little sympathy from the Reagan administration.[38]

Meantime, a series of federal court decisions in support of Chippewas' hunting and fishing rights in ceded areas of Wisconsin added significantly to the anti-Indian movement's constituency. The cases started in 1974 when Wisconsin game wardens arrested two members of the Lac Courte Oreilles band for spearing fish in a lake on ceded land in violation of state game regulations. The Lac Courte Oreilles and several other Chippewa bands sued, claiming that earlier cession treaties reserved their fishing, hunting, and gathering rights. Although the Indians lost in federal district court, in 1983 the Seventh Court of Appeals overturned the original ruling in a decision known as LCO I. Since 1983 the federal district court has ruled on various aspects of these reserved rights, including timber claims, and supplemented earlier decisions. In 1991 District Judge Barbara Crabb issued a "final judgment" that summarized and clarified LCO I through LCO VIII.[39]

Although Wisconsin state officials opposed the LCO decisions, they kept their fight within the judiciary. The same, however, was not true of white opponents in northern Wisconsin. Since 1983 anti-Indian leaders have charged that the Chippewa treaties are invalid and that unregulated Indian hunting and fishing would kill all the deer and fish and destroy the tourist industry. Their bumper stickers displayed such slogans as "Save a Deer,

Shoot an Indian," or "Spear an Indian, Save a Muskie." Wisconsin back-lashers appeared in force to protest at boat landings each spring when the Indians speared walleye and muskellunge during spawning season, a prac-tice permitted under the LCO rulings. Racial slurs, jeers, rock throwing, and threats, along with the displays of inflammatory posters and effigies, created what one reporter described as "a gauntlet of hate."

The organization of Protect Americans' Rights and Resources (PARR) in 1987 at Wausau was still another attempt to consolidate local anti-Indian groups into a regional or national organization. The prospects seemed en-couraging. The 500 Wausau delegates reportedly represented thirteen states and two Canadian provinces. They approved resolutions calling "for the abrogation of Indian treaties, the dissolution of Indian reservations, and an end to 'special privileges' for Indians."[40] Attendance dropped at PARR's second convention, and it remains largely a Wisconsin organiza-tion. More recently, the anti-Indian movement in Wisconsin suffered a staggering blow when a militant group known as Stop Treaty Abuse (STA) was sued by the Lac du Flambeau tribe in federal district court for violating Indians' civil rights and treaty rights. In January 1992, the court assessed STA $300,000 in court costs and attorney fees and granted the Indians in-junctive relief from white protestors.[41]

The organization of Citizens Equal Rights Alliance (CERA) in March 1988 constituted the fourth umbrella backlash group. CERA was old wine in a new bottle. Many of the officers of CERA and its constituent organizations were members of ICERR, S/SPAWN, and PARR. CERA may, however, come closer to achieving a truly national status. It claims a membership drawn from twenty-two states, and its approach is more comprehensive. CERA has also sent representatives to Washington for congressional hear-ings and lobbying activities.

William H. Covey of Big Arm, Montana, played a major role in founding CERA and continues as its president. Covey's extensive experience within the federal government gives him insights into how it operates. He served twice in the Army, first with the army engineers and later with counterin-telligence. He then spent thirty years in the Forest Service before his retire-ment in 1985 as a regional director. Covey afterward moved to the Flathead Reservation. The following year he purchased a recreation license from the Confederated Salish and Kootenai tribal government, and he became upset when he learned that he could be prosecuted in tribal courts if he violated either tribal or federal laws. Covey joined MOD, which was renamed All Citizens Equal (ACE). Covey as president of ACE met backlash leaders from Wisconsin and formed CERA.[42]

Although the literature issued by CERA addresses all the grievances of backlashers, the organization's central concern is tribal jurisdiction and In-dian claims of sovereign powers. Covey, for example, condemns the idea that "Indian Country" includes fee simple lands on reservations and that tribal governments possess jurisdiction over individuals living on such holdings. "Indian Country," he maintains, "means whatever the user wants it to mean." He condemns tribal sovereignty on the same grounds and notes that sovereignty changes meaning according to which legislation or court decision one reads.[43]

CERA's central goal involves a major legislative overhaul of the legal system for Indian affairs. Covey sees the present situation as a confused morass of statutes, case law, and treaties that are unfair for everyone. He wants a federal commission that will "impartially" review the existing legal structure of Indian affairs and then propose corrective legislation to remove sources of conflicts and confusion.[44] Covey and other backlash leaders clearly feel a sense of betrayal in recent actions of the federal, state, and local governments. Federal officials, for example, have permitted tribes to extend jurisdiction over private property owners on reservations. The Reagan administration proved especially disappointing when it announced its "government to government" statement and encouraged tribes to levy their own taxes. State and local governments, to worsen matters, have negotiated away non-Indians' rights in agreements with tribal governments. The acceptance of the Boldt decision and the LCO rulings by Washington State and Wisconsin officials were especially infuriating.[45] Covey's ideas reflect a typical western perspective: a dislike of government control but a desire for government help with problems.[46]

The charge of racism is an obvious stumbling block for CERA, and Covey, at least, approaches the subject carefully but with considerable candor. In an interview with a Missoula reporter in 1990, Covey conceded that "you'll find these [racist] types on both sides of the issue. But if an Indian admits that he is a racist, that's O.K. If a non-Indian says he's a racist, that's terrible." Covey also acknowledged that CERA might appear racist to outsiders, but its basic concern was legal jurisdiction.[47] Although Indian and white opponents of the anti-Indian movement frequently charge that it has ties with neo-Nazis or white supremacists, one human rights advocate believes that CERA and other backlash organizations are simply out to eliminate Indian rights.[48]

Obviously the outcome of the conflict between Indian autonomy and anti-Indian backlash remains unclear because it is ongoing. Tribal governments are usually made up of individuals who are moderate, educated, and prefer negotiation over serious confrontation. Perhaps as time passes and tempers cool, they and white opponents will resolve their differences. Although Covey and other backlash leaders have visited Washington several times, they have not yet succeeded in creating a national commission, let alone secured the legislative overhaul that they want. Covey discreetly maintains that CERA has "influenced" some legislation, and he believes that his organization will become more successful with experience.[49] A careful study of the existing legal structure of Indian affairs would take years to complete, and the results might well be less satisfactory to the backlashers than the current situation.

11.

Conclusions

The fact that an anti-Indian movement exists today in the West points to one of the major changes that occurred in the twentieth century. The achievement of greater tribal autonomy has transformed Indian-white relations, but its development was fitful. The establishment of tribal governments during the New Deal was a step toward increased self-government, but the more important advances started as a result of Indian hostility toward termination and tribes' eligibility for programs of the War on Poverty. Despite Indian success in tapping federal budgets, the intense poverty of most reservations automatically creates a continued economic and political dependency for Indians. The trust protection that Indians demand works to the same end. Full tribal autonomy remains unfulfilled.

Obviously, western regional development provided a context that deeply affected Indians and their affairs. This impact, like the development of tribal autonomy, has been uneven. The region started the century with relatively little voice nationally, but during the Progressive Era, its influence grew significantly. Theodore Roosevelt's "cowboy cabinet" and his conservation and reclamation programs represented important first steps, but real regional dominance started with the Woodrow Wilson administration when westerners gained greater control of the Departments of Interior and Agriculture and the Indian Affairs Committees. Perhaps the high point of western control over Indians was reached under Secretary of Interior Fall's tenure. Throughout the century, the federal government has increased its dominance over western development. The operations of agencies such as the Forest Service, the Bureau of Reclamation, and the Bureau of Land Management have deeply affected Indian affairs. These agencies have important white constituencies that have enabled them to control regional development. The BIA, in contrast, has seen its power diminish and has been increasingly less effective in protecting Indians and providing them with services.

The kinds of resources that whites wanted also shaped the regional influences. Acquiring Indian land remained the key motivation of whites during the first two decades of the twentieth century, but afterward the picture became much more complex. Other resources—timber, oil, natural gas, water, and the leasing of Indian land—grew more important after 1920 simply because the most desirable Indian agricultural and grazing lands had already fallen into white hands through allotment. Since World War II, westerners have had a diminished role in the quest for Indian resources. Instead, the chief seekers have usually been national or even multi-national corporations. In sum, the regional influence remains important, but it has become intermingled with other factors.

Exceptions to western domination of Indian affairs also deserve some mention. Although this study has not dealt much with Indian reform activities early in the century, the Indian Rights Association and other reform groups sometimes managed to obstruct western raids on Indian resources. Much more apparent, however, were the successes of Collier's reform crusades during the 1920s and the New Deal. Collier's western opponents during the New Deal, such as Senators Burton K. Wheeler and Dennis Chavez, may have had philosophical differences with his cultural pluralism, but their disputes with Collier also reflected western constituents' practical complaints against current Indian policies.

Although it is difficult, perhaps impossible, to document, the West itself has changed in its attitudes and behavior toward Indians since 1900. The century opened with the memory of recent Indian wars fresh in mind, and whites not only wanted Indian lands, but racial hostility made it easy for them to rationalize unethical methods of obtaining Indian property. Such attitudes have partially shifted. Perhaps the most basic element in the changed attitudes is that most westerners now vaguely accept what Collier preached—that the Indians' culture is worthy of respect and toleration. As the recent backlash indicates, anti-Indian elements remain, but they do not command much political power, either in the West or nationally.

If one can point to a central turning point for Indians in the West, it clearly involves the impact of World War II. This conflict opened major employment opportunities outside the reservations for Indians, and virtually an entire generation of young Indian males entered the military. Such major trends as off-reservation migration, more sophisticated leadership, and a sharpened sense of goals and identity had their origins in the Indians' wartime experiences.

The impact of twentieth-century events on Indian opinion and behavior has been perhaps less important than seems apparent. Today's Indian leaders are more articulate and sophisticated in dealing with outside interests, but their basic underlying ideas and goals remain the same as earlier Indian spokesmen. They want, in short, to deal with federal and state officials as equals and to achieve a reasonable degree of equity in relations with private business. Both past and present leadership realize that Indian treaty rights and federal trust obligations are fundamental. One of the potential dangers that current Indian leaders may face is their dependence on litigation. Although court victories have brought enormous gains, especially since World War II, the endless and repetitious suits and appeals have been expensive, and compliance has been problematic. From a layman's perspective, a greater threat is the tenuous nature of case law. Important judicial precedents exist for applying congressional plenary powers in cases, for example, and should the federal courts revert to that "line" of decisions, tribes will find themselves as powerless as in the past. The Indians' recent success with grants may present an equally problematic situation in the future if the federal government undergoes a major revision of its priorities.

In pursuing a regional approach, one of the most important (and unanticipated) results has been the realization that Indians and non-Indians in the West share much in common. The reaction of both groups to the two world wars affords one key example. Another was their common response to economic and demographical changes when agriculture became more mechanized and urbanization developed after World War II. Both Indians and whites reacted to the economic forces by leaving reservations and rural areas and taking up life in cities. Both groups share a peculiar love-hate set of attitudes toward the federal government, and the mere mention of the Bureau of Land Management raises the hackles of Indians and whites alike. More recently, reservation Indians and white ranchers responded to the energy crisis of the 1970s in a very similar fashion. Both sensed that massive coal strip mines and other energy proposals threatened their way of life and might destroy the land that both valued. If Indians and non-Indians can overlook their differences and concentrate on the basics that unite them, such as the land and a shared sense of place, perhaps the next century will offer better prospects for rapport.

Notes

Preface

1. *Abstract of the Twelfth Census, 1900* (Washington: Government Printing Office, 1902), 32, 34, 36, 40, 230, 250, 296, 331-33.
2. Ibid., 40. Indian Territory and Oklahoma Territory were combined in 1907 to form the present state of Oklahoma.

1. The Heritage of Severalty

1. 24 Stat. 388.
2. Earl Pomeroy, *The Pacific Slope: A History of California, Oregon, Washington, Idaho, Utah, and Nevada* (New York: Alfred A. Knopf, 1965), 71.
3. Wilcomb E. Washburn, ed., *The American Indian and the United States: A Documentary History*, vol. 3 (New York: Random House, 1973), 1703-1704.
4. D. S. Otis, *The Dawes Act and the Allotment of Indian Lands*, ed. Francis Paul Prucha (Norman: University of Oklahoma Press, 1973), 64-80, 99-103.
5. Ibid., 71-77. See also Frederick E. Hoxie, "Redefining Indian Education: Thomas J. Morgan's Program in Disarray," *Arizona and the West* 24 (Spring 1982): 5-18.
6. Leonard A. Carlson, *Indians, Bureaucrats, and Land: The Dawes Act and the Decline of Indian Farming* (Westport, Connecticut: Greenwood Press, 1981), 30-31.
7. Ibid., 57-75.
8. Otis, *The Dawes Act*, 145-46.
9. Congress revised the Dawes Act several times after 1887 to correct problems. The most significant change, except for leasing, was the allotment of land to both husbands and wives instead of only to heads of families. The new law was needed to prevent wives and their children from being dispossessed when couples divorced. This change was made part of the leasing legislation of 1891. See ibid., 112.
10. 26 Stat. 794.
11. Otis, *The Dawes Act*, 116-23.
12. Ibid., 128-31.
13. Roy Gittinger, *The Formation of the State of Oklahoma* (Norman: University of Oklahoma Press, 1939) offers a thorough accounting of the official side of the history of Indian Territory up to statehood. More recent interpretive works include Danney Goble, *Progressive Oklahoma: The Making of a New Kind of State* (Norman: University of Oklahoma Press, 1980) and John Thompson, *Closing the Frontier: Radical Response in Oklahoma, 1889-1923* (Norman: University of Oklahoma Press, 1986).
14. Muriel H. Wright, *A Guide to the Indian Tribes of Oklahoma* (Norman: University of Oklahoma Press, 1951) is a handbook which provides a general background and much information on the individual tribes. Rennard Strickland, *The Indians in Oklahoma* (Norman: University of Oklahoma Press, 1980) emphasizes the Indians' cultural contributions and is useful for the recent period.

15. Each tribe had a federal agent after their arrival in Indian Territory who acted as an intermediary between Washington and tribal governments. In 1874 federal administration was consolidated under the Union Agency at Muskogee. The federal district court at Fort Smith, Arkansas, maintained jurisdiction over white crimes or Indian crimes against whites, but tribal courts dealt with all cases involving Indians until 1889 when a federal court was established at Muskogee. See Wright, *Indian Tribes of Oklahoma*, 19.

16. Edwin C. McReynolds, *Oklahoma: A History of the Sooner State* (Norman: University of Oklahoma Press, 1964), 229-34.

17. H. Craig Miner, *The Corporation and the Indian: Tribal Sovereignty and Industrial Civilization in Indian Territory, 1865-1907* (Columbia: University of Missouri Press, 1976), 101. Miner's carefully researched work analyzes the complex interplay of corporate interests, tribal governments, and federal officials.

18. Ibid., 90.

19. Carl Coke Rister, *Land Hunger, David L. Payne and the Oklahoma Boomers* (New York: Arno Press, 1975).

20. Loren N. Brown, "The Establishment of the Dawes Commission for Indian Territory," *Chronicles of Oklahoma* 18 (June 1940): 176-77.

21. Ibid., 181.

22. Dawes, who was elderly, was not active after his first year on the commission.

23. Angie Debo, *And Still the Waters Run: The Betrayal of the Five Civilized Tribes* (Princeton: Princeton University Press, 1972), 24. Debo's study, originally published in 1940, remains a standard treatment on the subject.

24. Loren N. Brown, "The Dawes Commission," *Chronicles of Oklahoma* 9 (March 1931): 88-89.

25. Carlson, *Indians, Bureaucrats, and Land*, 115-30.

2. The Progressive Era, 1900-17

1. William T. Hagan, "Civil Service Commissioner Theodore Roosevelt and the Indian Rights Association," *Pacific Historical Review* 44 (May 1975): 187-200.

2. Garland grew up in Wisconsin and Iowa and lived briefly in Dakota Territory before reaching adulthood.

3. Frederick E. Hoxie, *A Final Promise: The Campaign to Assimilate the Indians, 1880-1920* (Lincoln: University of Nebraska Press, 1984), 103-107. Leupp's efforts to fit Indian affairs into western development included recruiting workers for private employers and various proposals to help whites start enterprises on reservations. On the Crow Reservation, for example, he attempted to arrange a long-term lease to promote sugar beet farming and a refinery.

4. Carlson points out that the number of allotments from 1881 to 1887 averaged 490 annually. From then to 1900 the figure increased to 2,733 per year. The average number then rose to 4,415 between 1900 and 1916 with peak years between 1907 and 1910. See Leonard A. Carlson, *Indians, Bureaucrats, and Land: The Dawes Act and the Decline of Indian Farming* (Westport, Connecticut: Greenwood Press, 1981), 73-75; J. P. Kinney, *A Continent Lost—A Civilization Won: Indian Land Tenure in America* (Baltimore: Johns Hopkins Press, 1937), 245.

5. 32 Stat. 275.

6. 34 Stat. 182.

7. See Felix S. Cohen, *Handbook of Federal Indian Law* (Washington: Government Printing Office, 1945), 354. The court reversed *Heff* in 1916.

8. 34 Stat. 1018.

9. 35 Stat. 444.

10. 36 Stat. 855.

11. A summary of the Omnibus Act can be found in Kinney, *A Continent Lost,* 249-63, 279-81.

12. Carlson, *Indians, Bureaucrats, and Land,* 185.

13. For the initial abuses and first safeguards, see Francis E. Leupp, *The Indian and His Problem* (New York: Charles Scribner's Sons, 1910), 66-69.

14. Kinney, *A Continent Lost,* 245-46.

15. 187 U.S. Reports 553-68. For background on the original agreement and the case, see William T. Hagan, *United States-Comanche Relations: The Reservation Years* (New Haven: Yale University Press, 1976), 281-84.

16. John Fahey, *The Flathead Indians* (Norman: University of Oklahoma Press, 1974), 296.

17. Ibid., 279.

18. Ibid., 256.

19. Burton M. Smith, "The Politics of Allotment: The Flathead Indian Reservation as a Case Study," *Pacific Northwestern Quarterly* 70 (July 1979): 132. Two other reservation openings which have been studied in depth allow comparisons with the Flathead experience. See Hagan, *United States-Comanche Relations,* 201-61 and Donald J. Berthrong, "Legacies of the Dawes Act: Bureaucrats and Land Thieves at the Cheyenne-Arapaho Agencies of Western Oklahoma," *Arizona and the West* 21 (Winter 1979): 335-54. Obviously additional research on openings is needed.

20. Smith, "The Politics of Allotment," 133-34.

21. Ibid., 134-35.

22. Ibid., 135; Fahey, *The Flathead Indians,* 295.

23. Smith, "Politics of Allotment," 134.

24. Dixon's worries were probably legitimate. In 1897 and 1900 a federal commission's attempts to secure Flathead lands failed badly when mixed bloods and Charlot, a traditionalist, united to block any agreement. Fahey, *The Flathead Indians,* 267, 277.

25. Smith, "Politics of Allotment," 137.

26. Ibid., 138.

27. Carlson, *Indians, Bureaucrats, and Land,* 30-31.

28. One facet of opening reservations, which scholars need to address, is how the process may have operated against the welfare of many white settlers. Lured by the prospect of cheap land and the false promises of dryland farming by real estate and newspaper interests, whites often settled geographic areas which did not permit a livelihood.

29. Janet A. McDonnell, "Land Policy on the Omaha Reservation: Competency Commissions and Forced Fee Patents," *Nebraska History* 63 (Fall 1982): 400.

30. Ibid., 400-401.

31. Ibid., 401-402.

32. Ibid., 402-405.

33. Ibid., 405-406.

34. Ibid., 406-407.

35. Keith W. Olson, *Biography of a Progressive: Franklin K. Lane, 1864-1921* (Westport, Connecticut: Greenwood Press, 1979), 59-71.

36. Janet Ann McDonnell, "The Disintegration of the Indian Estate: Indian Land Policy, 1913-1929" (Ph.D. diss., Marquette University, 1980), 100-106. See also McDonnell's "Competency Commissioners and Indian Land Policy, 1913-1920," *South Dakota History* 11 (Winter 1980): 21-34.

37. McDonnell, "The Disintegration of the Indian Estate," 106-13.

38. Ibid., 129.

39. The reservations included Cheyenne River, Coeur d'Alene, Crow, Flathead, Fort Hall, Fort Peck, Fort Totten, Santee, Sac and Fox, Shawnee, Shoshone, Sisseton, Standing Rock, Umatilla, Yankton, and Fort Berthold. Ibid., 113-19.

40. Francis Paul Prucha, *The Great Father: The United States Government and the American Indians,* vol. 2 (Lincoln: University of Nebraska Press, 1984), 881.

41. L. M. Gable to Lane, May 9, 1916, Department of Interior, Office of the Secretary, General Classified Files, 1907-1936, Competent Indians, National Archives, Record Group 48. Hereafter cited as NA, RG 48.

42. A transcript of the ceremony, which included an oath of citizenship and presentation of badges, is presented in McDonnell, "The Disintegration of the Indian Estate," 120-21.

43. *Washington Post,* June 13, 1906, 6.

44. W. O. Robert to Lane, June 26, 1916, Department of Interior, Office of the Secretary, General Classified Files, 1907-1936, NA, RG 48.

45. See Lane to McLaughlin and W. A. Meyer to Thackery, February 2, 1916, ibid.

46. Ibid.

47. Lawrence C. Kelly, *The Navajo Indians and Federal Indian Policy 1900-1935* (Tucson: University of Arizona Press, 1968), deals with the period under discussion. A recent tribal history is Garrick Bailey and Roberta Glenn Bailey, *A History of the Navajos: The Reservation Years* (Santa Fe: School of American Research Press, 1986).

48. Scabies are small mites which attach themselves to the skin of sheep. The parasites are not a serious health threat, but the irritation and scratching severely reduce wool yield.

49. David M. Brugge, *A History of the Chaco Navajos* (Albuquerque: National Park Service, Division of Chaco Research, 1980), 197.

50. Shelton to Commissioner of Indian Affairs, January 5, 1907, as quoted in Brugge, *Chaco Navajos,* 206.

51. Kelly, *The Navajo Indians,* 18-19. For more detail see J. Lee Correll and Alfred Dehiya, *Anatomy of the Navajo Reservation: How It Grew* (Window Rock, Arizona: Navajo Times Publishing Company, n.d.), 8-29.

52. Charles J. Kappler, comp., *Indian Affairs: Laws and Treaties,* vol. 3 (Washington: Government Printing Office, 1913), 699-70.

53. Ibid., 370.

54. Kelly, *The Navajo Indians,* 32.

55. Brugge, *Chaco Navajos,* 232.

56. Kappler, *Laws and Treaties,* vol. 3, 484. The frustration of finding quality land in national forests is discussed in the memoirs of two young field matrons stationed in a remote area of northern California. See Mary Ellicott Arnold and Mabel Reed, *In the Land of the Grasshopper Song: A Story of Two Girls in Indian Country in 1908-09* (New York: Vantage Press, 1957). The book was later reprinted by the University of Nebraska Press.

57. Stanley N. Murray, "The Turtle Mountain Chippewa, 1882-1905," *North Dakota History* 51 (Winter 1984): 32.

58. For a summary of the Papagos' experiences under United States rule, see Edward H. Spicer, *Cycles of Conquest: The Impact of Spain, Mexico, and the United States on the Indians of the Southwest, 1553-1960* (Tucson: University of Arizona Press, 1962), 134-46.

59. *Cong. Record,* 65th Cong., 2d sess., vol. 56: 4194.

60. 40 Stat. 562 and 41 Stat. 34.

61. Prucha, *Great Father,* vol. 2, 891-92.

62. Frederick E. Hoxie, "Beyond Savagery: The Campaign to Assimilate the Indians, 1880-1920" (Ph.D. diss., Brandeis University, 1977), 432.

63. Ibid., 423.

64. Ibid., 426-28.
65. For a summary of the Pimas' problems, see Alfonso Ortiz, "The Gila River Pima Water Problem: An Ethnohistorical Account," in Albert H. Schroeder, ed., *The Changing Ways of Southwestern Indians: A Historical Perspective* (Glorieta, New Mexico: Rio Grande Press, 1973), 245-57.
66. Larrabee to Secretary of Interior, July 17, 1905, Department of Interior Records, Office of the Secretary, NA, RG 48.
67. Leupp to Secretary of Interior, August 18, 1905, ibid.
68. Leupp to Secretary of Interior, August 18, 1905, ibid.
69. Norris Hundley, Jr., "The 'Winters' Decision and Indian Water Rights: A Mystery Reexamined," *Western Historical Quarterly* 13 (January 1982): 19-22. Hundley's earlier article, "The Dark and Bloody Ground of Indian Water Rights: Confusion Elevated to Principle," *Western Historical Quarterly* 9 (October 1978): 455-82, focuses more on the on-going debates which arose after the 1908 decision.
70. A miner's inch is a method of measuring the flow of water in cubic feet. It amounts to 2.5 cubic feet of flow per second. A more common (and understandable) measure is acre feet, which is the amount of water required to cover one acre to a one foot depth.
71. Riparian water rights are based on the theory only property owners along a stream can claim water from it. Their usage, however, requires they return the same volume and quality of water as was diverted.
72. Hundley, "The 'Winters' Decision," 23-25.
73. Ibid., 26-27.
74. *Winters et al. v. United States—Ninth Circuit Court of Appeals: Brief for Appellants* (n.p. [1905]), as quoted in ibid., 29.
75. The reserve rights doctrine had already been used by federal courts in a 1905 case involving Indian fishing rights in the Pacific Northwest, and it has become a cornerstone for all federally reserved lands. Hundley, "The Dark and Bloody Ground of Indian Water Rights," 469.
76. Ibid., 467-68. Hundley in his second article used agency records and the conventional legal wisdom of the period to conclude that Indians and the government both reserved water rights. See Hundley, "The 'Winters' Decision," f19.
77. Ibid., 40-42.
78. For a discussion of the congressional debates, see Hoxie, "Beyond Savagery," 477-80.
79. J. P. Kinney's writings have dominated the neglected field of Indian forestry. See Kinney, *A Continent Lost*, already cited and his *Indian Forest and Range: A History of the Administration and Conservation of the Redman's Heritage* (Washington: Forestry Enterprises, 1950). A more recent administration history, commissioned by the BIA, is Alan S. Newell, Richmond L. Clow, and Richard N. Ellis, *A Forest in Trust: Three-Quarters of a Century of Indian Forestry* (Washington: Bureau of Indian Affairs, 1986).
80. A matter of considerable importance on western reservations was the operation of agency sawmills during the post–Civil War. These typically were used to supply lumber for agency needs and to build houses for the Indians and not for commercial purposes.
81. Kinney, *Indian Forest*, 9.
82. Ibid., 7.
83. Ibid., 40.
84. Gifford Pinchot, *Breaking New Ground* (New York: Harcourt, Brace and Company, 1947), 411-12. One of the basic changes in Taft's administration was his "judicial style" which insisted upon statutory authority before executive action. This contrasted with Roosevelt's willingness to implement conservation whenever

no law prohibited action. See M. Nelson McGeary, *Gifford Pinchot: Forester-Politician* (Princeton, New Jersey: Princeton University Press, 1960), 113-26.

85. These frictions are best summarized in Newell et al., *A Forest in Trust,* 2-5 to 2-11.

86. Kinney, *Indian Forest,* 83-87.

87. Kinney, *A Continent Lost,* 265-68.

88. Ibid., 273.

89. Kinney, *Indian Forest,* 92-93. The underlying reasons for problems in 1910-1911 centered around Valentine and Assistant Commissioner Frederick H. Abbott's disagreement over the Ballinger-Pinchot controversy. Valentine's dismissal of the former superintendent of logging dealt with a troublesome timber sale in Wisconsin. Newell et al., *A Forest in Trust,* 2-20.

90. Kinney, *Indian Forest,* 183-90.

91. Kappler, *Laws and Treaties,* vol. 4, 636-53. For a summary of the episode, see Kinney, *Indian Forest,* 142-43.

92. An undated memorandum apparently details Roosevelt's position on the question. See Kappler, *Laws and Treaties,* vol. 4, 692-95.

93. Kinney, *Indian Forest,* 143.

94. Ibid.

3. Dissolving the Five Civilized Tribes

1. The standard treatment on the subject remains Angie Debo, *And Still the Waters Run: The Betrayal of the Five Civilized Tribes* (Princeton, New Jersey: Princeton University Press, 1972). Roy Gittinger, *The Formation of the State of Oklahoma* (Norman: University of Oklahoma Press, 1939) provides a carefully researched study of events leading to statehood. Two recent works include Danney Goble, *Progressive Oklahoma: The Making of a New Kind of State* (Norman: University of Oklahoma Press, 1980) and John Thompson, *Closing the Frontier: Radical Response in Oklahoma, 1889-1923* (Norman: University of Oklahoma Press, 1986).

2. Debo, *And Still the Waters Run,* 38-40.

3. Ibid., 31-60.

4. Ibid., 89-91.

5. Ibid., 117-19.

6. Ibid., 98-99.

7. Danney Goble's analysis of the leadership fits in with William A. Williams and James Williard Hurst's findings about the aggressive class of business leaders common between 1830 and 1890. Essentially, these men saw social interaction as a bruising individual struggle for personal achievement. The competition would result in moral progress, and the potential for success was, unlike Darwinian thought, infinite. John Thompson's interpretation relies more on cultural backgrounds. He sees eastern Oklahoma leaders as "lawless" southerners attempting to recreate the cotton economy and society of their native region. After they failed to develop a market economy in Oklahoma and depleted the soil by forcing tenants to grow cotton, their only source of profit was buying Indian land cheap and later selling it at higher prices. See Goble, *Progressive Oklahoma,* 38, and Thompson, *Closing the Frontier,* 10-11, 14-15.

8. Angie Debo to author, January 18, 1988, author's personal files.

9. For a summary of the Senate investigation, see Debo, *And Still the Waters Run,* 141-57. The hearings are available in U.S. Congress, Senate, *Report of the Select Committee to Investigate Matters Connected with Affairs in Indian Territory,* 59th Cong., 2d sess., November 11, 1906–January 9, 1907, 2 vols.

10. The circular letter, transcript of the Wewoka speeches, and a cover letter can

be found in R. S. Cate to Commissioner, June 27, 1911, File #58512-1911, General Files, 1907-1939, NA, RG 75.

11. Debo, *And Still the Waters Run*, 205-12.

4. The War to Assimilate All Indians

1. A. B. Genung, "Agriculture in the World War Period," in *An Historical Survey of American Agriculture* (Washington: Government Printing Office, 1941). This is a reprint from the *1940 Yearbook of Agriculture*, 277-96.

2. *Reports of the Department of the Interior, 1918*, vol. 2 (Washington: Government Printing Office, 1919), 16.

3. In my research, I encountered numerous published stories about hundreds of American Indians enlisting in the Canadian military before American intervention. Such enlistments seemed plausible because many tribes in the northern United States, especially in the Great Plains, had counterparts in Canada and both groups historically moved back and forth freely. Moreover, young men from plains tribes in the United States saw military service during the war as a means of gaining warrior status, and it seemed logical that some might have chosen to enlist in Canada before intervention. Despite a good deal of research, I found little evidence of this. Of the handful I could document, the best known was an impostor named Sylvester Long. A handsome mulatto from North Carolina, Long had attended Carlisle posing as a Cherokee. In 1916 he enlisted in the Canadian army, served in France, and claimed to have joined the British army. After the war he became a reporter in Calgary and eventually identified himself as Chief Buffalo Child Long Lance of the Canadian Bloods. Still later, I corresponded with Professor L. James Dempsey, a Canadian Indian scholar who earlier completed a thesis on the military participation of Indians from the prairie provinces. Dempsey agrees with my assessment that military service was a means of gaining warrior status, but he encountered no American Indians who enlisted in Canada. I finally concluded that some reporter wrote a false story on the subject during the pre-intervention phase, and later writers simply repeated it. For information on Sylvester Long, see Donald B. Smith, *Long Lance: The True Story of an Impostor* (Lincoln: University of Nebraska Press, 1983). L. James Dempsey to author, September 27, 1990, author's personal files.

4. *Reports of the Department of Interior, 1918*, vol. 2, 4-5.

5. Ibid., 4-5. See also David L. Wood, "Gosiute-Shoshone Draft Resistance, 1917-18," *Utah Historical Quarterly* 49 (Spring 1981): 174-75.

6. Sells's revisions seem unduly high. Even higher estimates, however, were given by Malcolm McDowell of the Board of Indian Commissioners who claimed that 15,000 Indians enlisted and "several thousand more" joined the Canadian military. McDowell's figures seem impossible since only 17,000 Indians registered for the draft in 1917, and a large number would have been rejected because of illiteracy or physical disabilities. See Malcolm McDowell, "Service as a Member of the United States Board of Indian Commissioners," in Frank C. Lockwood, *The Life of Edward E. Ayer* (Chicago: A. C. McClurg & Company, 1929), 227.

7. The controversy over integration vs. segregation is discussed in Michael L. Tate, "From Scout to Doughboy: The National Debate over Integrating American Indians into the Military, 1891-1918," *Western Historical Quarterly* 17 (October 1986): 417-37.

8. For background on Dixon, see the Records of the Third Wanamaker Expedition in the Records of the Bureau of Indian Affairs, File #3578-14-040, General Service, 1914, National Archives, Record Group 75. Hereafter cited as RBIA, NA, RG

75. Louis F. Phaller, "James McLaughlin and the Rodman Wanamaker Expedition of 1913," *North Dakota History* 44 (Spring 1977): 4-11 has additional information.

9. For Dixon's testimony, see U.S. Congress, House, Committee on Military Affairs, *North American Indian Cavalry*, 65th Cong., 1st sess., July 25, 1917, 3-27.

10. Tate, "From Scout to Doughboy," 428.

11. Ibid., 427.

12. *Reports of the Department of Interior, 1919*, vol. 2, 13-14.

13. Charles L. Davis to Commissioner, July 19, 1917, RBIA, General Services, File #49273-1917-926 (Part 2), NA, RG 75.

14. See RBIA, Orders, Circulars, Circular Letters, 1920-1921, Replies to Circular 1625, NA, RG 75.

15. Charley Peanum to Commissioner, May 11, 1917, RBIA, General Services, File #48831-1917-926, NA, RG 75.

16. W. M. Davis, F. Williams, T. Thompson to Commissioner, November 17, 1917, RBIA, General Services, File #107917-1917-926, NA, RG 75.

17. The Creek "uprising" started at a meeting at the Hickory Grounds near Mayetta, Oklahoma, on June 5, 1918. It is uncertain whether the meeting was to organize a Grand Army of the Republic unit, to resist the draft, or to secure a claim for loyalists of the Civil War. Ellen Perryman, a forty-year-old Creek, spoke at the meeting, and her behavior and statements led observers to question her rationality. A local reporter wrote a garbled and sensationalized account of the affair, and this touched off considerable hysteria in coming months. Rumors spread that the Creeks believed Germany would win the war and restore their land, that tribesmen would tear down whites' fences, torch barns and homes, and turn loose all livestock, or that the Indians were preparing to flee to Mexico. Perryman was finally arrested but later released without a hearing, and the hysteria apparently wore itself out. See RBIA, Classified Files, 1907-1939, Five Civilized Tribes, File #49330-1918-121, NA, RG 75.

18. Reports about German agents inciting Indians were fairly common and were indicative of the public wartime hysteria. For accounts of the events at the Goshute Reservation, see Richard Ellis, " 'Indians at Ibapah in Revolt': Goshutes, the Draft and the Indian Bureau, 1917-1919," *Nevada Historical Quarterly* 19 (Fall 1976): 163-70; and Wood, "Gosiute-Shoshone Draft Resistance," 173-88.

19. Ibid., 186.

20. *Arapaho Bee*, November 29, 1918.

21. *Calumet Cheftain*, March 27, 1919.

22. *Canadian Valley Record*, September 25, 1919.

23. *Thomas Tribune*, October 21, 1921 and January 12, 1922.

24. Garrick Bailey and Roberta Glenn Bailey, *A History of the Navajos: The Reservation Years* (Santa Fe: School of American Research Press, 1985), 118.

25. Hilda Faunce, *Desert Wife* (Lincoln: University of Nebraska Press, 1981), 289-94. David M. Brugge notes that Faunce used fictitious names in her book. She was married at the time to Winslow Wetherill, a member of a famous family of Navajo traders, and the owner of the post at Black Mountain was actually Lorenzo Hubbell whose main operation was at Ganado. Brugge agrees with me that Faunce's account probably exaggerated the actual danger of an uprising. Interview with David M. Brugge, June 23, 1993.

26. Ibid., 285-88.

27. "Annual Report: Office of the Superintendent of the Five Civilized Tribes, 1919," RBIA, NA, RG 75.

28. James McCarthy, *A Papago Traveler: The Memories of James McCarthy*, edited by John G. Westover (Tucson: University of Arizona, 1985), 68-87.

29. Ibid., 87-88.

30. Edgar K. Miller to Commissioner, January 27, 1921, RBIA, Orders, Circulars, and Circular Letters, Replies to Circular 1625, NA, RG 75.

31. *Reports of the Department of Interior, 1919,* vol. 2, 14-15.

32. Ibid., 15.

33. Robinson, *History of North Dakota,* 361.

34. Annual Narrative Report, 1918, Five Civilized Tribes, RBIA, NA, RG 75.

35. I encountered evidence that some Indians found jobs in automobile factories and that a crew of Hopis worked at a munitions plant in Tennessee. The Meriam Commission investigation in 1926-1927 found the remnants of "several hundred" Indians who worked at a steel plant in Torrance, California. The fifteen families who remained in the mid-1920s were regarded as skilled, intelligent, and ambitious working-class people who lived in neat bungalows. Charles Roberts's study of an Indian trade school in Tacoma indicates that local Indians took advantage of labor shortages and found high-paying jobs in shipbuilding and lumbering. See *The Problem of Indian Administration* (Baltimore: Johns Hopkins Press, 1928), 715-16 and Charles Roberts, "The Cushman Trades School and World War I," *American Indian Quarterly* 11 (Summer 1987): 224.

36. For a summary of World War I medical problems, see Diane Therese Putney, "Fighting the Scourge: American Indian Morbidity and Federal Policy, 1897-1928" (Ph.D. diss., Marquette University, 1980), 198-210. Roberts, "Cushman Trades School," 224-37, discusses both staffing shortages and the impact of influenza on students during the war and immediate postwar.

37. Funds rose to $14,500,000 in fiscal 1920 but dropped to $12,500,000 the following year. These figures reflect not only gratuitous appropriations but also reimbursable loans and money from tribal funds used for administration. See *The Annual Reports of the Department of Interior, II, 1917-1920.*

38. Ibid., *1917,* 3-4.

39. Ibid., 4.

40. Janet Ann McDonnell, "The Disintegration of the Indian Estate: Indian Land Policy, 1913-1929" (Ph.D. diss., Marquette University, 1980), 152-59.

41. *Annual Reports of the Department of Interior, 1917,* vol. 2, 336.

42. McDonnell, "Disintegration of the Indian Estate," 159-63.

43. *Annual Reports of the Department of Interior, 1919,* vol. 2, 3.

44. *Daily Oklahoman,* May 10, 1917, as quoted in David L. Wood, "American Indian Farmland and the Great War," *Agricultural History* 55 (July 1981): 250.

45. McDonnell, "Disintegration of the Indian Estate," 173-74.

46. Wood, "Indian Farmland and the Great War," 251.

47. Annual Narrative and Statistical Report, Cheyenne and Arapahoe Agency, 1917, Central Files, RBIA, NA, RG 75.

48. Annual Narrative Report, 1918, Rosebud Reservation, Central Files, RBIA, NA, RG 75.

49. For a general sketch on Campbell, see Hiram Drache, "Thomas D. Campbell—The Plower of the Plains," *Agricultural History* 51 (January 1977): 78-91.

50. This summary omits several details that are discussed in Wood, "American Indian Farmland," 256-57.

51. Ibid., 258.

52. Drache, "Thomas D. Campbell," 83. The corporation never operated on the Blackfoot and Shoshone reservations.

53. Wood, "Indian Farmland," 260.

54. *Annual Reports of the Department of Interior, 1917,* vol. 2, 29.

55. Gordon Macgregor, *Warriors without Weapons: A Study of the Society and Personality Development of the Pine Ridge Sioux* (Chicago: University of Chicago Press, 1946), 38-39.

56. Bailey and Bailey, *A History of the Navajos*, 118.
57. Faunce, *Desert Wife*, 278-79.
58. Bailey and Bailey, *A History of the Navajos*, 117.

5. From War to Depression, 1919-29

1. An interesting contrast can be seen in Gerald D. Nash's interpretation that "muted progressivism" typified western politics in the 1920s and Earl Pomeroy's view that conservatism dominated. In a sense both are right. Nash tends to deemphasize the immediate postwar, while Pomeroy concentrates on the conservatism of that period. See Gerald D. Nash, *The American West in the Twentieth Century: A Short History of an Urban Oasis* (Englewood Cliffs, New Jersey: Prentice-Hall, 1973), 109-20; and Earl Pomeroy, *The Pacific Slope: A History of California, Oregon, Washington, Idaho, Utah, and Nevada* (New York: Alfred A. Knopf, 1965), 215-45.

2. *Abstract of the Fifteenth Census of the United States, 1930* (Washington: Government Printing Office, 1933), 10. Oklahoma was an exception to population trends in the Great Plains as it added nearly 400,000 residents. Montana lost population.

3. Nash, *American West in the Twentieth Century*, 82.

4. Ralph C. Epstein, *The Automobile Industry: Its Economic and Commercial Development* (Chicago: A. W. Shaw Company, 1928), 13.

5. Nash, *American West in the Twentieth Century*, 91.

6. For a comparison of trucks to wagons for marketing, see John B. Rae, *The Road and the Car in American Life* (Cambridge: M.I.T. Press, 1971), 114, 129-30. The utility of trucks for transporting men and goods was demonstrated during World War I, and American production figures increased rapidly during the conflict and afterward. For a summary of the design changes that made trucks a more reliable and economical means of long-distance hauling, see James H. Thomas, *The Long Haul: Truckers, Truck Stops & Trucking* (Memphis: Memphis State University Press, 1979), 43-73. A useful overview is Merrill J. Roberts, "The Motor Transportation Revolution," *Business History Review* 30 (March 1956): 57-95.

7. *Fifteenth Census of the United States: 1930, Irrigation of Agricultural Lands* (Washington: Government Printing Office, 1932), 49-51.

8. Negotiation of the Santa Fe compact which divided the Colorado water among seven states and the legislation which authorized construction of Boulder Dam are covered in Norris Hundley, Jr., *Water and the West: The Colorado River Compact and the Politics of Water in the American West* (Berkeley: University of California Press, 1974), and Beverley Bowen Moeller, *Phil Swing and Boulder Dam* (Berkeley: University of California Press, 1971).

9. Ibid., 211-12, 341; Paul L. Kleinsorge, *The Boulder Canyon Project: Historical and Economic Aspects* (Palo Alto: Stanford University Press, 1941), 68-69.

10. See Donald L. Parman, "Inconstant Advocacy: The Erosion of Indian Fishing Rights in the Pacific Northwest, 1933-1956," *Pacific Historical Review* 53 (May 1984): 180.

11. Lawrence C. Kelly, *The Assault on Indian Assimilation: John Collier and the Origins of Indian Policy Reform* (Albuquerque: University of New Mexico Press, 1983), 151-57; *Dictionary of American Biography, Supplement Three, 1941-1945* (New York: Charles Scribner's Sons, 1973), 258-60.

12. *National Cyclopaedia of American Biography*, vol. 43 (New York: James T. White & Company, 1961), 141.

13. Kelly, *Assault on Assimilation*, 210-11.

14. Ibid., 213-16.

15. Ibid., 163-70.

16. Ibid., 170-71.

17. Ibid., 172.

18. Ibid., 173.

19. Ibid., 172-80.

20. Ibid., 180-81.

21. Ibid., 181-82. More detailed discussions of these council sessions can be found in Lawrence C. Kelly, *The Navajo Indians and Federal Indian Policy 1900-1935* (Tucson: University of Arizona Press, 1968), 48-55.

22. Ibid., 56-57. The normal distribution of revenues under the General Leasing Act was 52.5 percent to the reclamation fund, 37.5 percent to the states, and 10 percent to the federal government.

23. Ibid., 58. The legal rationale used by Fall paralleled that used when the Theodore Roosevelt administration transferred Indian timberlands on executive order reservations to the national forests in 1909.

24. Kelly, *Assault on Assimilation*, 185-87.

25. Ibid., 187-90, 246-51.

26. Collier's career before 1928 is discussed in detail by Kelly, *Assault on Assimilation*. Kenneth R. Philp, *John Collier's Crusade for Indian Reform 1920-1954* (Tucson: University of Arizona Press, 1977) covers Collier's entire career. Collier's autobiography, *From Every Zenith: A Memoir and Some Essays on Life and Thought* (Denver: Sage Books, 1963) and his other writings are useful but partisan.

27. Kelly, *Assault on Assimilation*, 110.

28. Collier, *From Every Zenith*, 126. Kelly points out that Collier's correspondence at the time is strangely silent on his impressions at Taos.

29. Ibid.

30. Stephen J. Kunitz, "The Social Philosophy of John Collier," *Ethnohistory* 18 (Summer 1971): 214-15.

31. Collier to Dr. Haynes, May 12, 1923 (1922?), John Collier Papers, Sterling Memorial Library, Yale University. Hereafter cited as Collier Papers.

32. Kelly, *Assault on Assimilation*, 355. Frear's support for Robert M. La Follette in 1924 cost him a seat on the Ways and Means Committee and assignment to the lowly Indian Affairs Committee, where he and Collier formed their alliance.

33. Ibid., 129-36. Collier claimed to have "read every report by each successive Indian commissioner since 1852 . . . " before taking up his new job. Collier, *From Every Zenith*, 131.

34. Kelly, *Assault on Assimilation*, 216-19.

35. Collier, *From Every Zenith*, 132. Collier's assertion is questionable.

36. Kelly, *Assault on Assimilation*, 220-21.

37. Ibid., 230-31, 236.

38. Ibid., 239-40.

39. Ibid., 241.

40. Ibid., 243-45.

41. Ibid., 245-46.

42. Ibid., 248-49.

43. Ibid., 252-53.

44. Ibid., 252-54.

45. Ibid., 295-99.

46. Ibid., 299-300.

47. Information on Hagerman, a former territorial governor and rancher, can be found in Kelly, *The Navajo Indians*, 62n.

48. Ibid., 61-72.

49. *Dictionary of American Biography, Supplement Three, 1941-1945* (New York: Charles Scribner's Sons, 1973), 845-46.

50. Kelly, *The Navajo Indians*, 72-75.

51. Ibid., 76-77.

52. Ibid., 77.
53. Ibid., 77-78.
54. Ibid., 78-81.
55. Ibid., 81-88.
56. Ibid., 88-103.
57. Philp, *John Collier's Crusade*, 85. The Newell tunnel was started in 1909 when a large-scale irrigation development was under way on the Flathead Reservation. The 2,000 foot tunnel was designed to divert water from the river to generate electricity to run pumps which would raise water to a higher level. After digging 1,700 feet at a cost of $101,685, the federal government abandoned the project two years later. J. F. McAlear, as told to Sharon Bergman, *The Fabulous Flathead* (Polson, Montana: The Reservation Pioneers, 1962), 98.
58. Cramton's involvement in the agreement was more than incidental. Sometime in 1925 he visited Polson where local whites feted him and encouraged his support of the power site development. Ibid., 99.
59. Philp, *John Collier's Crusade*, 86.
60. Collier and Representative Frear in 1926 visited the West to acquaint the latter with reservation conditions, and Collier wrote Wheeler requesting a meeting. Grorud was a Republican and former assistant state attorney general who had testified in favor of Wheeler when he was under indictment in 1924. Collier to Wheeler, August 22, 1926, Collier Papers. Burton K. Wheeler, with Paul F. Healy, *Yankee from the West: The Candid, Turbulent Life of the Yankee-born U.S. Senator from Montana* (Garden City, New York: Doubleday & Company, 1962), 237.
61. To Wheeler and many progressives, Anaconda, with its control over copper mining and smelting, as well as its interests in lumber, gas wells, and influential newspapers, ruled Montana politics and economy with a feudalistic control. Ibid., 316. Philp, *John Collier's Crusade*, 87.
62. See A. A. Grorud to Collier, November 2, 1927, Collier Papers. Wheeler was not related to the Montana senator, but was a well-known consulting engineer with interests in real estate, building, and investment. Collier's correspondence indicates that Wheeler represented other unnamed investors, which made his bid even more tenuous. *Who Was Who in America*, vol. 7 (Chicago: Marquis *Who's Who*, 1981), 608.
63. Philp, *John Collier's Crusade*, 101. Construction of a dam started in 1930 but was suspended a year later when the government granted an extension of the terms. The project was renewed in 1936 and completed two years later. The Kerr Dam was a major structure with a height of 204 feet and a top length of 450 feet. McAlear, *The Fabulous Flathead*, 108-11.
64. The Institute for Government Research in 1927 was incorporated into the Brookings Institution. Willoughby directed the Institute, and Meriam had conducted several major government retirement and job reclassification studies and served with the shipping board during World War I. For background on Meriam, see Donald T. Critchlow, "Lewis Meriam, Expertise, and Indian Reform," *The Historian* 43 (May 1981): 328-32.
65. Survey members and their backgrounds can be found in *The Problem of Indian Administration* (Baltimore: Johns Hopkins Press, 1928), 59. Field letters which Meriam wrote to Willoughby are in Donald L. Parman, ed., "Lewis Meriam's Letters during the Survey of Indian Affairs, 1926-1927 (Part I)," *Arizona and the West* 24 (Fall 1982): 253-80. For "Part II," see ibid. (Winter 1982): 341-70.
66. Lack of expertise on forestry did not seem to hamper survey members, but they recognized their lack of knowledge on irrigation called for a supplemental investigation by qualified personnel. A survey soon afterward produced a highly critical assessment. See Porter J. Preston and Charles A. Engle, "Report of Advisers on

Irrigation on Indian Reservations," *Hearings before a Subcommittee of the Committee on Indian Affairs, United States Senate,* 71st Cong., 2d sess., part 6, 2210-661.

67. The term *jurisdiction* covers various types of BIA facilities such as reservations, colonies, rancherias, hospitals, boarding schools, etc.

68 *The Problem of Indian Administration,* 87.

69. Ibid., 89-90.

70. Ibid., 346-429.

71. Ibid., 189-345.

72. Ibid., 433-34.

73. Ibid., 439-60.

74. Ibid., 472-80.

75. I strongly suspect that a fourth category, male migratory workers, could be added. The report does mention boarding school students who worked summers in sugar beet fields but makes little reference to adult laborers. For some idea of the latter, see James McCarthy, *A Papago Traveler: The Memories of James McCarthy,* ed. John G. Westover (Tucson: University of Arizona Press, 1985), 99-145.

76. *The Problem of Indian Administration,* 579-699.

77. Ibid., 699-705.

78. There were exceptions to this generalization, particularly in Sioux City, Phoenix, Albuquerque, and Santa Fe, where Indians had moved from local reservations or pueblos.

79. Ibid., 704-42. A revealing look at urban life is Anna Moore Shaw, *A Pima Past* (Tucson: University of Arizona Press, 1974), which traces her life from a reservation childhood through boarding school and rearing a family in Phoenix after World War I.

80. *The Problem of Indian Administration,* 736, 739-41.

81. Ibid., 689-90, 692.

82. Ibid., 113-28.

83. Collier apparently wanted some sort of investigation as early as January, 1927. See Collier to James W. Young, January 14, 1927, Collier Papers.

84. Philp, *John Collier's Crusade,* 83.

85. In a letter to Senator Frazier after the release of the Meriam report, Collier praised the findings on health, education, and economic self-support, but he believed that it overlooked or slighted reimbursable charges and the need for separate Indian courts and protection of Indian property. Collier to Lynn Frazier, May 23, 1928, Collier Papers.

86. The original group was chaired by Frazier of North Dakota, and included La Follette of Wisconsin, Wheeler of Montana, and W. B. Pine and Elmer Thomas of Oklahoma.

87. Louis R. Glavis of Pinchot-Ballinger fame acted as the first special investigator, and A. A. Grorud became the second around 1930 or 1931.

6. Depression and the New Deal

1. Earl Pomeroy, *The Pacific Slope: A History of California, Oregon, Washington, Idaho, Utah, and Nevada* (New York: Alfred A. Knopf, 1965), 294-97.

2. The most comprehensive treatment of the New Deal in the West is Richard Lowitt, *The New Deal and the West* (Bloomington: Indiana University Press, 1984). Gerald D. Nash, *The American West in the Twentieth Century: A Short History of an Urban Oasis* (Englewood Cliffs, New Jersey: Prentice-Hall, 1973), 139-91, contains a summary.

3. Lowitt, *The New Deal and the West,* 100-21.

4. Ibid., 226-27.

5. Joseph H. Cash and Herbert T. Hoover, eds., *To Be an Indian: An Oral History* (New York: Holt, Rinehart, and Winston, 1971), 152.

6. Ibid., 172-73.

7. Timber sales offers one example. The BIA restricted cutting after 1925 because of a slow market, but during 1931 lumber prices declined sharply when the construction industry went flat. Indian timber revenues fell from $2,313,644 in 1930 to $1,238,814 in 1931. *Annual Report of the Commissioner of Indian Affairs, 1931* (Washington: Government Printing Office, 1931), 24.

8. Donald L. Parman, *The Navajos and the New Deal* (New Haven: Yale University Press, 1976), 23-24.

9. A discussion of Oklahoma Indians' distress prior to the New Deal is B. T. Quinten, "Oklahoma Tribes, the Great Depression and the Indian Bureau," *Mid-America* 49 (January 1967): 29-43.

10. Scattergood was given unusual authority, which has prompted some writers to refer to this as the "Rhoads-Scattergood administration."

11. Donald T. Critchlow, "Lewis Meriam, Expertise, and Indian Reform," *The Historian* 43 (May 1981): 335-37. For a general summary, see William G. Robbins, "Herbert Hoover's Indian Reformers under Attack: The Failures of Indian Reform," *Mid-America* 63 (October 1981): 157-70.

12. Kenneth R. Philp, *John Collier's Crusade for Indian Reform 1920-1954* (Tucson: University of Arizona Press, 1977), 92-95.

13. *Annual Report of the Commissioner of Indian Affairs, 1931* (Washington: Government Printing Office, 1931), 3-4.

14. Critchlow, "Lewis Meriam," 339-40.

15. Philp, *John Collier's Crusade*, 96.

16. Critchlow, "Lewis Meriam," 338.

17. Philp, *John Collier's Crusade*, 111.

18. Ibid., 111-12.

19. For background on progressive Republicans in this period, see Ronald L. Feinman, *Twilight of Progressivism: The Western Republican Senators and the New Deal* (Baltimore: Johns Hopkins University Press, 1981).

20. Lawrence C. Kelly's account of Collier's appointment corrects Collier's misleading autobiographical account. See "Choosing the New Deal Indian Commissioner: Ickes vs. Collier," *New Mexico Historical Review* 49 (October 1974): 269-88.

21. Donald L. Parman, "The Indian and the Civilian Conservation Corps," *Pacific Historical Review* 40 (February 1971): 40-44.

22. A detailed discussion and analysis of the original bill is included in Vine Deloria, Jr. and Clifford M. Lytle, *The Nations Within: The Past and Future of American Indian Sovereignty* (New York: Pantheon Books, 1984), 66-79. The standard work on Indian reorganization is Graham D. Taylor, *The New Deal and American Indian Tribalism: The Administration of the Indian Reorganization Act, 1934-45* (Lincoln: University of Nebraska Press, 1980).

23. Deloria and Lytle, *The Nations Within*, 80-81.

24. Ibid., 101-21.

25. Ibid., 122-39.

26. The question of Papago mining had a considerable background, and Ashurst used the first day of Senate hearings to defend white mining rights even though the issue had nothing to do with the bill. Collier's acceptance of Ashurst's position sacrificed Wilbur's withdrawal order to secure passage of the reorganization bill. See ibid., 123.

27. Ibid., 142.

28. Parman, *The Navajos and the New Deal*, 67-78.

29. Laurence M. Hauptman, "The American Indian Federation and the Indian

New Deal: A Reinterpretation," *Pacific Historical Review* 52 (August 1983): 378-402. Hauptman's article emphasizes the AIF served as an umbrella organization and that the component groups did not entirely share the same outlook. All, however, shared the three basic goals discussed above.

30. 99 Stat. pt. 1: 378.

31. Peter M. Wright, "John Collier and the Oklahoma Indian Welfare Act of 1936," *Chronicles of Oklahoma* 50 (Autumn 1972): 347-71.

32. Thomas Biolsi, "Organizing the Lakota: The Indian New Deal" (Ph.D. diss., Columbia University, 1987), 144. The copy loaned to the author was an early draft, and the pages cited will not correspond to his final version. His revised diss. was recently published as *Organizing the Lakota: The Political Economy of the New Deal on the Pine Ridge and Rosebud Reservations* (Tucson: University of Arizona Press, 1992).

33. Ibid., 48-49.

34. Ibid., 56-57.

35. Ibid., Chapter 3, 31.

36. Ibid., 186.

37. Ibid., 186-208.

38. Ibid., 220-45.

39. Parman, *Navajos and the New Deal*, 160.

40. Ibid., 161-66.

41. Ibid., 166-68.

42. Ibid., 263.

43. Collier may have accepted the reductions for land purchases to avoid the hostility of western congressmen. See Taylor, *The New Deal and American Indian Tribalism*, 140.

44. Lawrence C. Kelly, "The Indian Reorganization Act: The Dream and the Reality," *Pacific Historical Review* 45 (August 1975): 302-305.

45. Taylor, *The New Deal and American Indian Tribalism*, 132.

46. Parman, *The Navajos and the New Deal*, 104-12.

47. For Wheeler's earlier ties with Roosevelt see his autobiography, *Yankee from the West: The Candid, Turbulent Life of the Yankee-born U.S. Senator from Montana* (Garden City, New York: Doubleday & Company, 1962), 294-95, 297-98, 302-305.

48. Ibid., 315. Philp, *John Collier's Crusade for Indian Reform*, 199.

49. Feinman, *Twilight of Progressivism*, 85-90.

50. David H. Dinwoodie, "Indians, Hispanos, and Land Reform: A New Deal Struggle in New Mexico," *Western Historical Quarterly* 17 (July 1986): 300-306.

51. Parman, *Navajos and the New Deal*, 132-59.

52. Ibid.

53. Hauptman, "The American Indian Federation," 393-99.

54. Philp, *John Collier's Crusade*, 198.

55. Donald Lee Parman, "The Indian Civilian Conservation Corps" (Ph.D. diss., University of Oklahoma, 1967), 217-19.

56. Parman, *Navajos and the New Deal*, 270.

57. Parman, "The Indian Civilian Conservation Corps," 222-29.

7. World War II

1. Gerald D. Nash, *The American West Transformed: The Impact of the Second World War* (Bloomington: Indiana University Press, 1985), 5-6.

2. Ibid., 17-23. Also see Leonard J. Arrington, *The Changing Structure of the Mountain West, 1850-1950* (Logan: Utah State University Press, 1963), 23.

3. "Indians Conserving and Rebuilding Their Resources through CCC-ID," *Indians at Work* 9 (November 1941): 33-34.

4. For an article that provides a great deal of insight into the importance of military installations, see Leonard J. Arrington and Archer L. Durham, "Anchors Aweigh in Utah: The U.S. Supply Depot at Clearfield, 1942-1962," *Utah Historical Quarterly* 31 (Spring 1963): 109-26.

5. Alison Ricky Bernstein, "Walking in Two Worlds: American Indians and World War Two" (Ph.D. diss., Columbia University, 1986), 120-21. Bernstein's revised dissertation has recently been published. See *American Indians and World War II: Toward a New Era in Indian Affairs* (Norman: University of Oklahoma Press, 1991).

6. Dover P. Trent, "The Use of Indian Manpower," *Indians at Work* 12 (January–February 1945): 6-9.

7. John Useem, Gordon Macgregor, and Ruth Hill Useem, "Wartime Employment and Cultural Adjustments of the Rosebud Sioux," *Applied Anthropology* 2 (January–March 1943): 1-9. The city in the original article was not named, but John and Ruth Hill Useem recall that it was Rapid City. Ruth Hill Useem to author, April 30, 1993, author's personal files.

8. "Indians in the News," *Indians at Work* 9 (March 1942): 21.

9. Garrick Bailey and Roberta Glenn Bailey, *A History of the Navajos: The Reservation Years* (Santa Fe: School American Research Press, 1986), 199.

10. Broderick H. Johnson, ed., *Navajos and World War II* (Tsaile, Arizona: Navajo Community College Press, 1977), 48-49.

11. Jeanne Clark, "Indian Women Harness Old Talents to New War Jobs," *Indians at Work* 10 (Nos. 2-6, 1943): 25-28; Bernstein, "Walking in Two Worlds," 124-26.

12. Katherine Archibald, *Wartime Shipyard: A Study in Social Disunity* (Berkeley: University of California Press, 1947), 105.

13. Bernstein, "Walking in Two Worlds," 275-81.

14. *Annual Report of the Secretary of Interior, 1945* (Washington: Government Printing Office, 1946), 249. The figure did not include officers or members of non-recognized tribes. For the 1944 survey, see Trent, "The Use of Indian Manpower," 6-9.

15. Bernstein, "Walking in Two Worlds," 35. Indians in Oklahoma, Kansas, Nebraska, Texas, and parts of California registered with county officials.

16. Donald L. Parman, *Navajos and the New Deal* (New Haven: Yale University Press, 1976), 281-82.

17. T. B. Hall to Collier, October 17, 1940, Records of the Bureau of Indian Affairs, Central Classified Files, 1907-52, National Defense Program, Sells Agency, National Archives, Record Group 75. Hereafter cited as RBIA, NA, and RG.

18. Clippings from the *Arizona Star*, May 21, 1941 and n.d. in ibid. Also see Elmer W. Flaccus, "Arizona's Last Great Indian War: The Saga of Pia Machita," *Journal of Arizona History* 22 (Spring 1981): 1-22.

19. Seth Wilson to William Zimmerman, Jr., May 2, 1941, RBIA, File no. 34976-1941-125, Hopi, NA, RG 75.

20. Wilson to Zimmerman, May 29, 1941, ibid.

21. Wilson to Collier, March 3, 1942, ibid.

22. Bernstein, "Walking in Two Worlds," 33-37. The army partly carried out Morgan's proposal by setting up a special camp at Fort Wingate, New Mexico, to teach Navajos sufficient English and basic military skills to permit their entry into service. This was obviously needed as Selective Service classified 88 percent of Navajos between eighteen and thirty-five as illiterate.

23. "U.S. Air Force Commander in Hawaii Is a Member of Osage Tribe of Oklahoma," *Indians at Work* 9 (January 1942): 13-15; James L. Crowder, Jr., "Osage Aviator: The Life and Career of Major General Clarence L. Tinker," *Chronicles of Oklahoma* 65 (Winter 1987-1988): 400-31.

24. Samuel Eliot Morison, *History of United States Naval Operations in World War II*, vol. 4: *Coral Sea, Midway and Submarine Operations* (Boston: Little, Brown and Company, 1949), 151.

25. Philip Johnston, "Indian Jargon Won Our Battles," *Masterkey* 38 (October–December 1964): 131-32.

26. Ibid., 132-33.

27. For the complete vocabulary, see Doris A. Paul, *The Navajo Code Talkers* (Bryn Mawr, Pennsylvania: Dorrance & Company, 1973), 23-29. Paul also includes several key documents dealing with the subject.

28. For two interviews of Navajos who served in the 200th, see Johnson, *Navajos and World War II*, 12-44, 123-27. Childer and Montgomery are mentioned in "Indian Heroism Honored," *Indians at Work* 12 (May–June 1944): 4-5 and "David from Oklahoma," ibid., 12 (January–February 1945): 30-31.

29. For a sampling of Indians' attitudes, see Margretta Stewart Dietrich, comp., *Doing Fine and Thanks a Million* (Santa Fe: N.p., 1943), and *Hello and Many Lucks* (Santa Fe: Santa Fe Press, 1945).

30. Johnson, *Navajos and World War II*, 12-44, 127.

31. James H. Howard, "The Dakota Victory Dance World War II," *North Dakota History* 18 (January 1951): 31-40.

32. Johnson, *Navajos and World War II*, 59-61.

33. Dietrich, *Hello and Many Lucks*, 38-39.

34. Bernstein, "Walking in Two Worlds," 63-65.

35. John Collier, [Editorial] *Indians at Work* 9 (January 1942): 1-4.

36. Bernstein, "Walking in Two Worlds," 176-77. For Collier's views on lowered morale, see [Editorial] *Indians at Work* 10 (July–September 1942): 1-5.

37. Hildegard Thompson, *The Navajos' Long Walk for Education: A History of Navajo Education* (Tsaile, Arizona: Navajo Community College Press, 1975), 74-77.

38. *Annual Report of the Secretary of Interior, 1944*, 249.

39. *Annual Report of the Secretary of Interior, 1946*, 366.

40. Alan S. Newell, Richmond Clow, and Richard N. Ellis, *A Forest in Trust: Three-Quarters of a Century of Indian Forestry* (Washington: Bureau of Indian Affairs, 1986), 4-13.

41. *Annual Report of the Secretary of Interior, 1946*, 351.

42. *Annual Report of the Secretary of Interior, 1945*, 239. The BIA remained concerned about overgrazing on the Navajo, Hopi, and Papago Reservations. On the Navajo Reservation, a continuation of livestock reduction and outside employment caused livestock numbers to drop below the grazing capacity.

43. *Annual Report of the Secretary of Interior, 1946*, 372.

44. Ibid., 365.

45. Bernstein, "Walking in Two Worlds," 142-44.

46. *Annual Report of the Secretary of Interior, 1943*, 278-79; *Annual Report of the Secretary of Interior, 1945*, 235.

47. *Annual Report of the Secretary of Interior, 1942*, 233-35; Bernstein, "Walking in Two Worlds," 144-46.

48. Dillon S. Myer, "An Autobiography of Dillon S. Myer" (Berkeley: University of California Oral History Office). Copy from the Truman Library.

49. Bernstein, "Walking in Two Worlds," 148-51.

50. Ibid., 169-73.

51. Ibid., 178.

52. Senate Committee on Indian Affairs, *Survey of Conditions among the Indians of the United States*, 78th Cong., 1st sess., 1943, S. Rept 310, 2:1-22.

53. Bernstein, "Walking in Two Worlds," 182-83. Collier was probably right because several key examples in the report were drawn from Montana, the home state of Grorud and his ally Wheeler.

54. Ibid., 187-90.

55. Mundt sponsored the resolution which created the House investigation, but James F. O'Connor of Montana chaired the select committee. Mundt, however,

served as acting chairman at times and showed the most interest in the proceedings.

56. The questions for tribal council and Indian leaders concerned local problems and government services, liquor laws, fish and game regulations, possible revotes on the IRA, law and order jurisdiction, removal of trust restrictions, elimination of unneeded services, and claims. The questions for superintendents dealt more with statistical data on their reservations.

57. House Committee on Indian Affairs, *Investigate Indian Affairs, Hearings before the Committee on Indian Affairs on H. R. 166*, 78th Cong., 2nd sess., 1944, parts 2-4.

58. House Select Committee to Investigate Indian Affairs and Conditions in the United States, *An Investigation to Determine Whether the Changed Status of the Indian Requires a Revision of the Laws and Regulations Affecting the American Indian*, 78th Cong., 2nd sess., 1944, H. Rept. 2091, 1-20.

59. Bernstein, "Walking in Two Worlds," 203-208; N. B. Johnson, "The National Congress of American Indians," *Chronicles of Oklahoma* 30 (Summer 1952): 140-43.

60. Bernstein, "Walking in Two Worlds," 206-207.

61. Ibid., 212-20. Part of my discussion is drawn from Dorothy R. Parker's "Choosing an Indian Identity: A Biography of D'Arcy McNickle" (Ph.D. diss., University of New Mexico, 1988). Parker's study has recently been published. See *Singing an Indian Song: A Biography of D'Arcy McNickle* (Lincoln: University of Nebraska Press, 1992).

62. N. B. Johnson, "The National Congress of American Indians," *The American Indian* 3 (Summer 1946): 1-4.

63. Kenneth R. Philp notes that Representative Jed Johnson of Oklahoma demanded that Collier resign because he remained on the payroll while establishing residence in Nevada. See Philp's *John Collier's Crusade for Indian Reform 1920-1954* (Tucson: University of Arizona Press, 1977), 210. See also John Leiper Freeman, "The New Deal for Indians: A Study in Bureau-Committee Relations" (Ph.D. diss., Princeton University, 1952), 456-61. Freeman tentatively suggests that Johnson and other members of the Subcommittee on Interior Appropriations threatened severe cuts in BIA funds for fiscal 1946 unless Collier resigned.

64. Collier's resignation letter and a general farewell statement are contained in *Indians at Work* 12 (January–February 1945): 1-5.

8. The Postwar Era, 1945-61

1. Donald L. Parman, "Inconstant Advocacy: The Erosion of Indian Fishing Rights in the Pacific Northwest," *Pacific Historical Review* 53 (May 1984): 182-83.

2. Gerald D. Nash, *The American West in the Twentieth Century: A Short History of an Urban Oasis* (Englewood Cliffs, New Jersey: Prentice-Hall, 1973), 233.

3. S. Lyman Tyler, "William A. Brophy 1945-48," in Robert M. Kvasnicka and Herman J. Viola, eds., *The Commissioners of Indian Affairs, 1824-1977* (Lincoln: University of Nebraska Press, 1979), 284.

4. Clayton R. Koppes, "From New Deal to Termination: Liberalism and Indian Policy, 1933-1953," *Pacific Historical Review* 46 (November 1977): 543-66.

5. Harry S. Truman, *Memoirs by Harry S. Truman, Year of Decisions*, vol. 1 (Garden City, New York: Doubleday & Company, 1955), 553-55; Larry J. Hasse, "Termination and Assimilation: Federal Indian Policy, 1943 to 1961" (Ph.D. diss., Washington State University, 1974), 73.

6. Ibid., n. 69.

7. Ibid., 81-86.

8. Ibid., 70-71.

9. Ibid., 100-104.

10. Ibid., 92-96; James E. Officer, "Termination as Federal Policy: An Overview," in Kenneth R. Philp, ed., *Indian Self-Rule: First-Hand Accounts of Indian-White Relations from Roosevelt to Reagan* (Salt Lake: Howe Brothers, 1986), 120-21.

11. Hasse, "Termination and Assimilation," 94-96.

12. John Adair and Evon Vogt, "Navajo and Zuni Veterans: A Study of Contrasting Modes of Cultural Change," *American Anthropologist* 51 (October–December 1949): 547-61. Also see John Adair, ed., *Life Histories of Six Zuni Young Men: Microcard Publication of Primary Records in Culture and Personality*, ed. Bert Kaplan, vol. 1, no. 23 (Madison, Wisconsin: Microcard Foundation, 1956), 108-25.

13. Adair and Vogt, "Navajo and Zuni Veterans," 551-54.

14. Alison Ricky Bernstein, "Walking in Two Worlds: American Indians and World War II" (Ph.D. diss., Columbia University, 1986), 84-86. See also Gerald Nash, *The American West Transformed: The Impact of the Second World War* (Bloomington: Indiana University Press, 1985), 145-46. Albert Hemingway, *Ira Hayes, Pima Marine* (Lanham, Maryland: University Press of America, 1988) contains background information about Hayes's military experiences.

15. Eric T. Hagberg and Robert Bunker, "Pueblo Sovereignty, Postwar," *New Mexico Quarterly Review* 18 (Summer 1948): 223-27.

16. Daniel McCool, "Indian Voting," in Vine Deloria, Jr., ed., *American Indian Policy in the Twentieth Century* (Norman: University of Oklahoma Press, 1985), 105-34, offers a summary of Indian voting rights. See also the Truman Papers, Files of Philleo Nash, Harry S. Truman Library, Independence, Missouri. Hereafter cited as Nash Files.

17. The most detailed discussion of the background of the 1946 claims act is Harvey Daniel Rosenthal, "Their Day in Court: A History of the Indian Claims Commission" (Ph.D. diss., Kent State University, 1976), 10-26. A summary can be found in the United States Indian Claims Commission, *Final Report* (Washington: Government Printing Office, 1979).

18. Rosenthal, "Their Day in Court," 26-60. Suits before 1946 produced awards of $49.4 million, but $29.4 million was deducted in gratuitous offsets, leaving $20 million for the tribes. Ibid., 55.

19. 60 Stat. 1049.

20. The first appointees included Chief Commissioner Edgar E. Witt of Texas and Commissioners Louis J. O'Marr of Wyoming and William M. Holt of Nebraska.

21. Rosenthal, "Their Day in Court," 156.

22. Ibid., 157-58.

23. Ibid., 170-71.

24. Ibid., 161-64.

25. Claims Commission, *Final Report*, 12-18.

26. Francis Paul Prucha, *Great Father: The United States Government and the American Indians*, vol. 2 (Lincoln: University of Nebraska Press, 1984), 1022.

27. The commission's refusal to allow interest followed an earlier Supreme Court ruling which held that "Congress, not this Court or other federal courts, is the custodian of the national purse." No doubt the commission also recognized that Congress would balk at interest payments costing several billion dollars. In one case, for example, the interest on a $3 million reward would have amounted to $15 million.

28. "Systematic Discrimination in the Indian Claims Commission: The Burden of Proof in Redressing Historical Wrongs," *Iowa Law Review* 57 (June 1972): 1300-19.

29. "Press Release from All-Pueblo Council of New Mexico," June 17, 1947, Nash Files.

30. "A Petition on Behalf of American Indians of New Mexico and Arizona," January 12, 1949, ibid.

31. The Hopi Reservation was solely in Arizona, but the Navajo Reservation was

divided between Arizona, New Mexico, and Utah. As critics quickly noted, confusion would have resulted for both states and Navajos if Fernandez's amendment had passed.

32. The 80 percent formula had been preceded by a conference in Santa Fe in April, 1949. Federal representatives and the two states agreed that Arizona and New Mexico would pay no more than 10 percent of public assistance costs. The Senate conferees objected to this because part of the funding was dependent on the availability of BIA appropriations. See William J. Cohen, "Public Assistance Provisions for Navajo and Hopi Indians: Public Law 474," ca. April 1950, Nash Files.

33. House Committee of Conference, *Conference Report*, 81st Cong., 1st sess., 1949, House Report 1338, 6: 1-8.

34. John Collier, "Hour of Crisis for American Indians," *New York Herald Tribune*, October 4, 1949, clipping in Nash Files.

35. Peter Campbell Brown to Stephen J. Springarn, October 14, 1949, and J. A. Krug to Frank Paw, Jr., October 15, 1949, ibid.

36. Senate Committee on Interior and Insular Affairs, *Message from the President of the United States*, 81st Cong., 1st sess., 1949, S. Document 119.

37. The total funds authorized under the Rehabilitation Act and related legislation were $108,570,000, but the amount actually appropriated was $89,946,240. See Garrick Bailey and Roberta Glenn Bailey, *A History of the Navajos: The Reservation Years* (Santa Fe: School of American Research Press, 1986), 234.

38. Parman, "Inconstant Advocacy," 182-85.

39. The dams built on the Columbia, Snake, and Missouri were not the only such projects completed after World War II. Other western reservations affected by river developments included Fort Mohave, Chemehuevi Valley, Colorado River, Yuma, and Gila Bend. See Michael L. Lawson, *Dammed Indians: The Pick-Sloan Plan and the Missouri River Sioux, 1944-1980* (Norman: University of Oklahoma Press, 1982), xxi-xxii.

40. Ibid., 17.

41. Ibid., 12-13.

42. Ibid., 15-16.

43. Ibid., 18-19. Additional background is provided by Roy W. Meyer, "Fort Berthold and the Garrison Dam," *North Dakota History, Journal of the Plains* 35 (Summer–Fall 1968): 239-44.

44. Lawson, *Dammed Indians*, 20-21, 27-29.

45. Ibid., 29-30.

46. Ibid., 59-60.

47. Ibid., 158-59; Meyer, "Fort Berthold," 321-25.

48. For a critical assessment of Myer, see Richard Drinnon, *Keeper of Concentration Camps: Dillon S. Myer and American Racism* (Berkeley: University of California Press, 1987).

49. Dillon S. Myer, "An Autobiography of Dillon S. Myer" (Berkeley: University of California Oral History Office, 1970), 185. Copy from the Truman Library.

50. Hasse, "Termination and Assimilation," 115.

51. Myer, "Autobiography," 257-70.

52. Hasse, "Termination and Assimilation," 127-29.

53. Myer, "Autobiography," 302-304.

54. Ibid., 258-59. Hasse, "Termination and Assimilation," 129-31.

55. Myer, "Autobiography," 261-66.

56. *Congressional Record*, 81st cong., 2nd sess., July 27, 1950, 11240-41, 11255-56.

57. Ibid., December 15, 1950, 16603-604.

58. Prucha, *Great Father*, vol. 2, 1032.

59. Hasse, "Termination and Assimilation," 144-47.

60. Clipping from *Salt Lake Tribune*, ca. May 13, 1950, in Files of Governors Patter-

son, McKay, and Hall, 1948-1955, Oregon State Archives Division, Salem, Oregon. Hereafter cited as Oregon Archives.

61. See "Committees" attached to "Governors' Interstate Indian Council, News Letter No. 1," July 21, 1950, Files of Governors Patterson, McKay, and Hall, 1948-1955, Oregon Archives. See also "Newsletter No. 4," November 21, 1951, ibid.

62. "News Letter No. 1," ibid.

63. A. H. Wright to Jarle Leirfallon, February 1, 1952, Files of Governors Patterson, McKay, and Hall, 1948-1955, Oregon Archives.

64. A. H. Wright to Douglas McKay, June 25, 1952, ibid.

65. According to Theodore W. Taylor, *The States and Their Indian Citizens* (Washington: Department of Interior, 1972), 89-90, 176-77, Colorado, Oregon, and Washington had no director or coordinator involved in Indian affairs. In his more recent book, *American Indian Policy* (Mt. Airy, Maryland: Lomond Publications, 1983), 108-20, Taylor lists the three states as having some form of organization.

66. For a transcript of Myer's speech, see "Press Release," December 9, 1952, in *John Collier Papers, 1922-1969* (Sanford, North Carolina: Microfilming Corporation of America, 1980), Reel 43.

67. Hasse, "Termination and Assimilation," 163-64.

68. For Eisenhower's general speeches, see *New York Times*, August 21, 1953, 12 and October 7, 1952, 22. Also see Elmo Richardson, *Dams, Parks & Politics: Resource Development & Preservation in the Truman-Eisenhower Era* (Lexington: University Press of Kentucky, 1973), 71-80. For his statements on Indian affairs, see *New York Times*, August 11, 1952, 1, 10 and "Excerpts from Remarks by Dwight D. Eisenhower . . . ," August 10, 1952, Intertribal Indian Ceremonial, Official Files, Box 618, Dwight D. Eisenhower Library, Abilene, Kansas. Hereafter cited as Eisenhower Library. This document also contains the Republican platform statement on Indian affairs and excerpts from other Eisenhower western speeches.

69. Lewis was a Phoenix attorney with background experience in irrigation and water rights litigation. He had little understanding of Indian affairs, although that, along with land management, fish and wildlife, and territories, made up his responsibilities. As a conservative, he readily agreed with Watkins and fellow terminationists. Hasse, "Termination and Assimilation," 175-76.

70. Lewis to William Langer, July 10, 1953, Official Files, Box 618, Eisenhower Library.

71. "Oral History Interview with Arthur Watkins in January 4, 1968, by Ed Edwin," Eisenhower Library.

72. "Oral History Interview with O. Hatfield Chilson, by Thomas F. Soapes, March 1, 1976," Eisenhower Library.

73. Leonard J. Arrington, *Brigham Young: American Moses* (New York: Alfred A. Knopf, 1985), 211. What adds to the puzzle is the fact that none of Watkins's records on Indian affairs were deposited with his papers.

74. Arthur V. Watkins, "Termination of Federal Supervision: The Removal of Restrictions Over Indian Property and Person," *Annals of the American Academy of Political and Social Science* 311 (May 1957), 47-55.

75. "Watkins Interview, January 4, 1968."

76. 67 Stat. B132. The House report offers a very full explanation of the resolution and its background reasoning. See House, *Expressing the Sense of Congress that Certain Tribes of Indians Should Be Freed From Federal Supervision, H. Rept. 841 to accompany H. Con. Res. 108*, 83d Cong., 1st sess., 1953.

77. Three reservations, Red Lake in Minnesota, Menominee in Wisconsin, and Warm Springs in Oregon, were exempted from the law. All were regarded as having adequate law enforcement.

78. 67 Stat. 588-90.

79. Hasse, "Termination and Assimilation," 188. Senator Hugh Butler of Ne-

braska was prominent in advocating termination well before the Eisenhower administration, but I was never able to establish any compelling reason for his actions. His personal papers indicate that a few constituents wrote him about Indian problems, but no major vested interest in Nebraska seemed interested. Butler's involvement may have been simply a quirk. See Hugh Butler Papers, Box 132, Nebraska State Historical Society, Lincoln, Nebraska.

80. George M. Tunison to Eisenhower, May 12, 1954, General Files, Box 1163, Eisenhower Library.

81. Press Release #295, August 15, 1953, Official Files, Box 618, Eisenhower Library.

82. Watkins to Bernard M. Shanley, July 9, 1954, Official Files, Box 612, Eisenhower Library.

83. Lewis to Charles F. Willis, Jr., June 5, 1953, General Files, Box 310, Eisenhower Library.

84. Charlie F. Willis to Sherman Adams, March 3, 1953, ibid., Box 311, Eisenhower Library.

85. Those who have examined the Emmons commissionership differ greatly. In "Termination and the Administration of Glenn L. Emmons as Commissioner of Indian Affairs, 1953-1961," *New Mexico Historical Review* 54 (October 1979): 287-304, Debra R. Boender virtually divorces Emmons from termination. Patricia K. Ourada in "Glenn L. Emmons 1953-61," in Kvasnicka and Viola, *Commissioners of Indian Affairs*, 301-10, implies that Emmons was strongly involved.

86. The twelve termination bills included Utah, Texas, Western Oregon, Klamath, California, Menominee, Flathead, Seminole of Florida, Makah, Nevada, Sac and Fox, Kickapoo, and Potawatomi of Kansas, and Turtle Mountain. The hearings for Nevada and part of those for the Klamath took place in the field. For transcripts, see Joint Committees on Interior and Insular Affairs, *Termination of Federal Supervision over Certain Tribes of Indians, Joint Hearings before the Subcommittees of the Committees on Interior and Insular Affairs*, 83rd Cong., 2nd sess., 1954, parts 1-12.

87. Steven C. Schulte, "Removing the Yoke of Government: E. Y. Berry and the Origins of Termination Policy," *South Dakota History* 14 (Spring 1984): 48-55.

88. *Termination of Federal Supervision*, 1585.

89. Ibid., 1541.

90. Ibid., 1451.

91. Ibid., 255, 891.

92. Ibid., 1463, 1467.

93. Ibid., 890.

94. Ibid., 895-98.

95. Ibid., 935.

96. Ibid., 919.

97. Ibid., 941-42, 967-70.

98. Lee to Hugh Butler, February 16, 1954, ibid., 52.

99. Ibid., 1582.

100. Crawford and his wife, Ida, had been fixtures in Klamath politics for several decades. Son of a tribal judge, he first became prominent around 1929 as an advocate of forming a tribal corporation. In 1933 John Collier appointed him as Klamath superintendent but dismissed him four years later. Crawford then became a bitter enemy of Collier and reorganization (which the Klamaths never approved). In Crawford's repeated lobbying for liquidation of Klamath property and distribution of proceeds, his main support was a relatively small group of "absentee" Klamaths who had left the reservation and wanted to convert their share of tribal assets into cash. Theodore Stern, *The Klamath Tribe: A People and Their Reservation* (Seattle: University of Washington Press, 1965), 249-50.

101. 68 Stat. 718.

102. Hasse, "Termination and Assimilation," 226-28.

103. Susan Hood, "Termination of the Klamath Indian Tribe of Oregon," *Ethnohistory* 19 (Fall 1972): 384-85. Elmo Smith to Sherman Adams, May 15, 1957, Official Files, Box 618, Eisenhower Library.

104. 71 Stat. 347.

105. 72 Stat. 816.

106. Hasse, "Termination and Assimilation," 293-94.

107. William Thomas Trulove, "Economics of Paternalism: Federal Termination of the Klamath Indians" (Ph.D. diss., University of Oregon, 1973), 176, 215.

108. Ibid., 233.

109. Ibid., 234-43.

110. Ibid., 244.

111. Ibid., 172, 180.

112. *Termination of Federal Supervision,* 76, 78.

113. Ibid., 1540.

114. Hasse, "Termination and Assimilation," 265-66.

115. Lee Metcalf's speech to the Indian Rights Organization details his thinking on the subject. See "The Need for Revision of Federal Policy in Indian Affairs," *Indian Truth* 35 (January–March 1958), 1-6.

116. Hasse, "Termination and Assimilation," 271.

117. "Oral History Interview with O. Hatfield Chilson, by Thomas F. Soapes, March 18, 1976," Eisenhower Library.

118. Fred A. Seaton, "Indian Policy," September 13, 1958, BIA (articles) file, Seaton Papers, Eisenhower Library.

119. Relocation offices also had operated in other cities but had closed by 1970.

120. Prucha, *Great Father,* vol. 2, 1082. These figures include not only direct participants but spouses and children.

121. 70 Stat. 986. See also Donald L. Fixico, *Termination and Relocation: Federal Indian Policy 1945-1960* (Albuquerque: University of New Mexico Press, 1986), 143.

122. Harry W. Martin, "Correlates of Adjustment Among American Indians in an Urban Environment," *Human Organization* 23 (Winter 1964): 294. Martin admits that Navajos' seemingly better adaptation may actually be that they were more timid and caused less trouble.

123. Joan Ablon, "Relocated American Indians in the San Francisco Bay Area: Social Interaction and Indian Identity," *Human Organization* 23 (Winter 1964): 296-304. Also see Elaine M. Neils, *Reservation to City: Indian Migration and Federal Relocation* (Chicago: Department of Geography, University of Chicago, 1971), 121-27.

124. For a general statement on Emmons's outlook, see his "Address," September 6, 1956, E. F. Bennett papers, Box 6, Eisenhower Library.

125. Kent Gilbreath, *Red Capitalism: An Analysis of the Navajo Economy* (Norman: University of Oklahoma Press, 1973), 111-16.

126. Larry W. Burt, "Factories on Reservations: The Industrial Development Programs of Commissioner Glenn Emmons, 1953-1960," *Arizona and the West* 19 (Winter 1977): 320-21.

127. Ibid., 322-23.

128. Gilbreath points out that leases needed to establish businesses on the Navajo Reservation involved twenty approvals from BIA and tribal offices. The process ran from one to five years, many applications were neither approved or disapproved, and successful applicants often had lost interest after long delays. Gilbreath, *Red Capitalism,* 40-49.

129. Burt, "Factories on Reservations," 328-30.

130. Schulte, "Removing the Yoke of Government," 61-63.

131. Burt, "Factories on Reservations," 332.

132. For Indians' outlook, see LaSalle Pocatello to E. J. Utz, September 19, 1956, Indian affairs file, Seaton papers, Eisenhower Library.

133. Glenn L. Emmons, "Address," E. F. Bennett papers, Box 6, Eisenhower Library. In his address Emmons claimed that a survey of relocated Indians in Los Angeles revealed that 80 percent had never owned land and the rest had kept theirs.

134. 68 Stat. 674.

135. See Ed Edmonson to Director US Public Health, May 22, 1954, Culp papers, Box 23, Eisenhower Library.

136. Debo to Lawrence Lindley, August 20, 1955, *Indian Rights Association Papers*, (Glen Rock, New Jersey: Microfilming Corporation of America, 1974), reel 61.

9. Self-Determination and Red Power

1. C. Matthew Snipp, *American Indians: The First of This Land* (New York: Russell Sage Foundation, 1989), 81, 83.

2. Ibid., 81.

3. Ibid., 88.

4. Margaret Connell Szasz, "Philleo Nash 1961-1966," in Robert M. Kvasnicka and Herman J. Viola, eds., *The Commissioners of Indian Affairs, 1824-1977* (Lincoln: University of Nebraska Press, 1979), 311.

5. Francis Paul Prucha, ed., *Documents of United States Indian Policy* (Lincoln: University of Nebraska Press, 1990), 246-47.

6. Ibid., 242-44. The commission later released a final report in book form. See William A. Brophy and Sophie D. Aberle, comps., *The Indian: America's Unfinished Business* (Norman: University of Oklahoma Press, 1966).

7. Edward C. Johnson's statement quoted in Kenneth R. Philp, ed., *Indian Self-Rule: First-Hand Accounts of Indian-White Relations from Roosevelt to Reagan* (Salt Lake City: Howe Brothers, 1986), 188.

8. D'Arcy McNickle, *Native American Tribalism: Indian Survivals and Renewals* (New York: Oxford University Press, 1973), 117.

9. Donald L. Parman, "Americans Indians and the Bicentennial," *New Mexico Historical Review* 51 (July 1976): 234-35.

10. Szasz, "Philleo Nash," 313-16.

11. For an example of these, see William L. Guy to Nash, March 23, 1962, Papers of Philleo Nash, Harry S. Truman Library, Independence, Missouri.

12. Nash, "Press Release," June 16, 1964, ibid. Richmond L. Clow points out that the legislation was of limited value to reservations because it was designed for depressed urban areas and not for reservations that were agriculturally based. Richmond L. Clow to author, November 1, 1992, author's personal files.

13. McNickle, *Native American Tribalism*, 118-19.

14. Robert Burnette and John Koster, *The Road to Wounded Knee* (New York: Bantam Books, 1974), 162.

15. Szasz, "Philleo Nash," 320.

16. See Richard N. Ellis, "Robert L. Bennett 1966-1969," in Kvasnicka and Viola, *Commissioners of Indian Affairs*, 325-31.

17. *Public Papers of the Presidents of the United States, 1968-69, Book I* (Washington: Government Printing Office, 1970), 335-44.

18. Josephy's study resulted in *Red Power: The American Indians' Fight for Freedom* (New York: American Heritage Press, 1971).

19. *Public Papers of the Presidents of the United States, 1970* (Washington: Government Printing Office, 1971), 564-76.

20. Unfortunately, the coverage in Richard Allan Baker's *Conservation Politics:*

The Senate Career of Clinton P. Anderson (Albuquerque: University of New Mexico Press, 1985) stops short of the Blue Lake controversy. For cultural perspectives on Blue Lake, see John J. Bodine, "Taos Blue Lake Controversy," *Journal of Ethnic Studies* 6 (Spring 1978): 42-48. For historical developments, see Robert A. Hecht, *Oliver La Farge and the American Indian: A Biography* (Metuchen, New Jersey: Scarecrow Press, 1991), 282-305.

21. For background on fishing rights, see Donald L. Parman, "Inconsistent Advocacy: The Erosion of Indian Fishing Rights in the Pacific Northwest, 1933-1956," *Pacific Historical Review* 53 (May 1984): 163-89 and Alvin M. Josephy, Jr., *Now That the Buffalo's Gone: A Study of Today's American Indians* (New York: Alfred A. Knopf, 1982), 177-211.

22. Ibid., 193-201.

23. AIM's reputation for criminal activities started with Dennis Banks and Clyde and Vernon Bellecourt who had been in prison before AIM was organized. The reputation was kept alive by AIM's many brushes with the law, endless threats, internal clashes, and allegations about members' improper use of funds.

24. The best analysis of AIM's philosophy and the reaction of Indians is Rachael A. Bonney, "The Role of AIM Leaders in Indian Nationalism," *American Indian Quarterly* 3 (Autumn 1977): 209-24.

25. Background on AIM activities in 1970-1972 can be found in Rolland Dewing, *Wounded Knee: The Meaning and Significance of the Second Incident* (New York: Irvington Publishers, 1985), 44-61.

26. Burnette and Koster, *Road to Wounded Knee*, 196-98.

27. Parman, "American Indians," 243-44.

28. Burnette and Koster, *Road to Wounded Knee*, 201.

29. For materials on the "Twenty Points" and related information, see Records of the National Council on Indian Opportunity, General Subject Files, Caravan, National Archives, Record Group 220.

30. Interview with Robert Robertson (former executive director of NCIO), Washington, January 9, 1976.

31. Burnette and Koster, *Road to Wounded Knee*, 215-16.

32. Dewing, *Wounded Knee*, 71-72.

33. Most scholars have used a full-blood vs. mixed-blood model in analyzing Pine Ridge factionalism. An interesting variation adds a third element, the cultural nationalists, in interpreting events leading to Wounded Knee II. See Philip D. Roos et al., "The Impact of the American Indian Movement on the Pine Ridge Indian Reservation," *Phylon* 41 (March 1980): 89-99.

34. Ibid., 95-96.

35. Rolland Dewing, "South Dakota Newspaper Coverage of the 1973 Occupation of Wounded Knee," *South Dakota History* 12 (Spring 1982): 48-64.

36. *The Harris Survey Yearbook of Public Opinion 1973* (New York: Louis Harris and Associates, 1976), 223-27.

37. Dewing, *Wounded Knee*, 276.

38. American Indian Policy Review Commission, *Final Report*, vol. 1 (Washington: Government Printing Office, 1977), 3-26. Hereafter cited as AIPRC, *Final Report*.

39. James G. Abourezk, *Advise and Dissent: Memoirs of South Dakota and the U.S. Senate* (Chicago: Lawrence Hill Books, 1989), 7-10.

40. Ibid., 10, 41-43.

41. AIPRC, *Final Report*, vol. 1, 3-26.

42. Ibid., 22-24.

43. Ibid., 15-23.

44. Ibid., 8-9, 12.

45. Ibid., 1.

46. Ibid., 4-9.

47. Ibid., 571.

48. Ibid., 610-11.

49. Ibid., 615-17.

50. Abourezk, *Advise and Dissent*, 4.

51. Mark Thompson, "Nurturing the Forked Tree: Conception and Formation of the American Indian Policy Review Commission," in *New Directions in Federal Indian Policy: A Review of the American Indian Policy Review Commission* (Los Angeles: American Indian Studies Center [UCLA], 1979), 5-18.

52. *New York Times*, July 16, 1978, Section 1, 22.

53. Ibid., July 19, 1978, A10.

54. Ibid., July 20, 1978, A21.

55. *Washington Post*, July 24, 1978, A6.

56. Charles F. Wilkinson, *American Indians, Time, and the Law: Native Societies in a Modern Constitutional Democracy* (New Haven: Yale University Press, 1987), 1-3.

57. Ibid., 1.

58. Ibid., 48.

59. Daniel L. Boxberger, *To Fish in Common: The Ethnohistory of Lummi Indian Salmon Fishing* (Lincoln: University of Nebraska Press, 1989), 154.

60. Ibid., 155-56. Richmond L. Clow suggests that this may be the first time that the Supreme Court has rejected a case and then taken it up later. Clow to author, November 1, 1992.

61. Wilkinson, *American Indians*, 66-67.

62. Prucha, *Great Father*, vol. 2, 1107.

63. For a list of the guarantees and their derivation, see Vine Deloria, Jr. and Clifford M. Lytle, *American Indians, American Justice* (Austin: University of Texas Press, 1983), 129.

64. Clow to author, November 1, 1992.

65. Chief of these was the national study of American Indian education, funded by the Office of Education, that used eight university centers in conducting a four-year investigation. In addition to the final report, Estelle Fuchs and Robert J. Havighurst published *To Live on the Earth: American Indian Education* (Garden City, New York: Anchor Books, 1973).

66. 86 Stat. 334.

67. 88 Stat. 2203.

68. 90 Stat. 1400.

69. 92 Stat. 1325.

70. Two of the schools, Oglala Lakota (Pine Ridge) and Sinte Gleska (Rosebud), offered four-year programs in 1989. Sinte Gleska also offered a master's degree in education.

71. Carnegie Foundation for the Advancement of Teaching, *Tribal Colleges: Shaping the Future of Native America* (Princeton, New Jersey: Carnegie Foundation for the Advancement of Teaching, 1989).

72. 92 Stat. 3069.

73. 92 Stat. 469.

74. Robert L. Bee, *The Politics of American Indian Policy* (Cambridge, Massachusetts: Schenkman Publishing Company, 1982).

75. Clow to author, November 1, 1992.

10. The New Indian Wars

1. American Indian Policy Review Commission, *Final Report*, vol. 1 (Washington: Government Printing Office, 1977), 338-39. Hereafter cited as AIPRC, *Final Report*.

2. Marjane Ambler, *Breaking the Iron Bonds: Indian Control of Energy Development* (Lawrence: University Press of Kansas, 1990), 59-60. For another appraisal of Indians' experience with energy companies and essays on several individual reservations, see Joseph G. Jorgensen, ed., *Native Americans and Energy Development II* (Boston: Anthropology Resource Center, 1984).

3. Ambler, *Breaking the Iron Bonds*, 66-67.

4. Ibid. and AIPRC, *Final Report*, I, 343.

5. Ambler, *Breaking the Iron Bonds*, 71-72.

6. Ibid., 79-80.

7. Ibid., 92-93.

8. Ibid., 94-95.

9. Ibid., 99-102.

10. Ibid., 105-106.

11. Ibid., 106-16.

12. Ibid., 89-90.

13. Lloyd Burton, *American Indian Water Rights and the Limits of Law* (Lawrence: University Press of Kansas, 1991), 36-37.

14. Ibid., 39-40. Richmond L. Clow believes that the increased number of westerners on the Supreme Court has influenced its decisions on Indian legal questions. This certainly deserves further study. Richmond L. Clow to author, November 1, 1992, author's personal files.

15. Burton, *American Indian Water Rights*, 41-42.

16. Ibid., 44.

17. Ibid., 46-47.

18. Ibid., 58-59.

19. Ibid., 71-73.

20. Ibid., 127. For a listing of contemporary water disputes, see ibid., 50-57.

21. For a more detailed treatment of these trends, see Stephen Cornell, *The Return of the Native: American Indian Political Resurgence* (New York: Oxford University Press, 1988).

22. Bee's study of Indian politics describes how a relatively small group of 900 Quechans on the Fort Yuma Reservation have managed, despite factionalism and frequent changes of leadership, to tap large amounts of federal funds and even to increase the tribe's land base. See Robert L. Bee, *The Politics of American Indian Policy* (Cambridge, Massachusetts: Schenkman Publishing Company, 1982), especially 38-48.

23. Jim Richardson and John Aloysius Farrell, "The New Indian Wars," *Denver Post* (Special Reprint, 1982), 17 and *Wotanin Wowapi*, June 25, 1992, 1-2.

24. *New York Times*, January 25, 1983, A16 and January 30, 1983, E9. For a copy of the "Statement," see *Public Papers of the Presidents of the United States, 1983, Book I* (Washington: Government Printing Office, 1984), 96-100.

25. Hazel W. Hertzberg, "Reaganomics on the Reservation," *New Republic* 187 (November 22, 1982): 15-18.

26. *New York Times*, January 19, 1983, A19 and January 25, 1983, A16.

27. *Spokesmen Review*, January 27, 1991, 1-2.

28. Ibid.

29. *Lac du Flambeau News*, June 1993, 14.

30. Much more economic analysis is needed on the impact of gambling on reservations. Ideally, non-Indians should bring outside money to the gaming operations and Indians and tribes should receive all the salaries and profits. If only Indians gamble, then essentially gaming is only a means of redistributing wealth.

31. 102 Stat. 2467-88.

32. *Lac du Flambeau News*, June 1993, 14.

33. *The Plain Dealer*, February 12, 1992.

34. Orlan J. Svingen's article on Indian voting rights in Big Horn County, Montana, examines voting discrimination against the Crows. More studies of a similar nature are needed. See "Jim Crow, Indian Style." *American Indian Quarterly* 11 (Fall 1987): 275-86.

35. American Policy Review Commission, *Report on Federal, State, and Tribal Jurisdiction, Task Force Four* (Washington: Government Printing Office, 1976), 21-24.

36. For information on the Sagebrush Rebellion, see Tom Matthews et al., "The Angry West vs. the Rest," *Newsweek* 94 (September 17, 1979): 31-40 and Michael P. Malone and Richard W. Etulain, *The American West* (Lincoln: University of Nebraska Press, 1989), 288-89. A study of the rhetoric of the Sagebrush Rebellion is C. Brant Short, *Ronald Reagan and the Public Lands: America's Conservation Debate 1979-1984* (College Station: Texas A. & M. Press, 1989). See especially chapter 2.

37. Rudolph C. Ryser, *Anti-Indian Movement on the Tribal Frontier* (Kenmore, Washington: Center for World Indigenous Studies, 1991), 15-16.

38. Ibid., 22-27.

39. Ronald N. Satz, *Chippewa Treaty Rights: The Reserved Rights of Wisconsin's Chippewa Indians in Historical Perspective* (Madison: Wisconsin Academy of Science, Arts, and Letters, 1991), 93-100, 195-97.

40. Ibid., 106.

41. Interview of Ronald N. Satz, October 6, 1992. Satz mentioned that the decision is currently under appeal, but several STA defendants have already settled out of court.

42. William H. Covey to author, January 15, 1991, author's personal files and *Missoulian*, January 28, 1990, B1-B2.

43. Covey to author, January 15, 1991.

44. Ibid.; Citizen Equal Rights Alliance, "Position Paper," March 1990, 26.

45. "This Is CERA," author's personal files.

46. Clow to author, November 1, 1992.

47. *Missoulian*, January 28, 1990, B1-B2.

48. Ibid. Ryser argues that Senator Metcalf and other right wingers joined the anti-Indian movement and helped it form links with such groups as the Populist Party, Christian Patriot, and Christian Identity. See Ryser, *Anti-Indian Movement*, 44-51.

49. Covey to author, January 15, 1991.

Bibliography

Manuscript and Microform Collections

Adair, John, ed. *Life Histories of Six Zuni Young Men: Microcard Publications of Primary Records in Culture and Personality*, vol. 1, no. 23.: Edited by Bert Kaplan. Madison, Wisconsin: Microcard Foundation, 1956, pp. 108-25.

Records of the Bureau of Indian Affairs. Record Group 75, National Archives.

Hugh Butler Papers. Nebraska State Historical Society, Lincoln, Nebraska.

John Collier Papers, 1922-1969. Sanford, North Carolina: Microfilming Corporation of America, 1980.

John Collier Papers. Sterling Memorial Library, Yale University, Archives and Manuscripts Division. New Haven, Connecticut.

Dwight D. Eisenhower Library. Abilene, Kansas.

Indian Rights Association Papers. Glen Rock, New Jersey: Microfilming Corporation of America, 1974.

Records of the National Council on Indian Opportunity. Record Group 220, National Archives.

Records of the Office of the Secretary of Interior. Record Group 48, National Archives.

Files of Governors Patterson, McKay, and Hall, 1948-1955. Oregon State Archives Division. Salem, Oregon.

Harry S. Truman Library. Independence, Missouri.

Books

Abourezk, James G. *Advise and Dissent: Memoirs of South Dakota and the U.S. Senate*. Chicago: Lawrence Hill Books, 1989.

Ambler, Marjane. *Breaking the Iron Bonds: Indian Control of Energy Development*. Lawrence: University Press of Kansas, 1990.

Archibald, Katherine. *Wartime Shipyard: A Study in Social Disunity*. Berkeley: University of California Press, 1947.

Arnold, Mary Ellicott, and Mabel Reed. *In the Land of the Grasshopper Song: A Story of Two Girls in Indian Country in 1908-09*. New York: Vantage Press, 1957.

Arrington, Leonard J. *Brigham Young: American Moses*. New York: Alfred A. Knopf, 1985.

_____. *The Changing Economic Structure of the Mountain West, 1850-1950*. Logan: Utah State University Press, 1963.

Bailey, Garrick, and Roberta Glenn Bailey. *A History of the Navajos: The Reservation Years*. Santa Fe: School of American Research Press, 1986.

Baker, Richard Allan. *Conservation Politics: The Senate Career of Clinton P. Anderson*. Albuquerque: University of New Mexico Press, 1985.

Bee, Robert L. *The Politics of American Indian Policy*. Cambridge, Massachusetts: Schenkman Publishing Company, 1982.

Berge, Wendell. *Economic Freedom for the West*. Lincoln: University of Nebraska Press, 1946.

Berkhofer, Robert F., Jr. *The White Man's Indian: Images of the American Indian from Columbus to the Present*. New York: Alfred A. Knopf, 1978.

Bernstein, Alison R. *American Indians and World War II: Toward a New Era in Indian Affairs*. Norman: University of Oklahoma Press, 1991.

Berthrong, Donald J. *The Cheyenne and Arapaho Ordeal: Reservation and Agency Life in Indian Territory, 1875-1907*. Norman: University of Oklahoma Press, 1976.

Biolsi, Thomas. *Organizing the Lakota: The Political Economy of the New Deal on the Pine Ridge and Rosebud Reservations*. Tucson: University of Arizona Press, 1992.

Boxberger, Daniel L. *To Fish in Common: The Ethnohistory of Lummi Indian Salmon Fishing*. Lincoln: University of Nebraska Press, 1989.

Brophy, William A., and Sophie D. Aberle, comps. *The Indian: America's Unfinished Business*. Norman: University of Oklahoma Press, 1966.

Burnette, Robert, and John Koster. *The Road to Wounded Knee*. New York: Bantam Books, 1974.

Burt, Larry W. *Tribalism in Crisis: Federal Indian Policy, 1953-1961*. Albuquerque: University of New Mexico Press, 1982.

Burton, Lloyd. *American Indian Water Rights and the Limits of the Law*. Lawrence: University Press of Kansas, 1991.

Carlson, Leonard A. *Indians, Bureaucrats, and Land: The Dawes Act and the Decline of Indian Farming*. Westport, Connecticut: Greenwood Press, 1981.

Carnegie Foundation for the Advancement of Teaching. *Tribal Colleges: Shaping the Future of Native America*. Princeton, New Jersey: Carnegie Foundation for the Advancement of Teaching, 1989.

Cash, Joseph H., and Herbert T. Hoover, eds. *To Be an Indian: An Oral History*. New York: Holt, Rinehart, and Winston, 1971.

Collier, John. *From Every Zenith: A Memoir and Some Essays on Life and Thought*. Denver: Sage Books, 1963.

Cornell, Stephen. *The Return of the Native: American Indian Political Resurgence*. New York: Oxford University Press, 1988.

Correll, J. Lee, and Alfred Dehiya. *Anatomy of the Navajo Reservation: How It Grew*. Window Rock, Arizona: *Navajo Times* Publishing Co., n.d.

Debo, Angie. *And Still the Waters Run: The Betrayal of the Five Civilized Tribes*. Princeton: Princeton University Press, 1972.

Deloria, Vine, Jr., ed. *American Indian Policy in the Twentieth Century*. Norman: University of Oklahoma Press, 1985.

———, and Clifford M. Lytle. *American Indians, American Justice*. Austin: University of Texas Press, 1983.

———, and Clifford M. Lytle. *The Nations Within: The Past and Future of American Indian Sovereignty*. New York: Pantheon Books, 1984.

Dewing, Rolland. *Wounded Knee: The Meaning and Significance of the Second Incident*. New York: Irvington Publishers, 1985.

Dictionary of American Biography, Supplement Three, 1941-1945. New York: Charles Scribner's Sons, 1973.

Dietrich, Margretta Stewart, comp. *Doing Fine and Thanks a Million*. Santa Fe: N.p., 1943.

———. *Hello and Many Lucks*. Santa Fe: Santa Fe Press, 1945.

Dippie, Brian W. *The Vanishing American: White Attitudes and U.S. Indian Policy*. Middletown, Connecticut: Wesleyan University Press, 1982.

Drinnon, Richard. *Keeper of Concentration Camps: Dillon S. Myer and American Racism*. Berkeley: University of California Press, 1987.

Dryden, Cecil Pearl. *Dryden's History of Washington*. Portland: Binfords & Mort Publishers, 1968.

Dyer, Thomas G. *Theodore Roosevelt and the Idea of Race*. Baton Rouge: Louisiana State University Press, 1980.

Epstein, Ralph C. *The Automobile Industry: Its Economic and Commercial Development*. Chicago: A. W. Shaw Company, 1928.

Fahey, John. *The Flathead Indians*. Norman: University of Oklahoma Press, 1974.

Faunce, Hilda. *Desert Wife*. Lincoln: University of Nebraska Press, 1981.

Feinman, Ronald L. *Twilight of Progressivism: The Western Republican Senators and the New Deal*. Baltimore: Johns Hopkins University Press, 1981.

Fixico, Donald L. *Termination and Relocation: Federal Indian Policy, 1945-1960*. Albuquerque: University of New Mexico Press, 1986.

Forbes, Jack D. *Native Americans and Nixon: Presidential Politics and Minority Self-Determination, 1969-1972*. Los Angeles: American Indian Studies Center (UCLA), 1981.

Fuchs, Estelle, and Robert J. Havighurst. *To Live on This Earth: American Indian Education*. Garden City, New York: Anchor Books, 1973.

Garnsey, Morris E. *America's New Frontier: The Mountain West*. New York: Alfred A. Knopf, 1950.

Gilbreath, Kent. *Red Capitalism: An Analysis of the Navajo Economy*. Norman: University of Oklahoma Press, 1973.

Gittinger, Roy. *The Formation of the State of Oklahoma*. Norman: University of Oklahoma Press, 1939.

Goble, Danney. *Progressive Oklahoma: The Making of a New Kind of State*. Norman: University of Oklahoma Press, 1980.

Gulliford, Andrew. *Boomtown Blues: Colorado Oil Shale, 1885-1985*. Niwot, Colorado: University Press of Colorado, 1989.

Hagan, William T. *The Indian Rights Association: The Herbert Welsh Years, 1882-1904*. Tucson: University of Arizona Press, 1985.

———. *United States–Comanche Relations: The Reservation Years*. New Haven: Yale University Press, 1976.

The Harris Survey Yearbook of Public Opinion, 1973. New York: Louis Harris and Associates, 1976.

Haystead, Ladd. *If the Prospect Pleases: The West the Guidebooks Never Mention*. Norman: University of Oklahoma Press, 1945.

Hecht, Robert A. *Oliver La Farge and the American Indian: A Biography*. Metuchen, New Jersey: Scarecrow Press, 1991.

Hemingway, Albert. *Ira Hayes: Pima Marine*. Lanham, Maryland: University Press of America, 1988.

Hertzberg, Hazel W. *The Search for an American Indian Identity: Modern Pan-Indian Movements*. Syracuse: Syracuse University Press, 1971.

Hoxie, Frederick E. *A Final Promise: The Campaign to Assimilate the Indians, 1880-1920*. Lincoln: University of Nebraska Press, 1984.

Hundley, Norris, Jr. *Water and the West: The Colorado River Compact and the Politics of Water in the American West*. Berkeley: University of Calfornia Press, 1974.

Iverson, Peter, ed. *The Plains Indians of the Twentieth Century*. Norman: University of Oklahoma Press, 1985.

Johansen, Dorothy O., and Charles M. Gates. *Empire of the Columbia: A History of the Pacific Northwest*. New York: Harper & Brothers, Publishers, 1957.

Johnson, Broderick H., ed. *Navajos and World War II*. Tsaile, Arizona: Navajo Community College Press, 1977.

Jorgensen, Joseph G., ed. *Native Americans and Energy Development II*. Boston: Anthropology Resource Center, 1984.

Josephy, Alvin M., Jr. *Now That the Buffalo's Gone: A Study of Today's American Indians*. New York: Alfred A. Knopf, 1982.

_____. *Red Power: The American Indians' Fight for Freedom*. New York: American Heritage Press, 1971.

Kelly, Lawrence C. *The Assault on Indian Assimilation: John Collier and the Origins of Indian Policy Reform*. Albuquerque: University of New Mexico Press, 1983.

_____. *The Navajo Indians and Federal Indian Policy 1900-1935*. Tucson: University of Arizona Press, 1968.

Kinney, J. P. *A Continent Lost, A Civilization Won*. Baltimore: Johns Hopkins Press, 1937.

_____. *Indian Forest and Range: A History of the Administration and Conservation of the Redman's Heritage*. Washington: Forestry Enterprises, 1950.

Kleinsorge, Paul L. *The Boulder Canyon Project: Historical and Economic Aspects*. Palo Alto: Stanford University Press, 1941.

Lamm, Richard D., and Michael McCarthy. *The Angry West: A Vulnerable Land and Its Future*. Boston: Houghton Mifflin Company, 1982.

Lawson, Michael L. *Dammed Indians: The Pick-Sloan Plan and the Missouri River Sioux, 1944-1980*. Norman: University of Oklahoma Press, 1982.

Leupp, Francis E. *The Indian and His Problem*. New York: Charles Scribner's Sons, 1910.

Limerick, Patricia Nelson. *The Legacy of Conquest: The Unbroken Past of the American West*. New York: Norton, 1987.

_____, Clyde A. Milner II, and Charles E. Rankin, eds. *Trails: Toward a New Western History*. Lawrence: University Press of Kansas, 1991.

Lockwood, Frank C. *The Life of Edward E. Ayer*. Chicago: A. C. McClurg & Company, 1929.

Lowitt, Richard. *The New Deal and the West*. Bloomington: Indiana University Press, 1984.

Macgregor, Gordon. *Warriors without Weapons: A Study of the Society and Personality Development of the Pine Ridge Sioux*. Chicago: Chicago University Press, 1946.

Malone, Michael P., and Richard W. Etulain. *The American West: A Twentieth-Century History*. Lincoln: University of Nebraska Press, 1989.

McAlear, J. F., as told to Sharon Bergman. *The Fabulous Flathead*. Polson, Montana: Reservation Pioneers, 1962.

McCarthy, James. *A Papago Traveler: The Memories of James McCarthy*. Edited by John G. Westover. Tucson: Sun Tracks and University of Arizona Press, 1985.

McDonnell, Janet A. *The Dispossession of the American Indian, 1887-1934*. Bloomington: Indiana University Press, 1991.

McGeary, M. Nelson. *Gifford Pinchot: Forester-Politician*. Princeton: Princeton University Press, 1960.

McNickle, D'Arcy. *Native American Tribalism: Indian Survivals and Renewals*. New York: Oxford University Press, 1973.

McReynolds, Edwin C. *Oklahoma: A History of the Sooner State*. Norman: University of Oklahoma Press, 1964.

Mezerik, A. G. *The Revolt of the South and the West*. New York: Duell, Sloan and Pearce, 1946.

Miner, H. Craig. *The Corporation and the Indian: Tribal Sovereignty and Industrial Civilization in Indian Territory, 1865-1907*. Columbia: University of Missouri Press, 1976.

Moeller, Beverley Bowen. *Phil Swing and Boulder Dam*. Berkeley: University of California Press, 1971.

Morison, Samuel Eliot. *History of United States Naval Operations in World War II*. Vol.

4: *Coral Sea, Midway and Submarine Actions, May 1942-August 1942*. Boston: Little, Brown, and Company, 1949.

Myer, Dillon S. "An Autobiography of Dillon S. Myer." Berkeley: University of California Oral History Office. (Copy from the Truman Library)

Nash, Gerald D. *The American West Transformed: The Impact of the Second World War*. Bloomington: Indiana University Press, 1985.

_____. *The American West in the Twentieth Century: A Short History of an Urban Oasis*. Englewood Cliffs, New Jersey: Prentice-Hall, 1973.

_____, and Richard W. Etulain, eds. *The Twentieth Century West: Historical Interpretations*. Albuquerque: University of New Mexico Press, 1989.

National Cyclopaedia of American Biography. Vol. 43. New York: James T. White & Company, 1961.

Neils, Elaine M. *Reservation to City: Indian Migration and Federal Relocation*. Chicago: University of Chicago, Department of Geography, 1971.

New Directions in Federal Indian Policy: A Review of the American Indian Policy Review Commission. Los Angeles: American Indian Studies Center (UCLA), 1979.

Olson, James S. and Raymond Wilson. *Native Americans in the Twentieth Century*. Provo: Brigham Young University Press, 1984.

Olson, Keith W. *Biography of a Progressive: Franklin A. Lane, 1864-1921*. Westport, Connecticut: Greenwood Press, 1979.

Otis, D. S. *The Dawes Act and the Allotment of Indian Lands*. Edited by Francis Paul Prucha. Norman: University of Oklahoma Press, 1973.

Parman, Donald L. *The Navajos and the New Deal*. New Haven: Yale University Press, 1976.

Paul, Doris A. *The Navajo Code Talkers*. Bryn Mawr, Pennsylvania: Dorrance & Company, 1973.

Philp, Kenneth R. *John Collier's Crusade for Indian Reform 1920-1954*. Tucson: University of Arizona Press, 1977.

_____, ed. *Indian Self-Rule: First-Hand Accounts of Indian-White Relations from Roosevelt to Reagan*. Salt Lake City: Howe Brothers, 1986.

Pinchot, Gifford. *Breaking New Ground*. New York: Harcourt, Brace and Company, 1947.

_____. *The Fight for Conservation*, with an introduction by Gerald D. Nash. Seattle: University of Washington Press, 1967.

Pomeroy, Earl S. *The Pacific Slope: A History of California, Oregon, Washington, Idaho, Utah, and Nevada*. New York: Alfred A. Knopf, 1965.

The Problem of Indian Administration. Baltimore: Johns Hopkins Press, 1928.

Prucha, Francis Paul, ed. *Documents of United States Indian Policy*. Lincoln: University of Nebraska Press, 1990.

_____. *The Great Father: The United States Government and the American Indians*. Vol. 2. Lincoln: University of Nebraska Press, 1984.

Richardson, Elmo. *Dams, Parks & Politics: Resource Development & Preservation in the Truman-Eisenhower Era*. Lexington: University Press of Kentucky, 1973.

Rister, Carl Coke. *Land Hunger: David L. Payne and the Oklahoma Boomers*. New York: Arno Press, 1975.

_____. *Oil! Titan of the Southwest*. Norman: University of Oklahoma Press, 1949.

Robinson, Elwyn B. *History of North Dakota*. Lincoln: University of Nebraska Press, 1966.

Rose, Mark H. *Interstate: Express Highway Politics, 1939-1989*. Knoxville: University of Tennessee Press, 1990.

Ryser, Rudolph C. *Anti-Indian Movement on the Tribal Frontier*. Kenmore, Washington: Center for World Indigenous Studies, 1991.

Satz, Ronald N. *Chippewa Treaty Rights, The Reserved Rights of Wisconsin's Chippewa*

Indians in Historical Perspective. Madison: Wisconsin Academy of Science, Arts, and Letters, 1991.

Schroeder, Albert H., ed. *The Changing Ways of Southwestern Indians: A Historical Perspective*. Glorieta, New Mexico: Rio Grande Press, 1973.

Shaw, Anna Moore. *A Pima Past*. Tucson: University of Arizona Press, 1974.

Short, C. Brant. *Ronald Reagan and the Public Lands: America's Conservation Debate 1979-1984*. College Station: Texas A. & M. Press, 1989.

Smith, Donald B. *Long Lance: The True Story of One Impostor*. Lincoln: University of Nebraska Press, 1983.

Snipp, C. Matthew. *American Indians: The First of This Land*. New York: Russell Sage Foundation, 1989.

Sorkin, Alan. *The Urban American Indian*. Lexington: University Press of Kentucky, 1978.

Spicer, Edward H. *Cycles of Conquest: The Impact of Spain, Mexico, and the United States on the Indians of the Southwest, 1533-1960*. Tucson: University of Arizona Press, 1962.

Stern, Theodore. *The Klamath Tribe: A People and Their Reservation*. Seattle: University of Washington Press, 1965.

Strickland, Rennard. *The Indians in Oklahoma*. Norman: University of Oklahoma Press, 1980.

Szasz, Margaret Connell. *Education and the American Indian: The Road to Self-Determination, 1928-1973*. Albuquerque: University of New Mexico Press, 1974.

Taylor, Graham D. *The New Deal and American Indian Tribalism: The Administration of the Indian Reorganization Act, 1934-45*. Lincoln: University of Nebraska Press, 1980.

Taylor, Theodore W. *American Indian Policy*. Mt. Airy, Maryland: Lomond Publications, 1983.

_____. *The Bureau of Indian Affairs*. Boulder, Colorado: Westview Press, 1984.

Thomas, James H. *The Long Haul: Truckers, Truck Stops & Trucking*. Memphis: Memphis State University Press, 1979.

Thompson, Hildegard. *The Navajos' Long Walk for Education: A History of Navajo Education*. Tsaile, Arizona: Navajo Community College Press, 1975.

Thompson, John. *Closing the Frontier: Radical Response in Oklahoma, 1889-1923*. Norman: University of Oklahoma Press, 1986.

Truman, Harry S. *Memoirs by Harry S. Truman*. Vol. 1: *Year of Decisions*. Garden City, New York: Doubleday & Company, 1955.

Washburn, Wilcomb E., ed. *The American Indian and the United States: A Documentary History*. Vols. 1-4. New York: Random House, 1973.

_____. *The Assault on Indian Tribalism: The General Allotment Law (Dawes Act) of 1887*. Philadelphia: Lippincott, 1975.

Wheeler, Burton K., and Paul F. Healy. *Yankee from the West: The Candid, Turbulent Life of the Yankee-born U.S. Senator from Montana*. Garden City, New York: Doubleday & Company, 1962.

Who Was Who in America. Vol. 7. Chicago: Marquis Who's Who, 1981.

Wiley, Peter, and Robert Gottlieb. *Empires in the Sun: The Rise of the New American West*. New York: G. P. Putnam's Sons, 1982.

Wilkinson, Charles F. *American Indians, Time, and the Law: Native Societies in a Modern Constitutional Democracy*. New Haven: Yale University Press, 1987.

Worster, Donald. *Rivers of Empire: Water, Aridity, and the Growth of the American West*. New York: Pantheon Books, 1985.

Wright, Muriel H. *A Guide to the Indian Tribes of Oklahoma*. Norman: University of Oklahoma Press, 1951.

Wyllys, Rufus Kay. *Arizona: The History of A Frontier State*. Phoenix: Hobson & Herr, 1950.

Dissertations

Bernstein, Alison Ricky. "Walking in Two Worlds: American Indians and World War Two." Ph.D. diss., Columbia University, 1986.
Biolsi, Thomas. "Organizing the Lakota: The Indian New Deal." Ph.D. diss., Columbia University, 1987.
Freeman, John Leiper. "The New Deal for Indians: A Study in Bureau-Committee Relations." Ph.D. diss., Princeton University, 1952.
Hasse, Larry J. "Termination and Assimilation: Federal Indian Policy, 1943-1961." Ph.D. diss., Washington State University, 1974.
Hoxie, Frederick E. "Beyond Savagery: The Campaign to Assimilate the Indians." Ph.D. diss., Brandeis University, 1977.
McDonnell, Janet. "The Disintegration of the Indian Estate: Indian Land Policy, 1913-1929." Ph.D. diss., Marquette University, 1980.
Parker, Dorothy. "Choosing an Indian Identity: A Biography of D'Arcy McNickle." Ph.D. diss., University of New Mexico, 1988.
Parman, Donald Lee. "The Indian Civilian Conservation Corps." Ph.D. diss., University of Oklahoma, 1967.
Putney, Diane Therese. "Fighting the Scourge: American Indian Morbidity and Federal Policy, 1897-1928." Ph.D. diss., Marquette University, 1980.
Rosenthal, Harvey Daniel. "Their Day in Court: A History of the Indian Claims Commission." Ph.D. diss., Kent State University, 1976.
Trulove, William Thomas. "Economics of Paternalism: Federal Policy and the Klamath Indians." Ph.D. diss., University of Oregon, 1973.

Articles and Book Chapters

Ablon, Joan. "Relocated American Indians in the San Francisco Bay Area: Social Interaction and Indian Identity." *Human Organization* 23 (Winter 1964): 296-304.
Adair, John, and Evon Vogt. "Navajo and Zuni Veterans: A Study of Contrasting Modes of Cultural Change." *American Anthropologist* 51 (October–December 1949): 547-61.
Arrington, Leonard J., and Archer L. Durham. "Anchors Aweigh in Utah: The U.S. Naval Supply Depot at Clearfield, 1942-1962." *Utah Historical Quarterly* 31 (Spring 1963): 109-26.
Berthrong, Donald J. "Legacies of the Dawes Act: Bureaucrats and Land Thieves at the Cheyenne-Arapaho Agencies of Western Oklahoma." *Arizona and the West* 21 (Winter 1979): 335-54.
Bodine, John J. "Taos Blue Lake Controversy." *Journal of Ethnic Studies* 6 (Spring 1978): 42-48.
Boender, Debra R. "Termination and the Administration of Glenn L. Emmons as Commissioner of Indian Affairs, 1953-1961." *New Mexico Historical Review* 54 (October 1979): 287-304.
Bonney, Rachael A. "The Role of AIM Leaders in Indian Nationalism." *American Indian Quarterly* 3 (Autumn 1977): 209-24.
Brown, Loren N. "The Dawes Commission." *Chronicles of Oklahoma* 9 (March 1931): 71-105.
_____. "The Establishment of the Dawes Commission for Indian Territory." *Chronicles of Oklahoma* 18 (June 1940): 171-81.
Burt, Larry W. "Factories on Reservations: The Industrial Development Programs of Commissioner Glenn Emmons 1953-1960." *Arizona and the West* 19 (Winter 1977): 317-32.

Clark, Jeanne. "Indian Women Harness Old Talents to New War Jobs." *Indians at Work* 10 (Nos. 2-6): 25-28.

Collier, John. "Editorial." *Indians at Work* 9 (January 1942): 1-4.

_____. "Editorial." *Indians at Work* 10 (July–September 1942): 1-5.

Critchlow, Donald T. "Lewis Meriam, Expertise, and Indian Reform." *The Historian* 43 (May 1981): 325-44.

"David from Oklahoma." *Indians at Work* 12 (January–February 1945): 30-31.

Dewing, Rolland. "South Dakota Newspaper Coverage of the 1973 Occupation of Wounded Knee." *South Dakota History* 12 (Spring 1982): 48-64.

Dinwoodie, David H. "Indians, Hispanos, and Land Reform." *Western Historical Quarterly* 17 (July 1986): 291-323.

Drache, Hiram. "Thomas Campbell—The Plower of the Plains." *Agricultural History* 51 (January 1977): 78-91.

Ellis, Richard N. "Robert L. Bennett 1966-1969." In Kvasnicka, Robert M. and Herman J. Viola, eds., *Commissioners of Indian Affairs, 1824-1977*. Lincoln: University of Nebraska Press, 1979.

_____. "'Indians at Ibapah in Revolt': Goshutes, the Draft and the Indian Bureau, 1917-1919." *Nevada Historical Society Quarterly* 19 (Fall 1976): 163-70.

Flaccus, Elmer W. "Arizona's Last Great Indian War: The Saga of Pia Machita." *Journal of Arizona History* 22 (Spring 1981): 1-22.

Genung, A. B. "Agriculture in the World War Period." In *An Historical Survey of American Agriculture*. Washington: Government Printing Office, 1941 (Reprint from the *1940 Yearbook of Agriculture*).

Hagan, William T. "Civil Service Commissioner Theodore Roosevelt and the Indian Rights Association." *Pacific Historical Review* 44 (May 1975): 187-200.

Hagberg, Eric T., and Robert Bunker. "Pueblo Sovereignty, Postwar." *New Mexico Quarterly Review* 18 (Summer 1948): 223-27.

Hauptman, Laurence M. "The American Indian Federation and the Indian New Deal: A Reinterpretation." *Pacific Historical Review* 52 (August 1983): 378-402.

Hertzberg, Hazel W. "Reaganomics on the Reservation." *New Republic* 187 (November 22, 1982): 15-18.

Hood, Susan. "Termination of the Klamath Tribe in Oregon." *Ethnohistory* 19 (Fall 1972): 379-92.

Howard, James H. "The Dakota Victory Dance World War II." *North Dakota History* 18 (January 1951): 31-40.

"How the West Was Really Won." *U.S. News & World Report* 108 (May 21, 1990): 56-65.

Hoxie, Frederick E. "Redefining Indian Education: Thomas J. Morgan's Program in Disarray." *Arizona and the West* 24 (Spring 1982): 5-18.

Hundley, Norris, Jr. "The Dark and Bloody Ground of Indian Water Rights: Confusion Elevated to Principle." *Western Historical Quarterly* 9 (October 1978): 455-82.

_____. "The Winters Decision and Indian Water Rights: A Mystery Reexamined." *Western Historical Quarterly* 13 (January 1982): 17-42.

"Indian Heroism Honored." *Indians at Work* 12 (May–June 1944): 4-5.

"Indians Conserving and Rebuilding Their Resources through CCC-ID." *Indians at Work* 9 (November 1941): 33-34.

"Indians in the News." *Indians at Work* 9 (March 1942): 21.

Johnson, N. B. "The National Congress of American Indians." *Chronicles of Oklahoma* 30 (Summer 1952): 140-48.

Johnston, Philip. "Indian Jargon Won Our Battles." *Masterkey* 38 (October–December 1964): 130-37.

Kelly, Lawrence C. "Choosing the New Deal Indian Commissioner: Ickes vs. Collier." *New Mexico Historical Review* 49 (October 1974): 269-88.

_____. "The Indian Reorganization Act: The Dream and the Reality." *Pacific Historical Review* 45 (August 1975): 291-312.

Koppes, Clayton R. "From New Deal to Termination: Liberalism and Indian Policy, 1933-1953." *Pacific Historical Review* 46 (November 1977): 543-66.

Kunitz, Stephen J. "The Social Philosophy of John Collier." *Ethnohistory* 18 (Summer 1971): 213-29.

Martin, Harry W. "Correlates of Adjustment among American Indians in an Urban Environment." *Human Organization* 23 (Winter 1964): 290-95.

Mathews, Tom, et al. "The Angry West vs. the Rest." *Newsweek* 94 (September 17, 1979): 31-40.

McCool, Daniel. "Indian Voting." In Deloria, Vine, Jr., ed., *American Indian Policy in the Twentieth Century*. Norman: University of Oklahoma Press, 1985.

McDonnell, Janet. "Competency Commissions and Indian Land Policy, 1913-1920." *South Dakota History* 11 (Winter 1980): 21-34.

_____. "Land Policy on the Omaha Reservation: Competency Commissions and Forced Fee Patents." *Nebraska History* 63 (Fall 1982): 399-410.

McDowell, Malcolm. "Service as a Member of the Board of Indian Commissioners." In Lockwood, Frank C., *The Life of Edward E. Ayer*. Chicago: A. C. McClurg & Company, 1929.

Metcalf, Lee. "The Need for Revision of Federal Policy in Indian Affairs." *Indian Truth* 35 (January–March 1958): 1-6.

Meyer, Roy W. "Fort Berthold and the Garrison Dam." *North Dakota History* 35 (Summer–Fall, 1968): 217-355.

Murphy, D. E. "Indians Conserving and Rebuilding Their Resources through CCC-ID." *Indians at Work* 9 (November 1941): 33.

Murray, Stanley N. "The Turtle Mountain Chippewa, 1882-1905." *North Dakota History* 51 (Winter 1984): 14-37.

Officer, James E. "Termination as Federal Policy: An Overview." In Philp, Kenneth R., ed., *Indian Self-Rule: First-Hand Accounts of Indian-White Relations from Roosevelt to Reagan*. Salt Lake City: Howe Brothers, 1986.

O'Reilly, Kenneth. "Progressive Era and New Era American Indian Policy: The Gospel of Self-Support." *Journal of Historical Studies* 5 (Fall 1981): 35-55.

Ortiz, Alfonso. "The Gila River Piman Water Problem: An Ethnohistorical Account." In Schroeder, Albert H., ed., *The Changing Ways of Southwestern Indians: A Historical Perspective*. Glorieta, New Mexico: Rio Grande Press, 1973.

Ourada, Patricia K. "Glenn L. Emmons 1953-61." In Kvasnicka, Robert M., and Herman J. Viola, eds., *Commissioners of Indian Affairs, 1824-1977*. Lincoln: University of Nebraska Press, 1979.

Parman, Donald L. "American Indians and the Bicentennial." *New Mexico Historical Review* 51 (July 1976): 233-49.

_____. "Inconstant Advocacy: The Erosion of Indian Fishing Rights in the Pacific Northwest, 1933-1956." *Pacific Historical Review* 53 (May 1984): 163-89.

_____. "The Indian and the Civilian Conservation Corps." *Pacific Historical Review* 40 (February 1971): 39-56.

_____, ed. "Lewis Meriam's Letters during the Survey of Indian Affairs, 1926-1927 (Part 1)." *Arizona and the West* 24 (Fall 1982): 253-80.

_____, ed. "Lewis Meriam's Letters during the Survey of Indian Affairs, 1926-1927 (Part 2)." *Arizona and the West* 24 (Winter 1982): 341-70.

Paxson, Frederic L. "The Highway Movement, 1916-1935." *American Historical Review* 51 (January 1946): 236-53.

Pfaller, Louis L. "James McLaughlin and the Rodman Wanamaker Expedition of 1913." *North Dakota History* 44 (Spring 1977): 4-11.

Philp, Kenneth R. "Stride toward Freedom: The Relocation of Indians to Cities, 1952-1960." *Western Historical Quarterly* 16 (April 1985): 175-90.

_____. "Termination: A Legacy of the Indian New Deal." *Western Historical Quarterly* 14 (April 1983): 165-80.

Pisani, Donald J. "Reclamation and Social Engineering in the Progressive Era." *Agricultural History* 57 (January 1983): 46-63.

Quinten, B. T. "Oklahoma Tribes, the Great Depression and the Indian Bureau." *Mid-America* 49 (January 1967): 29-43.

Robbins, William G. "Herbert Hoover's Indian Reformers under Attack: The Failures of Administrative Reform." *Mid-America* 63 (October 1981): 157-70.

Roberts, Charles. "The Cushman Indian Trades School and World War I." *American Indian Quarterly* 11 (Summer 1987): 221-39.

Roberts, Merrill J. "The Motor Transportation Revolution." *Business History Review* 30 (March 1956): 57-95.

Roos, Philip D., et al. "The Impact of the American Indian Movement on the Pine Ridge Indian Reservation." *Phylon* 41 (March 1980): 89-99.

Schulte, Steven C. "Indians and Politicians: The Origins of a 'Western' Attitude toward Native Americans in Wyoming, 1868-1906." *Annals of Wyoming* 56 (Spring 1984): 2-11.

_____. "Removing the Yoke of Government: E. Y. Berry and the Origins of Indian Termination Policy." *South Dakota History* 14 (Spring 1984): 48-67.

Smith, Burton M. "The Politics of Allotment: The Flathead Reservation as a Test Case." *Pacific Northwest Quarterly* 70 (July 1979): 131-40.

"Systematic Discrimination in the Indian Claims Commission: The Burden of Proof in Redressing Historical Wrongs." *Iowa Law Review* 57 (June 1972): 1300-1319.

Szasz, Magaret Connell. "Philleo Nash 1961-1966." In Kvasnicka, Robert M., and Herman J. Viola, eds., *The Commissioners of Indian Affairs, 1824-1977*. Lincoln: University of Nebraska Press, 1979.

Tate, Michael L. "From Scout to Doughboy: The National Debate over Integrating Indians into the Military, 1891-1918." *Western Historical Quarterly* 17 (October 1986): 417-37.

Thompson, Mark. "Nurturing the Forked Tree: Conception and Formation of the American Indian Policy Review Commission." In *New Directions in Federal Indian Policy: A Review of the American Indian Policy Review Commission*. Los Angeles: American Indian Studies Center (UCLA), 1979.

Trent, Dover P. "The Use of Indian Manpower." *Indians at Work* 12 (January–February 1945): 6-9.

Tyler, S. Lyman. "William A. Brophy 1945-1948." In Kvasnicka, Robert M., and Herman J. Viola, eds., *The Commissioners of Indian Affairs, 1824-1977*. Lincoln: University of Nebraska Press, 1979.

Useem, John, Gordon Macgregor, and Ruth Hill Useem. "Wartime Employment and Cultural Adjustments of the Rosebud Sioux." *Applied Anthropology* 2 (January–March 1943): 1-9.

"U.S. Air Force Commander in Hawaii Is a Member of Osage Tribe of Oklahoma." *Indians at Work* 9 (January 1942): 13-15.

Watkins, Arthur V. "Termination of Federal Supervision: The Removal of Restrictions over Indian Property and Person." *Annals of the American Academy of Political and Social Science* 311 (May 1957): 47-55.

"Westward Ho, Republicans!" *Newsweek* 116 (September 10, 1990): 33.

Wood, David L. "American Indian Farmland and the Great War." *Agricultural History* 55 (July 1981): 249-65.

_____. "Gosiute-Shoshone Draft Resistance, 1917-1918." *Utah Historical Quarterly* 49 (Spring 1981): 173-88.

Wright, Peter M. "John Collier and the Oklahoma Indian Welfare Act of 1936." *Chronicles of Oklahoma* 50 (Autumn 1972): 347-71.

Government Publications

American Indian Policy Review Commission. *Final Report.* Vols. 1-2. Washington: Government Printing Office, 1977.

_____. *Report on Federal, State, and Tribal Jurisdiction, Task Force Four.* Washington: Government Printing Office, 1976.

Brugge, David M. *A History of the Chaco Navajos.* Albuquerque: National Park Service, Division of Chaco Research, 1980.

Bureau of the Census. *Abstract of the Fifteenth Census of the United States, 1930.* Washington: Government Printing Office, 1933.

_____. *Abstract of the Twelfth Census, 1900.* Government Printing Office, 1902.

_____. *Fifteenth Census of the United States, 1930, Irrigation of Agricultural Lands.* Washington: Government Printing Office, 1932.

_____. *Fourteenth Census of the United States, 1920, Population,* Vol. 1. Washington: Government Printing Office, 1921.

_____. *Fourteenth Census, 1920, Irrigation and Drainage,* Vol. 7. Washington: Government Printing Office, 1920.

Cohen, Felix S. *Handbook of Federal Indian Law.* Washington: Government Printing Office, 1945.

Kappler, Charles J., comp. *Indians Affairs: Laws and Treaties,* 7 vols. Washington: Government Printing Office, 1904-1941.

Newell, Alan S., Richmond L. Clow, and Richard N. Ellis. *A Forest in Trust: Three Quarters of a Century of Indian Forestry.* Washington: Bureau of Indian Affairs, 1986.

Public Papers of the Presidents of the United States, 1968-69, Book I. Washington: Government Printing Office, 1970.

Public Papers of the Presidents of the United States, 1970. Washington: Government Printing Office, 1971.

Public Papers of the Presidents of the United States, 1983, Book I. Washington: Government Printing Office, 1984.

Secretary of Interior, *Annual Reports,* 1887-1945.

Taylor, Theodore W. *The States and Their Indian Citizens.* Washington: Department of Interior, Bureau of Indian Affairs, 1972.

Tyler, S. Lyman. *A History of Indian Policy.* Washington: Bureau of Indian Affairs, 1973.

United States Indian Claims Commission. *Final Report.* Washington: Government Printing Office, 1979.

United States Statutes at Large, 1887-1989. Washington: Government Printing Office, 1887-1991.

Congressional Hearings and Reports

House. Committee on Military Affairs. *American Indian Cavalry, Hearings on H.R. 3970.* 65th Cong., 1st sess., 1917.

House. Select Committee to Investigate Indian Affairs and Conditions in the United States. *An Investigation to Determine Whether the Changed Status of the Indian Re-*

quires a Revision of the Laws and Regulations Affecting the American Indian. 78th Cong., 2nd sess., 1944. H.R. 2091.

House. Committee on Indian Affairs. *Investigate Indian Affairs, Hearings before the Committee on Indian Affairs on H.R. 166.* 78th Cong., 2nd sess., 1944, Pts. 2-4.

House. *Expressing the Sense of Congress that Certain Tribes of Indians Should Be Freed from Federal Supervision, H. Rept. 841 to accompany H. Con. Res. 108.* 83d Cong., 1st sess., 1953.

House. Committee of Conference. *Conference Report, 81st Cong., 1st sess., 1949, H. Rept. 1338.*

Congress. Joint Committee on Interior and Insular Affairs. *Termination of Federal Supervision over Certain Tribes of Indians, Joint Hearings before the Subcommittees of the Committees on Interior and Insular Affairs.* 83rd Cong., 2nd sess., 1954, Pts. 1-12.

Senate. *Report of the Select Committee to Investigate Matters Connected with Affairs in Indian Territory,* (2 vols.), 59th Cong., 2d sess., November 11, 1906-January 9, 1907.

Senate. Committee on Indian Affairs. *Survey of Conditions among the Indians of the United States,* 78th Cong., 1st sess., 1943, S. Rept. 310.

Senate. Committee on Interior and Insular Affairs. *Message from the President of the United States,* 81st Cong., 1st sess., 1949, S. Doc. 119.

Senate. Committee on Indian Affairs. Subcommittee on Indian Affairs. Report prepared by Porter J. Preston and Charles A. Engle. "Report of Advisers on Irrigation on Indian Reservations." 71st Cong., 2d sess., 1928, part 6.

Newspapers

Arapaho Bee, 1917-1918.
Calumet Chieftain, 1919.
Canadian Valley Record, 1919.
Lac du Flambeau News, June, 1993.
Missoulian, 1990.
New York Times, 1952-1983.
Plain Dealer, 1992.
Richardson, Jim, and John Aloysius Farrell. "The New Indian Wars." *Denver Post* (Special Reprint) 1982.
Spokesman Review, 1991.
Thomas Tribune, 1921-22.
Wotanin Wowapi (Fort Peck Reservation), 1992.

Interviews

Brugge, David M. Interview with author. June 23, 1993.
Chilson, O. Hatfield. Interview by Thomas F. Scopes. Oral history interview. Eisenhower Library.
Robertson, Robert. Interview with author. January 9, 1976.
Satz, Ronald N. Interview with author. October 6, 1992.
Watkins, Arthur. Interview by Ed Edwin. Oral history interview. Eisenhower Library.

Index

Abourezk, James G.: South Dakota senator, involved with AIPRC, 159–62; personal background, 160

Acre feet, explained, 189n70

Adams, Hank: activist, negotiated clearing BIA, 156

Agnew, Spiro: mentioned, 152

Akeah, Sam: Navajo chairman, GIIC committee member, 134

Albuquerque Journal: published Ickes' telegram to Cutting, 104

Alcatraz occupation: settlement sought, 153; mentioned, 148, 159

All-Pueblo Council: opposed Bursum bill, 78; mentioned, 128

Allotment: statistics on, 3–4, 9–10; unallotted reservations, 4; procedures, 9; congressional openings, 14

American Association on Indian Affairs: started *The American Indian*, 120

American Indian Federation (AIF): founding of, 1934, 98; attacks on Collier, 104–105

American Indian Movement (AIM): founded, philosophy, 154; various protests, 1970s, 155; 1972 march, 155–57; Wounded Knee II, 157–58; impact, 159; criminal reputation, 209n23

American Indian Policy Review Commission (AIPRC): authorized, 1975, 159; makeup, 160; recommendations, Meeds-Abourezk clash, 161; Indian reactions, 162; mentioned, 178

American Indian Research Fund, created, 144

Americans for Indian Opportunity, founded, 154

Americans Before Columbus: NIYC publication, 150

Anderson, Clinton P.: New Mexico senator, cooperation with Myer, 132; opposed Blue Lake return, 153; mentioned, 141

Andrews, W. H.: New Mexico leader, protest against Navajo allotments, 20–21

Appropriation Act of 1902, provision on heirship lands, 12

Appropriation Act of 1907, allotted land sales permitted, 13

Appropriation Act of 1914, individual reimbursable loans, 25–26

Archibald, Katherine: writer, Indian workers in shipyard, 110

Area Redevelopment Act of 1961, reservation applications, 150–51

Arizona: admission, 1912, 12; denial of voting rights, 126

Arizona v. *California I:* upheld Winters, 165

Arizona v. *San Carlos Apaches:* upheld state water control, 172

Ashurst, Henry Fountain: Arizona senator, blocked executive order extensions, 21–22; mentioned, 82, 96

Atlantic and Pacific Railroad, mentioned, 19

Attorney-general, opinion on oil and natural gas leasing, 80

Atwood, Stella: reformer, ties with Collier, 73, 77, 78

Automobiles, 1920s statistics on, 71

Ayer, Edward E.: Chicago industrialist, proposed separate Indian units, 60

Backlash: traditional discrimination, 177; rhetoric, 178; ICERR, etc., 178–80; Wisconsin groups, 179–80

Baker, Newton D.: secretary of war, vetoed separate units, 61

Ballinger, Richard A.: headed Interior, canceled agreement with Forest Service, 26–27; vetoed oil leases, 75

Banks, Dennis: AIM leader, 157

Barnett, Jackson: scandal on, 87

Begay, Keats: Navajo, Bataan death march participant, 114

Bellecourt, Clyde: AIM leader, wounded by Carter Camp, 159

Belvin, Henry J. W.: Choctaw educator, commissioner candidate, 1953, 137

Bennett, Robert: commissioner, 151–52

Berle, Adoph A., Jr.: Collier ally in Pueblo lands legislation, 79–80

Berry, E. Y.: South Dakota representative, termination advocate, personal background, 137; Operation Moccasin, 145

Big Bend Dam, mentioned, 130–31

Blackfoot Reservation: early irrigation, 23;

DONALD L. PARMAN is Professor of History at Purdue University and author of THE NAVAJOS AND THE NEW DEAL and numerous articles on the history of Indians in the twentieth century.